Transforming One's Self

SUNY series in American Philosophy and Cultural Thought

Randall E. Auxier and John R. Shook, editors

Transforming One's Self

The Therapeutic Ethical Pragmatism of William James

Clifford S. Stagoll

SUNY
PRESS

Published by State University of New York Press, Albany

For information, contact State University of New York Press, Albany, NY
www.sunypress.edu

Library of Congress Cataloging-in-Publication Data

Name: Stagoll, Clifford S., 1965– author.
Title: Transforming one's self : the therapeutic ethical pragmatism of
    William James / Clifford S. Stagoll.
Description: Albany : State University of New York Press, [2023] | Series:
    SUNY series in American philosophy and cultural thought | Includes
    bibliographical references and index.
Identifiers: LCCN 2022041855 | ISBN 9781438493268 (hardcover : alk. paper) |
    ISBN 9781438493282 (ebook) | ISBN 9781438493275 (pbk. : alk. paper)
Subjects: LCSH: James, William, 1842–1910. | Pragmatism. | Philosophy. |
    Applied ethics.
Classification: LCC B945.J24 S68 2023 | DDC 144/.3—dc23/eng/20230301
LC record available at https://lccn.loc.gov/2022041855

10 9 8 7 6 5 4 3 2 1

Contents

Preface

William James's philosophy has been variously categorized, but rarely is he identified as an ethical theorist, much less one whose corpus comprises aspects of a comprehensive system of ethics. James is more often presented as *either* an epistemologist, *or* a philosophical (or experimental) psychologist, *or* a dispenser of homespun wisdom, *or* a philosopher of religion, *or* an ontologist. Indeed, most scholars of American pragmatism have considered his work in ethics to be minimal, or even slight.

Yet there has always been a contrary view, albeit in the minority. James's contemporary and peer John Dewey wrote that "James did not need to write a separate treatise on ethics, because in its larger sense he was everywhere and always the moralist."[1] James's student and interpreter Ralph Barton Perry believed that he had a "constant preoccupation with moral questions," reflected in consistent views on the subject over the course of his career.[2]

This book takes seriously these leads from Dewey and Perry, arguing that James's oeuvre contains a radical ethical theory addressing existential issues confronting his fellow Americans at the turn of the twentieth century. Responding to extraordinary changes in socioeconomic circumstances and established social mores, James proposes means for improving one's own self and life, a series of practical recommendations informed and justified by his philosophical psychology and philosophy. Turning away from the inadequacies of traditional philosophical ethics for addressing either the minutiae of daily decision-making or the most profound matters of self-conception, James argues that by adopting a positive (but realistic) attitude and paying careful attention to one's own habits and interests, it is possible to develop and maintain a richer, more satisfying existence than is possible by relying on either old forms of spiritualism or the new material science of his day. By considering together certain disparate aspects of James's corpus, it is possible to locate an action-oriented system of ethics that is consistent with American pragmatism's most representative themes.

That James has not usually been identified as an ethical theorist is hardly surprising: his diverse and changing interests, literary style, and impatience with argumentative and definitional consistency tend to make a thorough synthesis impossible. Furthermore, as Perry himself noted, James's utterances on ethics were occasional and scattered too loosely across his published works.[3] Often the significance of these statements becomes clear only when read in conjunction with arguments enunciated elsewhere, some of which are not obviously about ethics at all.

This is not to suggest that James's interpreters and champions in the academy have neglected his work on ethics altogether. His essay most obviously devoted to the subject, "The Moral Philosopher and the Moral Life," and another two that clearly invoke ethical themes ("On a Certain Blindness in Human Beings" and "What Makes a Life Significant") have been variously criticized, explicated, and championed and several of his works in philosophical psychology and presentations to lay audiences speak directly to either moral decision-making or pursuit of a rich and meaningful life, thereby engaging with the two disparate senses of philosophical ethics. Generally, though, these were understood as tangential to more significant themes in James's wonderfully diverse body of work.

Recently though, after years of relative neglect, there has been a resurgence of interest in James's ethics. These new studies form a more incisive incarnation of work that began in the 1960s: efforts that quickly faded from view in an era dominated by philosophies uninterested in first-personal human experience. Even after the apparent revival of pragmatism in the 1980s, little attention was paid to the earlier contributions of figures like Bernard P. Brennan and John K. Roth who had located important ethical themes within, and continuities between, apparently disparate aspects of James's work.[4] Only with these latest critical and constructive studies has the case been renewed for considering James a noteworthy figure in the history of ethics and various themes and ideas proposed as crucial for understanding his thoughts on the subject. Among these themes is the one pursued in this book: that "self-transformation"—making deliberate changes to one's own character—or one's most settled habits of thought and action—is the means for living a good life, thus constituting an ethics in the ancient Greek sense.

This book contributes to the minority view that James is indeed an ethical theorist through and through. It explains both his proposal that our conscious existence contains means for realizing a more rewarding life than we usually suppose and his concrete recommendations for realizing them. In James's ethics, moral theories are replaced by melioristic exhortations and practical advice for changing one's life, drawing upon his brilliant insights into the nature of consciousness and self. To change one's life entails changing one's self, and changing one's self is a matter of reorienting one's own experience and habits of thought and action. For James, then, improving one's life is a matter of the self working on the self rather than making judgments about (or being motivated toward) some factor *outside* the self.

Rather than explaining just the *thematic* unity among James's ideas that comprise his ethics (the purpose of much recent work on the matter), this book advances *interpretative* and *methodological* unity, too. It proposes a reading of James's ethics as a response to the socioeconomic circumstances of his day, derived from key themes in his metaphysics, philosophical psychology, philosophy of religion, and pedagogical theory. It shows that James's recommendations for a richer, more rewarding life—an ethics in the classical sense—are sustained by his theories of experience, consciousness, self, habit, and will, linked by a series of critical (though often overlooked) methodological decisions. Those decisions arise from James's distinctive commitments to first-person experience as philosophy's proper subject and actionable recommendations for future conduct as its product. Only by attending to intricate details from such disparate works as *The Principles of Psychology, Pragmatism, The Will to Believe,* and the various texts comprising *Talks to Teachers on Psychology; and to Students on Some of Life's Ideals* is it possible to grasp fully James's sophisticated ethics and its associated pedagogy.

As Charlene Haddock Seigfried has written, "Despite the realization that there are an infinite number of ways to reconstruct James's writings, not all ways are equally helpful, illuminative, or suggestive for further research."[5] The approach adopted here—comprising elements of intellectual history, interpretative exegesis, and practical philosophy—describes the main thrust of James's ethics of self-transformation and a justifiable way of understanding how its elements "fit together" while also pointing the way toward alternative constructions. As such, it tries to steer a path between being either too neat and systematic or too "loose" and inconclusive. Although it is unlikely that James meant for his work to cohere in precisely the manner proposed here (after all, time and again he was led in all kinds of different directions by his intellectual curiosity and propensity for reworking his ideas from different perspectives), this approach relies on some of his most well-developed ideas, explicitly stated assumptions, methodological choices, and deep commitments to experience and practice over philosophical abstraction and generalization.

Acknowledgments

Like so many students and scholars of American Pragmatism, I am grateful to the late John J. McDermott, whose learned and invigorating teaching, evocative yarns, and clouds of chalk dust at Texas A&M University introduced me to the delights of William James's work.

Stephen H. Daniel, also at Texas A&M, encouraged the joy of diving headlong into a text and was a wonderful teacher and kind friend for a student very far from home. At University of Western Australia, Michael Levine has been a most supportive and insightful colleague and a great lunch companion. Finally, John K. Roth was good enough to engage with a total stranger to discuss at length his work on James's ethics and its production during an "eclipse."

For their perceptive and helpful comments on a previous version of this work, I express my sincere thanks to Colin Koopman, Sarin Marchetti, Paul Stob, and two anonymous reviewers. I hope that I have done justice to your insightful observations and suggestions.

To Toad, Ming, Parrot, and Sloth, a lifetime of thanks for welcoming me into the Waples family.

In memory of my beloved parents, for whom curiosity, learning, and debate were essential aspects of daily life.

Abbreviations

The following sources are cited using abbreviations in parentheses within the text. All other references and bibliographical data are available in the endnotes and bibliography.

The Works of William James. 19 vols. Edited by Frederick H. Burkhardt, Fredson Bowers, and Ignas K. Skrupskelis. Cambridge, MA and London: Harvard University Press, 1975–1988.

ECR   Vol. 17. *Essays, Comments, and Reviews* (1987 [1865–1909])

EPh   Vol. 5. *Essays in Philosophy* (1978 [1876–1910])

EPs   Vol. 13. *Essays in Psychology* (1983 [1878–1906])

ERE   Vol. 3. *Essays in Radical Empiricism* (1976 [1912])

ERM   Vol. 11. *Essays in Religion and Morality* (1982 [1884–1910])

EPR   Vol. 16. *Essays in Psychical Research* (1986 [1869–1909])

MEN   Vol. 18. *Manuscripts, Essays and Notes* (1988 [1884–1910])

ML   Vol. 19. *Manuscript Lectures* (1988 [1872–1907])

MT   Vol. 2. *The Meaning of Truth* (1975 [1909])

P   Vol. 1. *Pragmatism* (1975 [1907])

PB   Vol. 14. *Psychology: The Briefer Course* (1984 [1892])

PP   Vols. 8–10. *Principles of Psychology* (1981 [1890]; 3 vols.)

PU   Vol. 4. *A Pluralistic Universe* (1977 [1909])

SPP   Vol. 7. *Some Problems of Philosophy* (1979 [1910])

TT   Vol. 12. *Talks to Teachers on Psychology; and to Students on Some of Life's Ideals* (1983 [1899])

VRE   Vol. 15. *The Varieties of Religious Experience* (1985 [1902])

WB   Vol. 6. *The Will to Believe and Other Essays in Popular Philosophy* (1979 [1897])

Introduction

William James's Ethics in the Pragmatist Tradition

Pragmatism's Contested History

Well over a century since its founders proclaimed American pragmatism to be a distinct philosophical school, there is still remarkably little general agreement about its unifying themes, styles, beliefs, and methods. It has been variously characterized as a theory of truth, meaning, or reference; a kind of metaphysics; some stance or attitude toward philosophical problems or practices; a way to free ourselves from philosophical obsessions (or disarm philosophical disputes); intellectual therapy; a generalized form of antiessentialism; "a way of thinking about thinking";[1] and much else besides. In a sense, this should not be surprising: the originators of the movement, Chauncey Wright, Charles Sanders Peirce, and William James (the so-called Golden Age pragmatists, together with John Dewey) held vastly different ambitions for philosophy, possessed diverse capabilities, and were educated in disparate professional fields. However, the amount of scholarly effort devoted to the matter in the years since, and the extent to which self-proclaimed pragmatists have been prepared to entertain even the broadest of characterizations, might have indicated the likelihood of progress. Instead, the divisions between pragmatism's various threads and the philosophers pursuing them are as wide as ever.

Of course, in intermural debates about which philosophy is superior, there are advantages and disadvantages to a position's being defined loosely. As Stanley Fish puts it, "A pragmatism so amorphous and omnivorous has the two advantages of being a very bad target—you feel that there is nothing to hit—and being a very bad substitute for the absolutes it tilts against—if

1

you don't know exactly what it is, it is hard to march under its banner. Pragmatism may be the one theory—if it is a theory—that clears the field not only of its rivals but of itself, at least as a positive alternative."[2]

But there is another view: that pragmatism's heterogeneity—the very reason that it has proved difficult to define—is in fact a sign of its adaptability to developments both within philosophy and outside it. Perhaps pragmatism's engagement with new issues and perspectives tests and stretches its explanatory resources, helping to maintain its philosophical relevance. One of the tradition's most eminent figures, Richard J. Bernstein, holds that pragmatism is properly understood as a "conflict of narratives," and that the working out of such conflict is crucial to its "continuity and vitality."[3]

There are perhaps two aspects of the debate about pragmatism's meaning and intent since James announced its birth in 1898 from which one might draw definitional succor. First is a general thematic consensus that, though broad and highly abstract, has allowed scholars to at least identify thinkers who might potentially be called "pragmatists": the understanding that pragmatism, in all its guises, examines philosophical concepts and problems in terms of human practices. The early pragmatists held that only if philosophy tested ideas in terms of practices and consequences could it move beyond generations of fruitless philosophical argument. In Nicholas Rescher's words, "The characteristic idea of philosophical pragmatism is that efficacy in practical application somehow provides a standard for the determination of truth in the case of statements, rightness in the case of actions, and value in the case of appraisals."[4] As such, there is no special dichotomy drawn by pragmatists between the realms of practice and theory; rather, theory is just one more practical tool for achieving human ends.

Second, uncertainty about pragmatism's meaning resolves to one principal issue over all others, such that, despite having set pragmatism in two very different directions, the nub of the issue is straightforward. As early as 1908, just a decade after pragmatism was so named and prior to either James's later excursions into metaphysics or Dewey's mature and protean works, Arthur Lovejoy famously located, in just the *epistemological* positions of the early pragmatists, thirteen different contentions "which are separate not merely in the sense of being discriminable, but in the sense of being logically independent."[5] Given the multitudinous directions in which pragmatism has developed since, one can but guess at how many more discriminable positions are afoot today. While it is unlikely that Lovejoy's despairing hope that "philosophers should agree to attach some single and stable meaning to the term" will be achieved anytime soon, it is true that most current definitional effort is committed to just one controversy rather than many.[6]

The dispute traces two distinct lines of development in the pragmatist genealogy; one characterized by Peirce's championing pragmatism as a means for settling philosophical (often definitional) disputes and another by James's conceiving it as a particular orientation toward the world. While Peirce and James agree that thought is always in the service of developing beliefs and producing actions, and although each was keen to dismiss Cartesian rationalism and appropriation of a priori categories for establishing episte-mological foundations, they did not agree on how these ambitions ought to be achieved, or the scope to which pragmatism ought to be applied. In its more recent guise, this misalignment has led to a schism between those who draw most strongly from Peirce and for whom pragmatism is principally a linguistic affair focused on epistemological matters (so-called neo-pragmatists or linguistic pragmatists) and those more concerned with reconstructing and expanding upon the work of such of the movement's other originators as James and Dewey, F. C. S. Schiller, Josiah Royce, Jane Addams, George Herbert Mead, George Santayana, and others (in my terminology, "recent classical pragmatists").

For Peirce, the meaning of a concept is identified by its future practical consequences. Seeking to establish a definitive means for deciding the meaning of scientific and philosophical notions, he expressed pragmatism's main tenet as follows: "that a *conception*, that is, the rational purport of a word or other expression, lies exclusively in its conceivable bearing upon the conduct of life; so that, since obviously nothing that might not result from experiment can have any direct bearing upon conduct, or if one can define accurately all the conceivable experimental phenomena which the affirmation or denial of a concept could imply, one will have therein a complete definition of the concept, and *there is absolutely nothing more in it*."[7] While Peirce's terminology is steeped in its late nineteenth-century intellectual context and imprecise by today's standards (Peirce acknowledged the maxim's vagueness), his emphasis on "a word or other expression" and his championing of the definitional potential of experimentation point the way toward a linguistic theory: that the meaning of an expression ought to be assessed on the basis of its consequences for human actions, which are determinable by formal scientific experimentation.

Only a close reading of Peirce's influential statement reveals the wider potential utility suggested by the expressions "rational purport" and "conduct of life" from which James takes his lead. James believed that by shifting the focus away from questions of how human experiences relate to a reality *outside* experience and toward relations *between* experiences, Peirce had delivered a way of avoiding philosophical skepticism and investigating what human experiences mean for behavior and a practical grasp of the world. The pragmatic method, James writes, "is to try to interpret each notion by tracing its respective practical consequences. What difference would it practically make to anyone if this notion rather than that notion were true?" (*P*, 28).

Pursuing this path, James gives pragmatism a humanistic and individualistic focus in place of Peirce's impersonal and objective one. By interpreting Peirce's maxim in terms of a psychology of action, setting aside the communal aspects of science's regulative processes, and referring pragmatism's general tenet to particular consequences and actions for a particular person, James makes of pragmatism a general theory of first-person meaning. The meaning of one's personal experiences is a matter of their impact upon how one thinks and acts, and pragmatism ought to focus on how one's thinking influences and is influenced by human practices. He contends that "if there were any part of a thought that made no difference in the thought's practical consequences, then that part would be no proper element of the thought's significance" (*P*, 259). Acting or "doing" becomes the aspect of human life most worthy of attention while "knowing" and "defining" are demoted, and so pragmatism ought to be less concerned with what is meant by calling a diamond "hard" or a table "flat" (the kinds of example used by Peirce) and more concerned with resolving issues in ethics, the down-to-earth decisions of daily life (for clarity, I shall refer to such matters as "practical" rather than "pragmatic"), religion, and psychology. As such, James claims, pragmatist philosophy is a "turn away from abstraction and insufficiency, from verbal solutions, from bad a priori reasons, from fixed principles, closed systems, and pretended absolutes and origins" and a "turn towards concreteness and adequacy, towards facts, towards action, and towards power" (*P*, 31).

The influence in the twentieth- and early twenty-first centuries of this schism between Peirce and James is much explored and greatly contested. Until recently, it had been explained in terms of "the eclipse narrative," an account of the influence of pragmatism taken as a single, clearly identifiable movement. This rendering begins with pragmatism in the ascendant at the time of James's death in 1910. In the United States its adherents—many of whom had been his students or acolytes—dominated senior faculty appointments at the most highly regarded universities, Dewey was becoming the best known and most influential academic in American public life, and a hearty appetite among the educated public for pragmatism's accounts of contemporary social issues saw it widely publicized in print and at public conferences.

But during this same period, the new logic of Gottlob Frege and Bertrand Russell was also attracting attention. The decline of Dewey's long and distinguished career was marked by his failure to adopt the techniques and nomenclature of the new mathematical logic and his continued emphasis on first-person experience rather than language. With Dewey's death in 1952, Jamesian pragmatism lost its greatest advocate and most able innovator without a successor in view. In place of experience-focused pragmatism came preoccupation with epistemological concerns, and successive waves of work inspired by Frege and Russell, Ludwig Wittgenstein's philosophy of language, Ernst Mach, Rudolf Carnap, Albert Tarski, and those various incarnations of positivism and logical empiricism loosely linked with the successes of experimental science. Even the style and language of philosophy moved on from "the quicksilver brilliance of James and [George] Santayana and toward . . . the technical virtuosity of philosophers like C. I. Lewis."[8] According to the eclipse narrative, pragmatism had virtually disappeared from university faculties and public view by the time that conceptual analysis and ordinary language philosophy had gained prominence in the 1950s, and only the rise to prominence of the bold and controversial Richard Rorty, with his 1979 work *Philosophy and the Mirror of Nature*, was pragmatism revived.

The eclipse narrative has been challenged of late in several ways. Louis Menand and others (inspired by the earlier work of Bruce Kucklick, Philip Weiner, and Edmund Wilson) have attempted to explain the shift in twentieth-century philosophical preoccupations in terms of extra-philosophical factors.[9] Other interpretations use cross-pollinations between thinkers in the pragmatist tradition to explain how it appears today: that is, as a loosely definable grouping exhibiting porous "boundaries" and the ongoing schism between Peirce's language-centric theory and James's focus on first-person meaning. Most notably, Cheryl Misak has argued that Peirce's ideas were adopted and adapted by such key figures in the dominant analytic tradition as Lewis, W. v. O. Quine, Frank Ramsay, and Wilfred Sellars.[10] On this account, rather than being "eclipsed," Peircean pragmatism developed into a discrete, antinaturalistic epistemology focused upon how meanings are communicated and acted upon in real-world settings.[11]

Such challenges to the eclipse narrative rely upon identifying and describing a continuous (or nearly continuous) lineage of pragmatist ideas appropriated by other traditions throughout the mid-twentieth century, becoming recognizably pragmatist again just in later years. As Tom Alexander points out, though, such approaches "resolutely ignore the way *discussion* of classical American Philosophy or the figures in that tradition nearly vanishes in mainstream philosophy, not to mention the open contempt shown to those who did show an interest in it."[12] Furthermore, although it has proved possible to construct such a lineage for Peircean pragmatism, the same can almost certainly not be done for the more naturalistic version advanced by James and Dewey. This tradition and its proponents were indeed "eclipsed," suffering a precipitous fall from prominence in the decades after Dewey's death. Compared with more technical philosophies engaged with epistemological matters, and their supposed (though often unrealized) ties with the explanatory tools of modern science, theories about human experience "in the round" might have seemed quaint.

Nonetheless, although engagement with James's work and themes in the 1950s, 1960s, and 1970s was limited to just a few philosophers, among them were some of the doyens of American philosophy; such "lonely laborers in the vineyard" (as Cornel West described them) as Bernstein, Max Fisch, James Gouinlock, Sidney Hook, John Lachs, Murray G. Murphey, Sandra Rosenthal, John K. Roth, John Smith, and Morton White.[13] At the State University of New York and then Texas A&M University, John J. McDermott interpreted James through an existentialist lens to encourage careful consideration of the transient and perilous nature of human lives.[14] At Rutgers, Bruce Wilshire used Jamesian resources interpreted phenomenologically to critique the "impersonal" nature of much analytic philosophy.[15] At Northwestern University, James M. Edie returned to James time and again in developing his phenomenological insights.[16] In the early 1960s, Duquesne University contributed a program on phenomenology that attracted such James scholars as Hans Linschoten.[17] Perhaps most significant for the future of James studies, the philosophy program at Yale—"out of touch with history and the particularity of human life," as one graduate student of the day writes—boasted several figures preoccupied with pursuing existential and historical questions by way of humanist philosophy: Smith, John Wild, and such highly capable graduate students as Bernstein, Rorty, and Roth.[18]

Significantly, these "laborers" were not content to treat the works of their Golden Age predecessors as mere source material for restatement or straightforward explication. Instead, they sought new directions by way of unexplored or underdeveloped themes, unstated assumptions, problems, and uncertainties, as well as ideas that could be brought into meaningful intercourse with other kinds of theory. They held that the very point of

James's pragmatism was about locating prospects for the future—new ways for addressing contemporary concerns, both theoretical and practical—rather than an endless cycle of review. For McDermott, this meant more than sixty years of writing about the pedagogical nature of experience and using it to aid the ill and dying; for Lachs, it meant bringing pragmatism into conversation with Stoicism and other schools of thought in terms of their recommendations for "styles" of living; for Smith, it was locating and publicizing lessons for American civil society; and for each of these figures, like James, it meant taking seriously an obligation to continue pragmatism's tradition of public philosophy through lectures outside the traditional university setting and engagements with other fields of study.[19] In this very broad sense—the imperative that pragmatism (indeed, all philosophy) ought to address the real-world problems of ordinary people and the purposes, meanings, and values of human lives—pragmatism in the Jamesian vein is rightly conceived as a *humanism*.

As James writes (referring to Kierkegaard), we must "live forward" even though we "understand backward" (*P*, 107). All our ideals and most important judgments are prospective rather than retrospective. If the future of pragmatism as a distinctive school was beholden to retellings of its past (to the original debate between Peirce and James, for instance), and if developments within the school were always to be attributed for their context and evaluation to one side or other of the divide, then how might pragmatism per se "live forward" while understanding its history backward?

There seems to me an opportunity—an obligation, perhaps—to rejuvenate and develop some of the themes that emerged during humanist pragmatism's darker days, when truly original interpretative work was conducted by a few scholars largely unnoticed by the philosophical firmament. This means returning to some of the issues and engagements extant at the time (specifically, from the late 1950s through to the 1970s) but left subsequently underdeveloped and without progeny. In terms of pragmatism's orientation toward the future, it means testing and elaborating on the work of both the Golden Age figures and West's "lonely laborers," using the latest ideas from the study of James's work to address contemporary circumstances and locate prospects for humanist pragmatism's development. I understand this kind of approach as consistent with James's imperative, quoted earlier, that "if there were any part of a thought that made no difference in the thought's practical consequences, then that part would be no proper element of the thought's significance": unless such rejuvenation as I propose moves pragmatism forward, then it would be well lost amid its contested history (*P*, 259).

By clarifying the meaning and context of this invocation of James's, we will in the first place be clearer about how the pragmatist test of practical usefulness ought to be applied to the interpretation and application of proposals for addressing life's challenges, and, in the second, locate among disparate interpretations of James's practical philosophy one particularly suggestive proposal: that various aspects of his oeuvre might productively be understood as elements of a set of ethical recommendations for living a richer, more fulfilling life than much Western philosophy would indicate as possible, even amid the complexities and confusions of contemporary socioeconomic circumstances.

James's Pragmatism as Applied Philosophy

In one sense, James's belief that philosophy ought to "make a difference" is too general to distinguish humanist pragmatism from other schools of thought. As H. S. Thayer points out, "To be committed to a preference for useful over useless" is not to mark oneself out as a pragmatist but to just restate a position "as old as the human race," adopted not just in philosophy but by magic and religion, too.[20] But James clearly *does* mean to propose a distinctive philosophical position when couching pragmatism as an alternative to styles of philosophy more concerned with intricate analytical puzzles (which he refers to as "intellectual gymnastics"). He means that philosophy ought to return to praxis as the best means for engaging with one's circumstances from moment to moment: more thoughtful and consistent testing of one's beliefs in pursuit of a better path through life than can be offered by merely extending one's knowledge or applying some universal prescription to every case.

On this account, a philosophy's justification is found in the consequences of adopting it rather than the authoritative power of those pronouncing it, and its meaning is located "in the living" rather than in the pages of a persuasive text. James summarizes his hopes for simple, earthy pragmatism over highfalutin theory this way: "The really vital question for us all is, What is this world going to be? What is life eventually to make of itself? The centre of gravity of philosophy must alter its place. The earth of things, long thrown into shadow by the glories of the upper ether, must resume its rights" (*P*, 62). This is not to suggest that James's pragmatism ought to be understood *just* in terms of its applicability to real-world problems and practices; on the contrary, he brings to his theorizing a range of praxeological commitments. But he is always concerned with testing and applying these commitments in practice.

The real-world setting for James's work was in some ways quite like our own, with individuals and societies under intense pressure and changing rapidly. Communities were fracturing and values changing: the rich were becoming richer and the poor relatively poorer; political divisions were evident in increasingly polarized agenda and uncivil means for pursuing them; scientific and technological changes proceeded with unprecedented scale and speed; new and powerful economic forces were emerging; interpersonal alienation was encouraged by the rapid breakdown of traditional modes of engagement; there was rampant growth in materialism and materialistic pursuits; and, the reach of government and corporate organizations into personal lives was increasing. Such changes challenged the human capacity not merely to accommodate them in the daily course of events but to make sense of one's own self, life, and place in the world, too.

According to James, philosophy had failed to respond appropriately. He recorded that philosophy had developed a poor reputation because of three problems in particular: first, in the eyes of its potential public audience, "philosophy makes no theoretic progress, and shows no practical applications"; second, it is "dogmatic, and pretends to settle things by pure reason"; and third, it is "out of touch with real life for which it substitutes abstractions. The real world is various, tangled, painful. Philosophers almost without exception have treated it as noble, simple, and perfect" (SPP, 12, 18, 19). Philosophy tended to go on constructing and refuting conceptual differences without having an impact on real lives. James's hope was that the new generation of scholars might have become sufficiently dissatisfied with a "philosophic atmosphere" that was "too abstract and academic" that they would be motivated to pioneer a more engaged philosophy: "Life is confused and superabundant, and what the younger generation appears to crave is more of the temperament of life in its philosophy, even though it were at some cost of logical rigor and purity" (ERE, 39).

In fact, we have seen that with rare exceptions, philosophy would become even more technical, obtuse, and inward-looking. Even at the time of pragmatism's rejuvenation in the late 1970s, Rorty expressed his dismay at philosophical argument that comprised "shoptalk" and "mere logic chopping," and a profession "which looks back only a few decades, and finds its principal justification in the sheer intelligence of the people who are part of it."[21] Dewey, who of all the pragmatists engaged most directly with the realm of daily events, expressed humanist pragmatism's hope in this way:

"Philosophy recovers itself when it ceases to be a device for dealing with the problems of philosophers and becomes a method, cultivated by philosophers, for dealing with the problems of men."[22] It is significant, then, that he thought that "it is pragmatism as method which is emphasized . . . [and] uppermost in Mr. James's own mind."[23]

Like McDermott, Lachs, and other recent classical pragmatists, James understood that pragmatism's concern with real human lives meant that he was a public philosopher de facto, whether or not he cared to claim that title.[24] Following Ralph Waldo Emerson's example, James addressed issues of public concern in language and locations accessible to a nonacademic audience. From the mid-1890s until the end of his life, James participated in public debates about issues as diverse as American imperialism in the Philippines (he was vice president of the Anti-Imperialist League), regulation of big business, care of the mentally ill, the awful problem of lynching, racism, homogenization of university teaching qualifications, medical licensing, and the status accorded new and heterodox approaches in science and medicine (especially psychology), and he sometimes engaged with the issues of particular professional groups (as in his *Talks to Teachers on Psychology; and to Students on Some of Life's Ideals*, where he also touched upon the "duty, struggle, and success" of farmers in dealing with the challenges of their land [*TT*, 134]).[25] By involving himself in the social, economic, and political issues of his day, and applying insights from his technical specialities to the realm of public affairs, James meant to return philosophy to a more practical engagement with the world.

Most often, though, James's pragmatism focused upon the lives and circumstances of individuals, deploying philosophical reasoning and argument (sometimes in conjunction with scientific observation and psychological speculation) to either undermine philosophical presuppositions that place untenable limits on human existence, or propose new ways for thinking about and living one's life. He considered matters ranging from whether life is worth living at all to the limits of knowledge about the world, and from the nature of human psychological resources to prospects for a system of ethics and the proper place of religion, in almost every case exemplifying his commitment to the confluence between theoretical and practical philosophy.

In framing his advice, James is usually careful to acknowledge that we find ourselves subject in everyday life to a wide range of circumstances over which we have no direct control. As Rorty observes, "The world can blindly and inarticulately crush us," revealing the "brute power and . . . naked pain" inherent in human life.[26] Yet even in the face of this reality, James believes that our only option is to act. Complaining about human powerlessness is frivolous and pointless: "The return to life can't come about by talking. It is an *act*. . . . [T]he concepts we talk with are made for purposes of *practice* and not for purposes of insight" (*PU*, 131). As such, the question "what ought I to do?" is the pragmatist equivalent of that used to frame ethical theorizing since the ancient Stoics and Epicureans: "How ought I to live?"

To the extent that James proposes ways of thinking in the cause of acting, he is also proposing an ethics for defining one's life. Our ever-changing circumstances impose an unavoidable labor: to decide how to think and act differently in the future from how we have previously, thus laying out a direction for one's life. With repetition, our responses become ingrained, revised just when they fail to yield the expected or optimal outcome. This is an inevitably first-person project, for only an individual—acting within a social context perhaps, but deciding alone—can "feel at home," determine how she ought to behave, and develop habits of action. As one deals with life's challenges more or less successfully, one develops one's self by way of habitual dispositions, creative responses, and resignation to the limits on human power. James locates in these three aspects of selfhood prospects for meaningful exercise of human agency; that is, for understanding and coping with the events of the world and transforming one's self while doing so.

For James, the ability to create and change one's self by thinking and acting gives hope for real progress in life. As Roberto Unger puts it, for the pragmatists, "everything in the context—our context—can be changed, even if the change is piecemeal. And the change, in the form of an endless series of next steps, can take a direction, revealed, even guided by ideas. We can develop practices and institutions that multiply occasions for our exercise of our power of resistance and reconstruction."[27] This opportunity, James believes, ought to give rise neither to blind optimism and the temptation to overlook or dismiss the vagaries of circumstance (which he describes as "indiscriminate hurrahing for the Universe" [*ERM*, 114]), nor to suffocating pessimism (and consequent downplaying of the powers of human agency), but instead to realistic hope, or "meliorism": provided that one is willing to commit sufficient effort and risk a turn in the wrong direction, a poor choice, or a habit with unfortunate consequences, then one has "a fighting chance" of living well and creating a self to be proud of.

Consequently, for James, the task for a philosophy properly engaged with human lives is not to construct a system that "defines away" the moment of decision, encompasses it within a universal teleology, subordinates it to a particular value-set, or reduces it to an instantaneous quest for epistemological certainty, but instead to inspire and instruct, thereby aiding resolve, commitment, and action. Philosophy "makes a difference" when it inspires commitment of energy and risk taking that is sufficient not just for coping with the world's exigencies but also for living life well. James means to provide an ethics that will guide selection of actions from the range of options, a theory of selfhood that explains the import of those actions, a psychology that makes sense of the habituation of such actions, and a philosophy that inspires energetic commitment to particular courses of action in a moment and over a lifetime. As such, his work ought to be assessed less in terms of its consistency, rigor, and thematic continuity than its potential impact upon people's lives in the face of life's unavoidable challenges.

Hidden in Plain View: Uncovering James's Ethics of Self-Transformation

Although James's commentators have often acknowledged the extent to which his concern with practical issues guided his development of theory, they have not typically highlighted the point in regard to his prescriptions for how individuals might best live their lives.[28] But in the 1960s, two figures in particular—Bernard Brennan in 1961 and John K. Roth in 1969—argued that James's whole oeuvre ought to be understood in terms of his abiding interest in moment-to-moment decisions of practical import, such that James ought to be considered first and foremost as an ethicist. Furthermore, they contended that his ethics is derived from (and best explained in terms of) his ontology, epistemology, and psychology.

As James Campbell has observed, "to maintain that William James was essentially a moralist is hardly a controversial claim. Josiah Royce, for example, wrote that James was 'profoundly ethical in his whole influence'; and this viewpoint has been echoed over the years by Ralph Barton Perry, John Wild, Thayer, and Abraham Edel."[29] West writes that James "is first and foremost a moralist obsessed with heroic energies and reconciliatory strategies available to individuals," a "restless patrician of the street" who favored "a specific way of life" over epistemology and science.[30] But Brennan and Roth go further than merely championing James's credentials as an ethical theorist, with each of them advancing an interpretation of his work in terms of its guidance for the practical, everyday decisions that together comprise a life.

Brennan begins his book *The Ethics of William James* by claiming that "any attempt to understand [James's] moral thought requires, first of all, the construction of an outline of his ethical views, synthesizing the moral implications of his statements on metaphysics, religion, and epistemology, and, of course, his statements on explicitly ethical topics" since "any systematic exposition predominately in terms of one or two of his principal angles of vision, to the exclusion of others, will produce a distortion that is utterly false to James's general intentions."[31] According to Brennan, the most valuable texts for this purpose are "*The Will to Believe*, which affirms the basic importance of moral questions and affirms also the existence of morality; *A Pluralistic Universe*, which develops an ethics-oriented metaphysics; *The Principles of Psychology* (hereafter, *Principles*), which supports James's effort to find an objective basis for ethics by introducing the doctrine of necessary ideas; and *The Varieties of Religious Experience*, which concludes that Christian sainthood embodies the highest morality yet attained."[32]

Despite this holistic approach, Brennan's analysis is missing any consideration of the self, so that, although he builds an intricate picture of interrelationships between James's ethics and wider philosophy, it is not clear why one should *care*, at least in terms of understanding or adopting his recommendations. By contrast, such matters are "front and center" for Roth, who contends that James's philosophy begins with the realization that human life "is a search for meaning. It is an attempt to find and to give sense to existence. Ethical reflection seeks to establish guidelines that will establish an environment where the chances for finding a meaningful pattern of life are enhanced for each individual . . . [and] the norms that a man may follow do not become norms without a man's active participation in their establishment."[33] James's ethics is meant "to help people make good judgments and good decisions and to assist us in determining what is most important and valuable. Doing these things involves paying close attention to experience, engaging in critical inquiry, recognizing fallibility, and taking risks, including the risks that go with admitting error and striving for correction."[34] Roth contends that James's philosophy is framed by his belief that "our lives are permeated by a freedom that gives us the chance to shape the world that we inhabit" and so is an attempt to answer the following question: "If I am free to act in a variety of ways, how should I act and what values should I take to be the most important? Human freedom forces this moral question upon us."[35]

Yet the imperative of individual freedom doesn't stand alone: "James's ethical philosophy revolves around his assumption that the most important values . . . are those of freedom, on the one hand, and personal and social unity, on the other."[36] For James's ethics to be complete requires not just recommendations for how best to exercise one's freedom but for how that might cohere with one's community. According to Roth, his answers are not to be found in any "fully systematic ethical theory" or "system of rules," but instead in "a general ethical stance towards existence" that is "scattered throughout his writings."[37]

Like so much of the extraordinarily innovative and insightful mid- to late-twentieth-century scholarship on pragmatism, the work by Brennan and Roth was ignored by the philosophical mainstream and even by most scholars working on pragmatism. Only in the last decade or so has it reemerged, initially in footnotes to studies of James's works most obviously concerned with ethics, and then among philosophers pursuing more holistic analyses. Of the latter, four figures in particular have been central to renewed interest in James's ethics, although several others have contributed mightily.[38] Foremost among them, Sarin Marchetti agrees that James's ethics relies on a series of disparate ideas located across a range of books and lectures, including some that don't relate to ethics in any obvious way.[39] He interprets James as conducting a radical critique of the presuppositions, methods, and goals of traditional ethics, both as a field of philosophical inquiry and as personal practice.[40] Marchetti argues that for James, we should give up ethics conceived as a search for certainty realized in projects of foundationalist system-building and focus instead on the particular moral problems that we encounter and our practices in response. For James, our habits carry potential both for "stiffening" behaviors to the point where they constitute "the very mortification and deadening of the self" but also "the key, vital activity through which we constitute ourselves as purposeful and effective subjects."[41] Whether particular habits are of the first kind or the second is decided, Marchetti argues, by the extent of one's therapeutic self-criticism and self-training—those "practices of the self" presaged in James's early publications—which together constitute a form of "self-transformation." Although Marchetti does not attempt a systematic explication of these various threads, his general approach to reinterpreting James's corpus and his emphasis on the dynamics of habit are central to this book, too.

Colin Koopman explores the relationship between James's "will to believe" and ethics in greater detail.[42] He studies James's theories of habit and will in terms of the human capacity for self-reflexive self-review, and argues that the concept of the will to believe—often misunderstood by James's critics as a weak justification for wishful thinking—is actually "a naturalistic account of the value of sculpting our habits."[43] Since habits define much of what is distinctive about a person, Koopman concludes that James's "contributions to moral psychology and normative ethics are both . . . oriented around self-transformation," his response to the difficulties of indecision, and the need to act on moral probabilities rather than certainties.[44] Although Koopman's interpretation is not too concerned with either the intricate psychological dynamics of self-transformative activity or practical exercises for achieving it (both of which are central to this book), he does a fine job of explaining how, for James, "volition is not primarily a relation between our Self and extra-mental matter . . . , but between our Self and our own states of mind" (*PP*, 1172).

Like Marchetti and Koopman, Lucas McGranahan emphasizes the philosophy of self-transformation in his work on James's use of concepts from Darwin's biology to explore the nature of individuality.[45] For McGranahan, too, "James's philosophy is ethical to its marrow," and the ethics is realized primarily by his accounts of individual agency and the selective nature of will."[46] Although McGranahan is more concerned to show that James's philosophy relies on a "Darwinian functionalist model of volition" than with the methodological imperatives, metaphysics, and psychology emphasized in this book, he agrees that "the result [of James's theory of the will] is the outline of a viable moral philosophy with concrete consequences for pedagogy—taken both in the narrow sense of educational theory and in the broadest sense in which philosophy is intended to offer a general theory of living and dying well."[47]

The fourth key figure in the recent renewal of interest accorded James's ethics is Trygve Throntveit, whose thematic emphasis is slightly different again. He proposes that James's disparate works can be read as elements of a single project describing how freedom is possible, such that "the multistranded philosophy of knowledge, truth, and experience that came to be known as pragmatism was originally, and remained essentially, a tool in the quest to imbue human life . . . with moral significance."[48] Throntveit conducts his investigation at the nexus between morality and politics, with less emphasis on the philosophical and psychological particulars of James's ethics and more on the various ways in which his conceptions of freedom play out in diverse practices and institutions.

This book takes its lead from the interpretative start-points provided by figures like Brennan and Roth, advancing a line of study from those darker days of James scholarship preceding pragmatism's renaissance. It is intended to "put flesh on the bones" of the minority view that James ought to be understood as an ethical theorist (among very many other things), not just for his insightful criticisms of traditional normative ethics but for advancing a constructive theory for how to live a good life. The position advanced here—that it is not merely ethical *themes* that James provides us but a holistic and comprehensive theory—is meant as a step forward in reinterpreting James's humanistic pragmatism. It shows that even some of James's more obscure and technical analyses contribute to a conception of the self that is consistent with the first-personal experience of selfhood and the undervalued capacity to change one's self and life in small but significant ways. Like those "lonely laborers" working during the dark decades of the "eclipse," I aim to honor the classical pragmatists, not by rehearsing their philosophy but by "putting it to work," encouraging changes to philosophical practices and individual lives.

Specifically, I construct an orderly version of James's therapeutic pragmatism by weaving together his more substantial commentaries with those that McDermott describes as "aperçus, gleanings, quick shots of wisdom that strike at the heart of the everyday: that is, the fabric in and through which we live our lives" and then to test them according to pragmatist criteria: the practical differences that they can make.[49] For James, a good reader gives sympathetic consideration to an author's context and worldview, placing themselves "at the centre" of the author's "philosophic vision" in order to "understand at once all of the different things it makes him write or say" (*PU*, 117).[50] Regarding James's ethical recommendations, a critical point of context is the scattering of relevant ideas across numerous works written over the course of a lengthy career, so that a representation and interpretation of them means *necessarily* drawing from disparate works intended for disparate audiences. "Since human action is a response to some vision of the world, it cannot be sharply separated from the other . . . branches of philosophy," and so James's various theorizations of that vision contribute to and are components of his ethics.[51] By reading together James's early works on scientific and philosophical psychology with later ones on the metaphysics of experience, pedagogy, and ethics, and emphasizing thematic and conceptual continuities, I intend to do justice to James's restless and ambitious spirit. My point is not that James *intended* these works to be "of a piece" but that they can be productively and helpfully interpreted as if they were—and that such an interpretation gets to the center of James's vision for pragmatism. To use James's own words: "I have sought to unify the picture as it presents itself to my own eyes, dealing in broad strokes" (*P*, 5).

Chapter 1 situates James's philosophy within the radical socioeconomic and intellectual circumstances of his time, highlighting the extent to which they undermined long-established certainties of American life. It shows that James meant his philosophy to be a response to the consequent questioning of extant beliefs, values, and conceptions of the world; or more precisely, a philosophically founded therapeutic recommendation not just for coping with such changes but also for exploiting them in pursuit of a richer, more rewarding life.

As interpretative exegesis, this book emphasizes how James's methodological decisions led him to surmount traditional disciplinary boundaries (sometimes despite himself) such that the various aspects of his work together lay the foundation for his ethics. Chapter 2 shows how James relies on introspection to access and describe the dynamism, richness, and complexity of experience. Taking his lead from David Hume's empiricism (but pressing well beyond it), he describes the relational character of conscious life both phenomenologically and ontologically as a "field" on which relations between ideas are constantly made and changed. In terms of ethics, James's account of experiential dynamism highlights the importance of novelty and context for one's decisions and indicates the potential to change the configuration of one's ideas—and thus one's lived reality.

James's phenomenological and ontological perspectives on the self are considered in chapter 3. Both of these are evident in his early work, *Principles*, where they indicate ambiguity between a purely descriptive project and a search for the very structures of consciousness and mind. Chapter 3 contends that the ambiguity is best resolved by a phenomenological reading of James's texts, as it enables his various conceptions of self-identity to be reconciled with his account of how we respond freely and creatively to experiential circumstances. On this view, selfhood has a "felt quality" describable as the arrangement of one's ideas around an ever-changing point of focus. Usually, that focus is decided by chance circumstances and one's immediate habitual response, and we pay it little heed. But at other times, it is determined by careful, deliberate attention to matters of special interest. Concentrated attention allows us to intervene in the moment between a stimulus and an otherwise habitual response and to create new configurations of ideas that, over time and with repetition, harden into new habits of thought.

Chapter 4 examines James's pedagogical recommendations for changing habits of thought and action in pursuit of a richer existence aligned with one's interests. It lays out his account of habit in detail, highlighting the extent to which conscious life relies upon deeply engrained patterns of thought. But the psychological mechanisms for habit formation bring associated risks, too: one might overlook or ignore new ways of appreciating one's circumstances and capabilities or adopt simplistic conceptions of the world such as those offered by some sciences and religions, leaving one blind to other possibilities. James shows that life-enhancing ethics requires us to avoid ways of thinking that are simplistic or too rigidly patterned. By concentrating deliberately on one interest rather than another, or pursuing new relationships between ideas, one can not only respond to the world effectively but also challenge habits of thought that have come to define one's character. For James, character development, or self-transformation, is a lifelong project of reflective decision-making, risk taking, and habit formation. As soon as we stop paying attention to our habits, we tend to avoid energetic pursuit of our interests, thus ceding the potential for a more satisfying life.

The work concludes by recalling James's place in pragmatism's history as a philosophy of practice. James provides a pragmatist ethics oriented toward self-betterment. He does not propose that we can take complete control over our lives by sheer effort or "the power of positive thinking," as some self-help theories suggest. For James, our fate is neither completely in our own hands nor entirely out of our control. His sophisticated, subtle, and nuanced analyses—not always consistent, and sometimes difficult to piece together—show that we have some capacity for influencing the kind of person that we become and the kind of life that we lead, however constrained we are by the vagaries of circumstance.

In his celebrated and controversial work, *The Self Awakened: Pragmatism Unbound*, Unger writes of Golden Age pragmatism:

> Its promise of freedom from many-sided dogma, its abandonment of the claim to see the world from the stars, its embrace of the awkward situation of the human agent, struggling against the institutional and conceptual structures that shackle him, its offer to help him loose and reinvent these structures so that he may become greater and more vital as well as less deluded—none of this would have been enough to make pragmatism what it is today: the philosophy of the age.[52]

For Unger, classical pragmatism is in the ascendant because it has not been denuded of a primary focus upon self-conscious human agency, the context sensitivity of our decisions and actions, or prospects for changing one's own life. These elements, rejected during philosophy's "emasculation" and "retreat to more defensible lines," are pragmatism's richest and most important, loaded with potential for better understanding of how lives and communities might be improved.[53] I hope to show that Unger is right. After all, James tells us, our "ideals ought to aim at the *transformation of reality*—no less!"[54]

Chapter 1

Locating James's Therapeutic Project

It is something to be able to paint a particular picture, or to carve a statue, and so to make a few objects beautiful; but it is far more glorious to carve and paint the very atmosphere and medium through which we look, which morally we can do. To affect the quality of the day, that is the highest of arts.

—Henry David Thoreau, *Walden; or, Life in the Woods*

An Ethics of and for Its Time

William James lived "on the fulcrum between two historical worlds: the gentility of late Victorian New England and the cosmopolitan currents of modernity."[1] The scale and impact of changes undergone by America in the years that James devoted to philosophy (from the late 1870s until his death in 1910) make them among the most significant in the nation's history. Construction of the railroads, introduction of industrial manufacturing, and the rise of sophisticated financial markets transformed the domestic economy and brought radical changes to ways of life that had evolved over centuries. The natural environment was transformed and exploited in ways that challenged the image of the American pioneer battling against nature. The scale of industry, business transactions, education, and administration increased dramatically, encouraging managerialism and increasing work-skill specialization. Ownership of the means of production became more concentrated, and the products of personal labor increasingly passed to industrial barons rather than the family table. New theoretical accounts of the world

21

rested upon forecasting and the statistics of probability rather than inherited authority.[2] Finally, the rise of modern science enabled machinery to replace human power, and necessitated faster problem-solving, production, communication, and transmission of information and goods.

These changes represented the triumph of material progress over American's spiritual and religious foundations. Mechanistic science generally, and the new Darwinian understanding of nature particularly, undermined some of the most deeply held assumptions of American religion and individualism, such that, as James put it, "The nature-lore [science] and the individual-fate-lore or religion have become so differentiated as to be antagonistic."[3] Human beings were newly theorized by scientists and artists alike in terms of biological forces. Simultaneously, the growing human sciences—anthropology, experimental psychology, behavioral and market economics, and sociology among them—shifted focus from explanatory to applied knowledge in the cause of progress.

As James observed, such "mutations of intellectual climate . . . make the thought of the past generation seem as foreign to its successor as if it were the expression of a different race of men. The theological machinery that spoke so livingly to our ancestors . . . sounds as odd to most of us as if it were some outlandish savage religion" while "the vaster vistas which scientific evolutionism has opened . . . have changed the type of our imagination" (*PU*, 18). Rather than humble worshippers, Americans realized to a greater extent their capacity for altering and controlling their world. Natural theology and religious spiritualism fell into relative neglect, conceived less as reliable means for determining human value than as last resorts for those holding out in a struggle against "the final challenge of Matter, live, terrible, steel-fingered, boiler-souled, to the manhood of the earth."[4]

Paul Croce has written that "uncertainties in other departments of cultural and intellectual life may come and go, but religious and scientific uncertainty is doubt at its most profound."[5] James was keenly aware that such doubt could generate feelings of passivity and helplessness: the belief that one could not influence things for the better, whether by way of action or prayer. In response, he made it his business to convince his peers that their actions really could improve their lives, regardless of the challenges they had to face.

Newfound confidence in science and mechanism also damaged assumptions on which rested belief in freedom of the will and the emotional need for meaningful interactions with the demystified natural world. As early as 1869, preoccupied with his inability to improve his poor health, James wrote that "we are wholly conditioned, that not a wiggle of our will happens save as the result of physical laws."[6] Nearly forty years later, he placed his observation in a historical context:

> For a hundred and fifty years past the progress of science has seemed to mean the enlargement of the material universe and the diminution of man's importance. The result is what one may call the growth of naturalistic or positivistic feeling. Man is no lawgiver to nature, he is an absorber. She it is who stands firm; he it is who must accommodate himself. Let him record truth, inhuman tho' it be, and submit to it! The romantic spontaneity and courage are gone, the vision is materialistic and depressing. (*P*, 15)

On this view—one that James would challenge and reject throughout most of his career—it might *seem* that we are "in control" of the world by means of our scientific understanding and ability to manipulate it, but science reveals that even our means of manipulation are defined and limited by natural laws and mechanisms. Despite appearances to the contrary, the material world has a "final say" in what we can and cannot do. If this were the whole story, then free will and all that it entails (including moral responsibility) would be illusory.

The consequences of science's undermining traditional beliefs and values extended beyond humankind's self-image into another kind of materialism, too. It came to be reflected in peoples' assessment of themselves and others on the basis of their possessions, as James notes in a public lecture:

> We should be ashamed of our lack of spirit if we were from the outset content to be financial failures. So we load up with houses, goods, servants, furniture, bric a brac, responsibilities, a burden all assumed for the sole purpose of making ourselves like other people, correct in their eyes, we become mean, dishonest, cruel, everything that the market-war demands, and die vitiated and satiated, and bored, without knowing why we were created. If the other people had been simpler, we should have been so too; If none of us had been so rich, we all would have been happier; but of the spirit of the age . . . we all are both accomplices and victims. (*ML*, 106)

By diminishing such traditional human values as social unity, faith, and moderation, scientific materialism encouraged the rise of consumerism. Consequently, the romantic ideal of the independent and heroic individual was overrun on all sides by materialism, constituting a "crisis of individual autonomy": on the one hand, the ability to influence one's circumstances was brought into doubt by scientific materialism; on the other, consumerist materialism meant that one was assessed by others according to what one owned rather than one's efforts and achievements.[7] Modern civilization had become, in James's words, a "big, hollow, resounding, corrupting, sophisticating, confusing torrent of mere brutal momentum and irrationality" (*ECR*, 157).

Just as the way these changes impacted upon the devout believer deviated from the experience of the scientifically inspired empiricist, so, too, the various strata of American society felt them in disparate ways. The working classes were "too busy trying, in strenuous fashion, to survive the economic and social roller-coaster ride that defined the era" to bother very much with "any generalized ideology."[8] By contrast, the wealthy New Englanders among whom James was raised and educated, and with whom he most often mixed, experienced a different kind of crisis; a "cultural turmoil" arising from, and reflected in, preoccupation with the new psychology, widely adopted in religion's stead. Their growing wealth and power were reflected in what seemed a meaningless life; an easy existence requiring little zest, commitment, or effort that James called "*tedium vitae*"; tedium as a way of life. It was evidenced by a range of symptoms typifying "nervous exhaustion" (fatigue, headache, neuralgia, anxiety, uncertainty in decision-making, inability or unwillingness to work, and depression), and demarcated by a diagnosis of "neurasthenia."[9] James called it, alternatively, "Americanitis," which he described as a national tendency toward "over-tension and jerkiness and breathlessness and intensity and agony of expression" that handicapped efficiency and spiritual well-being (*TT*, 123).

Suffering his own misfortunes, and as sensitive as anyone to the impacts of materialism, James felt keenly the effects of the new socioeconomic circumstances. Like many of his peers, he agonized about finding a meaningful occupation, flitting between academic and professional fields after abandoning a passion for painting, arguing with his domineering father about the matter, and struggling with the urgency of the new work ethic.[10] On top of this, he experienced poor physical health for much of his life, lost close and much-loved family members (including his sister, two brothers, and an adored cousin) to illness and despair, was burdened by his father's imposition in childhood of a demanding God, and struggled with the conflict between science and faith, two of the most potent forces in his life. It is hardly surprising that James should experience his own version of the crisis of the individual (first and most dramatically in 1860, but again, it seems, several times in later years), lending urgency to his philosophical endeavors.[11]

James believed that his own travails typified those of many Americans, and if he could formulate means for coping with his own challenges, these same approaches might be taken up by others: he could "cure" Americans of *tedium vitae* one person at a time. This would prove typical of James's first-person approach to philosophy, for "much of James's mature work was devoted to finding the words to construct persuasive arguments out of the templates of the hard-won beliefs of his own life."[12]

Links between the private worries of philosophers and the issues pursued in their public works are much remarked. Regarding the pragmatists' responses to the crises of late nineteenth- and early twentieth-century America, Bruce Kuklick notes that "it is possible to show that . . . the concerns of the cultural elite determined what problems would be philosophically viable and the men who became philosophers did so to resolve personal crises": after all, Harvard philosophy had focused on the problems of Bostonian gentry since at least the mid-nineteenth century.[13] Furthermore, James declared openly that he perceived on behalf of his own "class" (that is, the "educated class" corresponding "to the aristocracy in older countries") an obligation to utilize its education and good judgment "to divine the worthier and better leaders" in the cause of saving democracy (*ECR*, 110, 106).

This aside ought not to diminish the urgency and extent of the public problems that James meant to address. In much of America, people were struggling to come to terms with rapidly changing values and circumstances and adopt social roles and behaviors that placated new familial and communal expectations.[14] Nor should James's personal concerns detract from his intention to aid the wider community. As Patrick Dooley points out, James "remained adamant that his calling was to respond to a general audience of men and women who were understandably concerned with the inroads that science and the rise of Darwinism seemed to be making on the secure place that religion, free will and personal responsibility had had," a task that he pursued even in the face of fierce criticism from more technically minded philosophers.[15] In this spirit, James writes: "It seems to me that the fraternity of the intellectual have got to resist *this* craze [of 'market-war demands' and 'success-worship']. . . . Intellectual men must stand for the dignity of smaller worldly successes, or of worldly failures. Later generations will recognize the wisdom, history will vindicate it, when the present success-craze, born of our material expansion, shall have spent its vitality" (*ML*, 107). We seem to still be waiting for that vindication.

It is debatable whether James's responses were therapeutic in the sense attributed to that term today; that is, as means for healing disease. James refused to conceive of his philosophy as "specific for low spirits" and displayed little obvious interest in the details of healing (even when training as a doctor).[16] Yet there is strong evidence that James intended his work to be therapeutic in *some* sense. Daniel Bjork, whose biography of James explores how his self-examinations influenced his work, notes that James not only "wanted to be healthy" but that, for him, "health was the natural state and disease should yield to the proper therapeutics. Disease was not to be simply accepted as part of the human condition."[17] Throughout James's corpus are proposals for restoring wellness and avoiding ill health, as in his recommendations for saving young men from excessive drinking, discussion of the merits of hypnotism, and overt support for the "mind cure" movement of his day (*TT*, 110; *PP*, 1194; *VRE*, 114). Consequently, while it might not be correct to attribute to James a proposal for healing *disease*, it does seem right to conclude that his philosophy is therapeutic in a more general sense: intended to have positive impacts on mind and body.

As such, we ought not to read James's humanist philosophy as a purely intellectual undertaking but rather a therapeutic one: "never a mere theory," to use Perry's words, "but always a set of beliefs which reconciled him to life and which he proclaimed as one preaching a way of salvation."[18] For James, philosophy ought to enable one to improve one's lot by enunciating, justifying, and enabling productive approaches to "self-help." Although such a conception of philosophy has fallen from favor (to be replaced by vacuous pop psychology on the one hand and abstruse technical philosophy on the other), it seemed to James entirely appropriate for the circumstances of his time.

James's therapeutic intent is evident not just in his concern to salve (or indeed, save) his peers but in his approach to solving the issues underlying their problems. With his fellow pragmatists, James believed that "eliminating the obstacles of outmoded philosophical and political doctrines would free Americans to solve the problems they faced."[19] Yet he found "dismal shallowness" in both "the spiritualistic systems" and "the free-thinking tendency which the *Popular Science Monthly* . . . represents" (*EPh*, 4). Whether recommendations for action relied upon religious doctrine or experimental science, "the result in both cases alike is mediocrity," either acceding to religious orthodoxy or turning towards "an equal but opposite dogmatism about scientific answers" (*EPh*, 4).[20] It was obvious to James that neither religion nor science can explain the world *in toto*. On the one hand, an overreliance on science can lead toward a deterministic worldview that diminishes belief in human agency, just as it had once for James himself. On the other, overreliance on religion can encourage retreat from the sometimes harsh and difficult realities of the world as it is experienced. As James observes, both positions can prove demoralizing, even paralyzing.

Although James was reluctant to countenance religion's irrationalism or set aside science's capacity to explain and manipulate the physical realm, neither could he ignore science's challenges to human longings, values, and hopes. Scientific rationality "is so superbly complete in *form*" as to reconcile "the thinker to the notion of a purposeless universe, in which all the things and qualities men love . . . are but illusions of our fancy attached to accidental clouds of dust which will be dissipated by the eternal cosmic weather as carelessly as they are formed" (*PP*, 1260). A wholly scientific picture of the world contains no sense of nature's mystery or purpose, diminishes its awe-inspiring grandeur, and undermines "a sense of the importance and purposiveness of human life."[21] Furthermore, it is at odds with other precious values, some of which (devotion to righting injustice, selflessness, and so on) have made people with strong religious beliefs "impregnators of the world, vivifiers and animaters of potentialities of goodness which but for them would lie forever dormant" (*VRE*, 285).

Consequently, the starting point for James's therapeutic philosophy is at odds with that of such champions of science as his contemporaries W. K. Clifford, Hermann von Helmholtz, T. H. Huxley, Herbert Spencer, John Tyndall, and Wilhelm Wundt, for whom *only* evidence wrought of the scientific method was admissible in formulating a worldview. For James, we ought to avoid any form of explanation that eliminates or explains away the surprise and possibility that we experience routinely. Instead, "If we are finite, if our experiences are finite, and if there is no higher meaning which transforms these experiences into something other than the way in which we undergo them, then the affairs of time, our things and events, are to be taken at face value," as McDermott puts it, and we should take it that "the transcendent and infinite are abstractions, ways of compensating for the opacity and ambiguity in our human experience."[22]

As such, philosophy's modernization ought not to involve veering toward mathematicized logic (thereby aligning philosophy with the rise of the sciences in much the same way that psychology had done in declaring independence from philosophy) but instead working out what Emerson called "an original relation to the universe"; a new way for conceiving and situating human lives. Freed from both religious doctrine and scientific closure, philosophy's "educational essence lies in the quickening of the spirit to its *problems*," redescribing the challenges of human life in ways that encourage new intellectual and other perspectives and solutions (*EPh*, 5).

James situated his other great philosophical preoccupation, the confrontation between free will and determinism, in similar terms to that between religion and science. If science is considered the only way of properly explaining our existence, and granted that it explains more phenomena over time, then it seems reasonable to suppose that it will eventually reveal the mechanisms behind our decision-making, in much the same way as it has the mechanisms of biological functioning. If this were so, then free will could be considered "free" in no meaningful human sense, and it would become impossible to account for ethical claims in terms of an individual's values, choices, and actions. "Pessimism must then be fatalism," James concluded, extinguishing human autonomy and the possibility of individualistic morality.[23]

Yet as with the dispute between religion and science, everyday experience reveals a counter-position: that there *is* in fact "active originality and spontaneous productivity" in our lives, evident as "mental fact" (*ML*, 136). Our experience indicates that we *do* exercise free will in everyday life and that circumstances are altered by our having done so. This realization provides James with a lead for his subsequent work because "a philosophy whose principle is so incommensurate with our most intimate powers as to deny them all relevancy in universal affairs, as to annihilate their motives at one blow, will be even more unpopular than pessimism," and so "better face the enemy than the eternal Void!" (*WB*, 70–71). Philosophy ought to begin with the evidence of everyday experience—including evidence of free will and the commensurate causal efficacy of our decisions—and then work toward answering the challenges posed by materialism and determinism, rather than assuming away such evidence to accommodate the claims of science.

While James's therapeutic pragmatism sought to resolve the contemporary conflicts between religion and science and free will and determinism, it was a general observation about their *form* that led to his distinctive philosophical ambitions and method. Time and again, James observed, philosophy tended to approach complicated problems by establishing and arguing for each of two directly opposed and simplifying positions: knowledge (or certainty, or fact) against ignorance (or uncertainty, or fiction), good against evil (or bad), "is" against "ought," strong against weak, true against false, and being against nonbeing were other examples. Often, it seemed to him, such disputes resolved to differences merely of philosophical style. On one side were "tender-minded," "rationalistic, dogmatic, system-building" philosophers like Aristotle, Descartes, Spinoza, Leibniz, Kant, and Hegel, who resorted to "optimistic theories, supplementing the experienced world by clean and pure ideal constructions"; on the other were "men of hard facts"—such "tough-minded" philosophers as Socrates, Locke, Berkeley, Hume, and Mill—who had an "empiricist, critical, sceptical" bent and were "more in touch with actual life . . . but less inspiring" (*ML*, 381–82). Whether the consequent bifurcations in philosophy were the products of conceptual framing or intellectual style, they seemed to James never to be resolved, so that debates about them contributed little in the way of practical guidance for how real human lives might (or ought) to be conducted.

James held loftier ambitions for pragmatism, claiming that "philosophic study means the habit of always seeing an alternative, of not taking the usual for granted, of making conventionalities fluid again, of imagining foreign states of mind" (*EPh*, 4). Rather than arguing on behalf of either "the scientific loyalty to facts" or "the old confidence in human values and the resultant spontaneity, whether of the religious or of the romantic type," James wished instead to *reconcile* them; to make them congruent in a way that enabled both philosophical progress and practical guidance for a lay audience (*P*, 17).[24]

Reading James today, the "salvation" to which he commits might seem relatively modest: to at least make life "worth living" (*WB*, 34–56). "It surely is a merit in a philosophy to make the very life we lead seem real and earnest," he writes, and "nothing could be more absurd than to hope for the definitive triumph of any philosophy which should refuse to legitimate, and to legitimate in an emphatic manner, the more powerful of our emotional and practical tendencies" (*PU*, 28; *PP*, 943). Reading him from the imagined perspective of James's own time, however, his ambition seems urgent and significant. Whether siding with religion or science, free will or determinism, one's most fundamental beliefs are capable of constraining engagement with life's problems and opportunities; to "*obstruct* action and literally *stifle* the flow of life" in ways that "most definitely affect our behavior."[25] James intends to provide means for releasing thoughts and actions from the constraints of dominant paradigms old and new so that people not merely *cope* with extant circumstances but *thrive*, realizing a fuller range of life's possibilities.

Ethics Reconsidered

For James, then, philosophy is more than intellectual puzzling or a professional calling. Instead, it is a means for resolving personal doubts and troubles and propagating therapeutic recommendations of value to those Americans struggling with challenges to established conceptions of themselves and the world. James writes, "If thought is not to stand forever pointing at the universe in wonder, if its movement is to be diverted from the issueless channel of purely theoretic contemplation, let us ask what conception of the universe will awaken active impulses capable of effecting this diversion" (WB, 65–66). In this spirit "the really vital question for us all is, What is this world going to be? What is life eventually to make of itself?" (P, 62). For him (as for Dewey, and such later figures as Wittgenstein, Michel Foucault, and Rorty), philosophy is a practice of reflecting upon the mode and activities of individual lives in order to improve them, rather than, say, a process of abstraction or concept-creation in pursuit of knowledge, and so his philosophy generally and his ethics specifically are of a piece.

Perry, a student of James's and his most celebrated early biographer and interpreter, was crucial for establishing the conventional understanding of his ethics.[26] Not only was he first into print on the subject (in his *The Thought and Character of William James*), but he provided such a confident and competent assessment that his views went largely unchallenged for decades.[27] Yet because Perry's account is largely biographical, it fails to draw out the complexity and viability of James's ethics as a whole. Instead, it considers a single essay, "The Moral Philosopher and the Moral Life" (hereafter "Moral Philosopher") from 1891 (reprinted six years later in *The Will to Believe and Other Essays in Popular Philosophy*), James's "only published discussion of theoretical ethics" and "only systematic discussion of . . . ethical theory," according to Perry, as his final say on the subject.[28] As Edie points out, this exclusive focus meant that Perry (together with Dewey) remained not "at all sensitive to James's notion of the free act and, when they read all he was writing about it, they tended simply to cancel it out in their own minds as just another sign of 'his neurasthenia' which would best be passed over in silence."[29] Because James never resiled from positions recorded in his essay, left nothing in his unpublished papers to indicate dissatisfaction with it, and didn't publish anything further that addressed ethics overtly, acceptance of the piecemeal analysis presented by Perry and others became commonplace.

"Moral Philosopher" is James's attempt to justify a humanistic and secular ethics that disposes of the need for a transcendent source or measure of ethical value. He proposes a wholly naturalistic approach whereby all questions about ethical value ought to be resolved by referring to empirical facts, or, more specifically, the experiences of thinking beings. Beyond these "bare bones," much about the essay is contested. Perry interprets it through the lens of some lecture notes that preceded it, an approach that has the advantage of highlighting themes carried over from James's earlier *Principles* but the disadvantage of assuming that the essay is a *conclusion* to James's ethics rather than a starting point.[30]

Perry considers James to be advancing "an eclectic version of consequentialism which stresses the interest[s] of human beings as the proper target of moral concern," and the maximization of those interests as its prescriptive principle.[31] He amplifies four contentions in James's essay that he takes to be decisive. First, that it is impossible to construct any proof of goodness or badness free from presuppositions about what defines "good" and "bad." As Perry puts it, for James, "to *prove* a thing good, we must conceive it as belonging to a genus already admitted good. Every ethical proof therefore involves as its major premise an ethical proposition; every argument must end in some such proposition admitted without proof."[32] Second, that there is no morality *inherent* within the nature of things (or events), leaving us with no option but to resort to the selectivity of human consciousness and feeling to make moral judgments (*WB*, 147).

Third, since direct conflicts between moral claims make it impossible for all of them to be realized, we should as a general rule make decisions that realize as many as possible.[33] It is not the case that everything anointed by human reason as "good" is compossible; in James's words, "There is hardly a good which we can imagine except as competing for the possession of the same bit of space and time with some other imagined good" (*WB*, 153–54). To cope, we ought to "consider *every* good as a real good, and *keep as many as we can*. That act is the best act which *makes for the best whole*, the best whole being that which prevails at least cost, in which the vanquished goods are least completely annulled."[34] Of course such a (highly contestable) principle will not resolve all ethical conflicts, and so, fourth, disputes ought to be decided by dismissing claims that are "not organizable"—that is, inconsistent with socially established traditions—in favor of others that "fit" with communal expectations. Taking these themes together, Perry concludes that James's "principle is clear: value derives ultimately from the interests of the individual; and the social whole is justified by the inclusion and reconciliation of the individual parts."[35]

Perry's brief account, and the prominence it accords James's earlier lectures, led commentators to a particular understanding of "Moral Philosopher." In the first place, many have set aside the extent to which it ranges across philosophical fields. James tells us that he is interested in three questions that arise in ethics: the "psychological question" concerning the "historical *origin* of our moral ideas and judgments"; the metaphysical question, concerning the meaning of ethical words like "good" and "obligation"; and the casuistic one, regarding how we might measure goods and decide what we ought to do in practice when there is a conflict between moral claims (*WB*, 142). Not only do these questions take him well beyond the bounds of traditional moral philosophy, but they also engage him in a wide-ranging interpretative project unaccounted for by Perry. For example, as Hilary Putnam points out, James tackles the "metaphysical question" not by seeking after a *definition* of extant terms but by inquiring into the *nature* of obligation, good, ill, and the like, often from a first-person perspective.[36] For James (as for pragmatists generally), it is impossible to solve metaphysical and ethical issues independently of one another, since metaphysical notions of self must account for conduct, and metaphysical investigations will always be conducted from a perspective defined by first-person interests.

In the second place, commentators have tended to overlook James's stated aim for the essay. "The main purpose of this paper," he tells us, "is to show that there is no such thing possible as an ethical philosophy dogmatically made up in advance. We all help to determine the content of ethical philosophy so far as we contribute to the race's moral life. In other words, there can be no final truth in ethics any more than in physics, until the last man has had his experience and said his say" (*WB*, 141).[37] James will argue that there are no universal moral rules or fixed principles, valid always and in all circumstances. Human values are always developing, with each person and moral decision as relevant as the next.

Perry, too, overlooks the significant implications of James's opening gambit, for if "there can be no final truth in ethics," then "the nature of existence demands that we use our freedom to take a stand on questions about the nature of existence and moral values, and all of us do deal with these questions somehow, even though the decisions may not be fully articulated."[38] Had Perry pursued this point, his rendition of the essay (and selection of its key themes) would likely have been very different. For example, James holds that the moral philosopher's task "is to find an account of the moral relations that obtain among things, which will weave them into the unity of a stable system, and make of the world what one may call a genuine universe from the ethical point of view" (*WB*, 141). If we read James's quote about the moral philosopher's task with emphasis on human freedom and the contingency of moral rules, then he can be taken as highlighting a need for ongoing assessments of unique moral circumstances in an attempt to balance social unity with the maximization of individual freedom, whereas if with Perry we downplay both of these themes, it seems to suggest a simpler ordering of moral claims according to a single "right" assessment of moral relations.

None of this is meant to suggest that Perry's selective reading of James's essay is wholly to blame for the little interest and respect accorded his ethics. James's exposition is problematic of its own accord, largely because he sometimes seems to adopt an unqualified utilitarianism, as in these quotes:

> Since everything which is demanded is by that fact a good, must not the guiding principle for ethical philosophy (since all demands conjointly cannot be satisfied in this poor world) be simply to satisfy at all times *as many demands as we can*? That act must be the best act, accordingly, which makes for the *best whole*, in the sense of awakening the least sum of dissatisfactions. In the casuistic scale, therefore, those ideals must be written highest which *prevail at the least cost*, or by whose realization the least possible number of other ideals are destroyed. (*WB*, 155)

> There is but one unconditional commandment, which is that we should seek incessantly, with fear and trembling, so to vote and to act as to bring about the very largest total universal good which we can see. (*WB*, 158)

Here, James is arguing for a principle of maximizing either the number of moral demands satisfied or the "total universal good," matters of simple arithmetic rather than moral effort. This has led some commentators to suggest that "James's moral theory should be understood as a *demand-satisfaction* version of utilitarianism since demands are, properly speaking, what his version of the principle of utility aims to maximize," while "satisfying as many demands as we can at the least cost . . . should be understood as James's moral *ideal*—and he seems to understand this utilitarian ideal as the highest and most inclusive one that we can imagine."[39] At the very least, it seems to indicate that James is inconsistent, endorsing both qualitative moral diversity and straightforward quantitative optimization.

However, on a more holistic reading of "Moral Philosopher," it can be argued that James is not in fact championing a traditional utilitarianism. One reason for maintaining that James's principle differs from the utilitarianism of Alexander Bain and Hume is because it neither proposes the maximization of pleasure over pain or happiness over unhappiness, nor holds the satisfaction of demands to be an intrinsically valuable first-order *property* (as are knowledge, beauty and happiness, for example, in traditional utilitarian dicta). Although James agrees that *some* of our moral evaluations are of such a "brain-born kind," he thinks that things become more complex once we look beyond the "coarser and more commonplace moral maxims" (*WB*, 143). Then we find what James considers to be *innate* preferences, claims, and demands that also are worthy of moral consideration. He provides such diverse examples as a "sense for abstract justice," a passion for music or philosophy, a "feeling of the inward dignity of certain spiritual attitudes, as peace, serenity, simplicity, veracity," and an aversion to "querulousness, anxiety, egoistic fussiness" (*WB*, 143). Such "purely inward forces" cannot be reduced to quanta of happiness and utility, James argues, and yet their status as moral claims means that they must be taken into account when making moral decisions.

James's recognition of the diversity of our moral demands also explains why he is not obviously susceptible to one of the key criticisms of utilitarianism: that unless the maximization principle is sufficiently qualified, it is possible to imagine cases where satisfaction of a particular moral demand could outweigh the value of many others, or where morally unconscionable outcomes would follow from strict adherence to the principle. For example, we might imagine a case where maximization of utility would favor the demands of millions of people "on the simple condition that a certain lost soul on the far-off edge of things should lead a life of lonely torture" (*WB*, 144). That our moral intuition, innate sense of justice, and natural repulsion speak so strongly against unquestioning application of the utilitarian metric in such a case supports James's inclusion of them among factors relevant for moral decision making.

Another reason favoring the revisionist reading is that the context of James's remarks on maximal satisfaction of demands shows him to be defining a *communal* arrangement in which opportunities for self-expression are maximized, rather than an ethics founded solely on the utility or happiness of each individual. Although he considers utilitarian ethics right to focus on the preferences and needs of individuals, he thinks that it fails to account adequately for inevitable clashes between people over whose preferences (and which of them) should be realized and whose should be "butchered" (*WB*, 154). As McGranahan points out, "The Jamesian demand may be for literally anything under the sun. Since no demand is absolutely disallowed, a demand can only be called into question by being incompatible with other demands. Given this metaethical framework, James concludes that our only "categorical imperative" is to work toward a cooperative universe that allows for the greatest possible satisfaction of mutually compatible demands."[40] There is simply no way of "quantifying away" the qualitative diversity of moral claims, as strict adherence to the utilitarian calculus would have it. As such, James says, "that act must be the best act . . . which makes for the *best whole*" in terms of minimizing the demands (including those intuitive demands mentioned above) left unsatisfied (*WB*, 155).

To this point, James still seems susceptible to charges of being overly subjectivistic and perhaps even relativistic. If there is no authoritative standard by which to differentiate better moral judgments from worse ones, and if all the desires of disparate individuals are accorded equal weight in seeking the best communal outcome, then his moral philosophy seems problematic indeed. Apparently, any actions, even awful ones, might be justifiable for a theory concerned above all with satisfying the most demands. In the case of deliberate self-transformation specifically, it might seem as if certain selfish or even destructive decisions might be justified even if they cause great upset or damage to one's family, friends, and community, provided that they are consistent with maximizing demands overall.

But James thinks that his theory addresses such concerns by favoring decisions and actions that minimize the extinguishment of other moral demands. A murderer would extinguish all the future demands of his victim and damage the ability of the victim's loved ones to realize their goals, at least insofar as they involved interactions with the victim. Someone who leaves behind their family to pursue a selfish life unfettered by commitment would "butcher" the interests of family members, including various affections, dependencies, trust, hopes and expectations for the future, and so on. Stealing the property of another person would eliminate all those benefits associated with the owner's use of, pride in, and reward from the item's acquisition and possession.

As such, the idea that the property and person of other people ought to be respected enables more moral claims to be realized than would commission of violence or theft, for example, and so is consistent with James's position. In fact, he contends that his position tends to favor conventional morality. The moral ideals adopted and adapted by a community over time are the products of a kind of long-term "experiment" into how human beings best accommodate one another's interests and tend to be more inclusive and supportive of self-expression than those guided just by the happiness or utility of individuals (*WB*, 155–56). An ethical person tends to consider the impacts of their decisions on the interests of the people around them by referring to moral conventions. Although this will certainly be difficult on occasion and might even give rise to uncertainty about the right course, "over the long run, persons of good will, who are not blind to the needs and desires of others, will enact values that promise to enhance human life."[41]

As we shall see, James makes such arguments relevant to an ethics of self-transformation by translating them into the language of individual experience and the moderating effects of social relations but not in "Moral Philosopher."[42]

Revisionist readings of "Moral Philosopher" have often questioned such interpretations as Perry's by emphasizing James's declaration that it was meant as a critical work rather than a proposal for a new ethical system. Franzese, for instance, contends that it "does not work as an outline of a moral theory because it was certainly not intended to be one. On the contrary, it was intended to show the futility of that traditional philosophical task."[43] James's declared intent—"to show that there is no such thing possible as an ethical philosophy dogmatically made up in advance" (*WB*, 141)—is consistent with his critique of ethical theories that propose or rely on a final principle or univocal definition of the good. (James criticizes explicitly Kant's deontology; the utilitarianism of Jeremy Bentham, James and John Stuart Mill, and Herbert Spencer; and ethics founded in "serving God.") Such theories prescribe which facts are relevant for moral assessment and how and by what criteria they ought to be assessed. For James, such reductionism is patently inadequate for the complex moral circumstances of the real world, where, as James puts it, "every real dilemma is in literal strictness a unique situation; and the exact combination of ideals realized and ideals disappointed which each decision creates is always a universe without a precedent, and for which no adequate previous rule exists" (*WB*, 158). Human freedom and life's novel and ever-changing circumstances preclude universal moral codes, and so "slavish adherence to rules needs to be replaced with a critical analysis of facts and problems that can lead to forms of moral action that are creative and tailored to fit particular situations."[44]

Furthermore, universalized principles tend to downplay the distinctively *human* elements of any moral challenge. They tend to be inconsistent with ordinary moral phenomenology (for example, awareness of a tendency to employ different moral criteria from one judgment to the next, or to favor one's own welfare over that of others) and to ignore the intricate mental processes by which individuals assess their circumstances, make ethical decisions, and consequently commit to actions. "Goodness, badness, and obligation must be *realized* somewhere in order really to exist," James writes, "and the first step in ethical philosophy is to see that no merely inorganic 'nature of things' can realize them. Neither moral relations nor the moral law can swing *in vacuo*. The only habitat can be a mind which feels them" (*WB*, 145). Our experience does not provide predetermined evaluative criteria for deciding moral insights and judgments but rather we establish such criteria in the course of deciding and acting, according to the circumstances. In this regard, James is especially scathing of utilitarianism—the theory with which his own ethics is sometimes mistaken—for relying upon a needlessly pessimistic moral psychology and an overly narrow conception of consequences and for venerating utility, pleasure, and happiness as the only (and correct) criteria of moral goodness.

When James emphasizes the specific conditions that situate any moral judgment—the fact that every moral decision is for this person, under these circumstances, here and now—he is also saying that no *other* person or system of ethics can decide the case on that person's behalf. As Roth puts it, for James, "The universe and human values are in the process of development. He takes this to mean that each existing person contributes to the character of the world and to its value. Each man is entitled to hold a view about the universe and to make free choices about moral values."[45] Since moral decisions are a matter for the individual, informed by definite psychological traits in particular circumstances, there is no place for a *system* that dictates the process or decides the outcome. To utilize a moral guideline established in advance would require each moral case or question to be molded to its language and criteria, something that James thought "deadening" and inadequate.

The implications of James's critique of traditional moral philosophy are profound. When he argues that any adequate system of ethics must account for the phenomenological and psychological aspects of actual moral judgments, he is taking a severely naturalistic stance. For James, words like "good," "bad," "right," and "obligation" do not refer to the "absolute natures" of acts, but to "objects of feeling and desire" having "no foothold or anchorage in Being, apart from the existence of actually living minds," so that "nothing can be good or right except so far as some consciousness feels it to be good or thinks it to be right" (*WB*, 150, 147). As such, one's acts will count as evidence of the thinking that led to and decided them, rather than being "right" or "wrong," "good" or "bad" in and of themselves. To express the idea baldly, morality for James is all about thinking.

In terms of his specific therapeutic project, James's discussion of the particularity of each ethical judgment highlights the error of moral determinations based on the edicts of either the churches (for whom moral guidance is grounded in or derived from some infallible work or supernatural being) or scientists (many of whom rejected outright the possibility of a spiritual dimension to human lives):

> Everywhere the ethical philosopher must wait on facts. The thinkers who create the ideals come he knows not whence, their sensitivities are evolved he knows not how; and the question as to which of two conflicting ideals will give the best universe then and there, can be answered by him only through the aid of the experience of other men. . . . In point of fact, there are no absolute evils, and there are no non-moral goods; and the highest ethical life—however few may be called to be its burdens—consists at all times in breaking rules which have grown too narrow for the actual case. (*WB*, 158)

For James, there is conflict not only between the prescriptions of the two then-dominant credos but also between the realities of human moral life and *any* worldview that prescribes moral values. Values are always relative to a context and best decided by careful, intelligent reflection on extant circumstances. As Croce records, "Most people [in James's time], when they thought about scientific or religious truths, simply ignored the growing mountains of professional research and instead looked to non-intellectual justifications of their beliefs and convictions and to uncomplicated expressions of information."[46] But for James, such moral dogmatism and conservatism were expressions of the absolutism that he criticized.

A situation in which univocal moral codes undercut established mores without providing an acceptable alternative was intolerable for James, having led Americans to their crisis and diminished the human capacity for sensible and rational moral decision-making in complex circumstances. For him, "The recognition and acknowledgement of the concrete, practical point of view of human beings in the world would eliminate the many tragedies caused by blind insistence on reducing all explanations to the one assumed to underlie and account for all the rest, whether this is ultimately thought to be physical, political or religious."[47] The way forward was not to provide more conclusive scientific evidence or more authoritative religious dogma, but to give up the idea of foundational ethics altogether and rely instead on sound human reasoning.

In this regard, James urges us to take seriously a similarity between ethics and science. Both confront the facts of existence by experimental testing of hypotheses about the nature of the world and predictions about the outcomes that will follow from a decision or interpretation. Since each experiment might theoretically produce an unexpected result, it would be wrong to adopt any epistemological or ethical stance as final and absolute. Reliance on a moral principal that is supposed to be immune from life's organic reality "changes a growing, elastic, and continuous life into a superstitious system of relics and dead bones" (*WB*, 158). Consequently, James writes, "so far as the casuistic question goes, ethical science is just like physical science, and instead of being deducible all at once from abstract principles, must simply bide its time, and be ready to revise its conclusions from day to day" (*WB*, 157). We simply must remain open to the possibility of amending our moral values and judgments over the course of a lifetime.

Life, Character, and Experimentation

James's rejection of moral certainty and the traditional quest for a supreme and comprehensive moral theory does not indicate his abandonment of the broad question of how best to live. On the contrary, he writes that "this life *is* worth living . . . *since it is what we make of it, from the moral point of view*; and we are determined to make it from that point of view . . . a success" (*WB*, 55). James made clear in "Moral Philosopher" the need for general principles to help us mediate personal satisfaction with social harmony. But rather than universal rules, James's guidance for his troubled peers will take the form of principles informed by each person's own, unique experiences, applied according to the particular characteristics of the moral challenge faced; a set of "*theories* [that] *become instruments, not answers to enigmas, in which we can rest*" (*P*, 32).

Central to James's multifaceted approach to ethics is his rejection of the idea that moral life is distinctively different from other aspects of human existence. James thinks that "moral life is just that, life, or a process of feeling, activity, and growth. Desires lead to activities that lead to experiences that lead to new desires, and 'The pure philosopher can only follow the windings of the spectacle.'"[48] Traditional ethics has failed to provide an adequate account of actual moral thought and practice because it has failed to acknowledge continuity between morality and the rest of human interests and actions. Given the experimental nature of human existence—the process of ongoing adaptation to new circumstances, informed by an ever-growing fund of experiences—this observation opens the way for considering our moral decisions and actions in the same kinds of ways as other decisions and actions.

It is tempting under the influence of traditional moral philosophy to conceive of such an approach (and James's general moral principles) in terms of moral "ideals" that are relatively consistent in the long term. If we consider life's various experiments in terms of achieving, expressing, or advancing toward a preconceived end, then, it seems, a kind of moral unity is attainable, notwithstanding the challenge of deciding on an ideal (or set of ideals) appropriate to the length and complexity of most human lives.

But James considers such an approach deficient in two respects: one practical and the other theoretical. He thinks that ideals as they are usually conceived—that is, as a kind of abstract goal to pursue whenever the opportunity presents—are "the cheapest things in life," and that "the most worthless sentimentalists and dreamers, drunkards, shirks and verse-makers, who never show a grain of effort, courage, or endurance, possibly have them on the most copious scale" (TT, 163). On the practical deficiency, James writes, "The more ideals a man has, the more contemptible, on the whole, do you continue to deem him, if the matter ends there for him, and if none of the laboring man's virtues are called into action on his part,—no courage shown, no privations undergone, no dirt or scars contracted in the attempts to get them realized" (TT, 164). On the theoretical shortcoming, he observes that ideals are not only too abstract to reliably unite one's moral judgments with other purposes, interests, drives, thoughts, actions, and decisions, but there is not even a clear distinction to be drawn between ideals and these other phenomena: determination of an ideal necessitates a judgment, for instance, and to refer to an ideal means invoking a context defined by one's momentary interests.

James's position exemplifies one of pragmatism's most decisive claims: that the lived world is characterized by interpenetration (and integration) of facts, values, and theories.[49] The relevant facts in the case of moral judgments are *all* those that inform and provide context, whether psychological, physical, cultural, historical, or whatever. The relevant values are not just those to which the decision-maker refers deliberately, but all of those adopted over the course of one's life (not always deliberately or even consciously), together with those that any action consequent to the decision might substantiate.

Pertinent theories are not just those that might explain the decision in ret-rospect by providing an account of the relationship between fact and value, but the very nature of the connections between fact and value constructed by the decision-maker.

Consequently, James contends, we ought not to consider ideals and values as abstract principles to guide or decide particular judgments but as *instantiations* of a judgment in a particular set of circumstances. It is not the case that one first adopts a value like "honesty," say, and then seeks to act according to that abstract ideal in every instance (even those where honesty is patently *not* the best policy), but rather that we act in a manner that we decide is appropriate in the circumstances and, over time, we recognize a pattern of truth-telling that we call honest, together with a range of con-sequences. Our moral welfare is not determined by a relationship between our judgments and some preordained external standard but rather by the way that one's judgments and actions "hang together" to define one's moral character. Furthermore, since every choice and action is a component of life's ongoing but piecemeal experimentation, moral philosophy ought to account as much for one's ambitions, visions, attitudes, habits, plans, and circumstances as for the actions in which they issue. As such, the moral philosopher's guiding question ought not to be "What are the right rules to follow?" or "Which ideals ought we to pursue?" but rather "What general approaches to moral judgments and actions will lead to our betterment?"

It is possible also to read James as suggesting a merely retrospective role for ethics, a kind of "genealogy" of moral decision-making that traces a path from decisions and actions to the values that they instantiate. Plainly this would be inadequate for a theory intended to guide moral thinking and action. But in fact, James's approach is informed by his meliorism—the future-oriented belief that, if one goes about life carefully and thought-fully, and is "willing to live on possibilities that are not certainties," then improvement is possible—and he intends his pragmatist advice for all those capable of such an attitude (*MT*, 124). On a melioristic view, the absence of universal values ought not to recommend nihilism or hopelessness ("the nightmare view" of life [*WB*, 54]), but rather the realization, reminiscent of twentieth-century existentialism, that we are free to make the most of life's myriad possibilities; to realize "the zest, the tingle, the excitement of reality" from within the "teaming and dramatic richness of the concrete world" (TT, 135; *WB*, 62). As James observes, "Where a process of life communicates an eagerness to him who lives it, there the life becomes genuinely significant" (*TT*, 134).

For James, the moral person "must vote always for the richer universe" (*WB*, 158). Each new opportunity that we encounter is a part of life's potential, and pursuing these opportunities is what makes for a "rich" life. Each exploration and realization of a new way of thinking and living forces the "growing, enlarging, liberated self . . . to meet new demands and occasions" and to readapt and remake itself in the process.[50] Whether or not we achieve our life's potential—whether we *grow* to a greater or lesser extent—rests upon the series of such decisions over the course of a life. As such, for James, the ethical significance for a person of each moment is not limited to "what act he shall now choose to do," but rather what we "shall *become* is fixed by the conduct of this moment" (*PP*, 277). Not only is there no way to tell what other opportunities pursuing this one might lead to, but each acceptance or rejection of an opportunity entrenches one's commitment to a life of either energetic engagement, growth and enrichment, or relative passivity and stagnation. Although the richer life will entail some losses and failures, these are as nothing, James thinks, compared to the wasted potential of a poorer one.

Understood this way, ethics becomes an exercise in positivity and creation rather than prohibition and rulemaking, one rewarded by a satisfying and energizing life rather than by the consolations of asceticism or an after-life. Like his predecessor Emerson, James intends his ethics as reflexive guidance for improving one's own existence by realizing more of life's potential good (he mentions self-esteem, mental well-being, relaxation, development of personal capabilities, creativity, and appreciation of the richness of life's meanings, satisfactions, and fulfillments),[51] rather than, say, by tackling the "theoretical" problem of avoiding evil.

Of course, for James, what precisely one ought to make of life's possibilities is not decidable on the basis of an ethical imperative, authoritative direction, or epistemological or ontological certainty. Instead, he encourages us to think and act in ways that decide and promote our own purposes and sense of fulfillment, whatever they might be. The aim is not "to make war against one's self," as with traditional proscriptive ethics, but "to fashion a style of existence, a mode of the self, in which we lower our defenses enough to strengthen our readiness of the new, our attachments to life, and our love of the world."[52]

Robert Roth summarizes the relationship that James establishes between ethics and human developmental potential in this way: "Morality has to do with acts that further one's development as a human being in a creative [or experimental] way. One makes free choices and performs free acts that lead to one's self-fulfillment and in that very process becomes a good moral person."[53] It is not that we aspire to some idealized moral version of ourselves or that there is some aspect or form of ourselves somehow separate from real-world decisions, guiding life's experiments, but rather that we realize (or fail to realize) our moral potential in our experiences. As such, the good life ought to be conceived as a series of experimental self-creative engagements with life's myriad possibilities rather than a series of activities projected toward a predetermined ideal.

As Smith points out, "That we are unfinished beings living in a world as yet unfinished means that we have practical work to do in shaping our world and the transforming of ourselves."[54] Whether one is engaging more energetically with life's opportunities, adopting and committing to different ideals, taking a different approach to balancing one's own interests with those of others, or even deliberately setting aside traditional ethical rules inculcated in youth, one is *changing* something about one's self. (To emphasize the deliberate nature of the project, I will call it "self-transformation" in preference to such alternatives as "self-realization," "self-development," or "self-experimentation.") As we shall see, James's ethics is much concerned with the nature of such changes and the nature of self.[55]

The prospect of improving individual lives through the gradual accretion of patterns of thought and action is crucial for the Golden Age pragmatists. Dewey provides the most succinct summaries, as in an 1893 essay that begins with an observation about the theory's prevalence:

> In the newer contentions regarding the moral end, the idea of "self-realization" insists upon its claims. The idea seems to me an important one, bringing out two necessary phases of the ethical ideal: namely, that it cannot lie in subordination of self to any law outside itself; and that, starting with the self, the end is to be sought in the active, or volitional side rather than in the passive, or feeling, side. Yet with those who use the phrase, there is often a tendency, it seems to me, to rest in it as a finality, instead of taking it as a statement of a problem. As warning off from certain defective conceptions, in pointing to an outline of a solution, it is highly serviceable; whether it has any more positive and concrete value depends upon whether the ideas of self and of realization are worked out, or are left as self-explaining assumptions.[56]

It is James who tackles most completely and vigorously the "working out" that Dewey considers so important, providing an alternative to moral theories where the self is either the moral end (as in Kantian deontology) or merely the means for producing consequences (utilitarianism) by showing how the self might be both morally responsible for, and a product of, decisions made and interests pursued.[57]

For James, moral guidance must be informed by a philosophical understanding of how human beings make sense of experience and a metaphysical account of experience itself. Since the meaning and context attached to moral decisions are psychological phenomena, moral theory ought to attend to the workings of the mind, too; and because one's physical presence in a world of objects and other people provides much of this context by way of sensory input (and often demands a bodily response), James feels an obligation to address that as well. Indeed, James's "working out" of the ethics of self-transformation ranges far and wide, from his theory of habit to the metaphysics of self, and from the nature of will to the workings of education.

Unsurprisingly, such a broad scope means that aspects of James's ethical "workings out" are scattered across his many works, major and minor, their relevance to moral theory rarely signaled. Marchetti is right that James gives voice to his "peculiar overall moral perspective . . . in the interplay" between disparate works, some of which are "expressively dedicated to moral *issues*," others addressing "arguments of moral *relevance*," some "whose *intention* is moral," and yet others "with moral *implications*."[58] It is left to his interpreters to piece together the disparate components into a cohesive and coherent whole, a project conducted here in the coming chapters. Of James's contemporaries, Dewey best characterized his therapeutic ethics, highlighting the need to "fight against induration and fixity" in one's self in order to "realize the possibilities of [its] recreation" experimentally: "The growing, enlarging liberated self . . . goes forth to meet new demands and occasions, and readapts and remakes itself in the process. It welcomes untried situations" because they provide the best opportunities for growth, and "*the* end is growth itself."[59] Among recent philosophers, McDermott has provided brilliantly evocative presentations, some of which will be called upon later.[60]

A positive assessment of the completeness of James's ethics is not universally shared. Edel, for instance, believed that "James's moral philosophy remains sketchy," and that while he did "produce material on the subtle human emotions and feelings that enter into morality . . . and of the sanctions that operate in human conduct," he nowhere provided an ethics proper, by which Edel means "technical answers to technical questions of moral philosophy."[61] As such, Edel rejects the kind of approach to James's work taken by Brennan and Roth—and by implication, the one taken here—on the grounds that they focus too much on "the cognitive orientation, metaphysical and epistemological, as well as [on] bringing out the values and virtues that emanate from the cognitive orientation" and not enough on defining and explaining distinctively *moral* decision-making.[62]

A rejoinder to Edel and others who object to James's "shifting the ground" of moral inquiry rests upon acceptance or otherwise of the argument in "Moral Philosopher" that moral theory ought to give an adequate account of the psychological practices underlying our ethical judgments and practices. If James's position is accepted, then a "cognitive orientation" seems entirely appropriate for his therapeutic project: consciousness is the realm in which one's circumstances and experiences coalesce in moral decisions and consequent actions. As Marchetti puts it, "By giving up a detached, third-personal description of the various facets of our selfhood in favor of an engaged, first-personal one, James makes room for a different picture of the way in which psychological considerations might be relevant for ethics. . . . Rather than one of *foundation*, the relationship between ethics and psychology would thus be for James one of *emergence*."[63]

The mismatch between James's approach and Edel's preference for "technical" moral theory seems to resolve to this: Edel overlooks or rejects the critical tenor of "Moral Philosopher" and expects James's alternative account to address the same kind of issues as those approaches that he rejects. But as we shall see, James pursues "technical answers to technical questions" in ethics by using philosophical psychology because he thinks that the answers are to be found in the mind's dynamism rather than in abstract philosophical reasoning.

For James, "books upon ethics . . . so far as they truly touch the moral life, must more and more ally themselves with a literature which is confessedly tentative and suggestive rather than dogmatic. . . . Treated in this way ethical treatises may be voluminous and luminous as well; but they never can be *final*, except in their abstractest and vaguest features; and they must more and more abandon the old-fashioned, clear-cut, and would-be 'scientific' form" (*WB*, 159). For ethics to be relevant beyond the philosophical firmament, it must forgo preoccupation with, and reliance upon, idealized circumstances and judgments, and deal instead with the messy circumstances, barely visible opportunities, and ongoing experimentation typical of real life. Although costly in terms of philosophical brevity and precision, James's approach will prove its worth in day-to-day realization of the potential of one's own life and self. As McDermott expresses James's conception of the ethical project, "The self that we accept ourselves to be is but one tenuous shaping, which is vulnerable to forces that can up-end it and cause us to present ourselves to the world in a multiple number of profoundly different ways. The task is obvious. We must seize the world on behalf of our own version and it is this version that is to become our self."[64]

Chapter 2

Uncovering Life's Potential

Relational Experience

The psychology of the self has succeeded so well that it is now the instinct of most of us to turn for a cure for our ills back within ourselves rather than to the nature of things.

—Allan Bloom, *The Closing of the American Mind*

Experience and Ethics

James's insistence that moral theory ought to account for, and incorporate, the psychological and practical realities of human decision-making represents a bold philosophical move founded in the pragmatist commitment to collapsing traditional distinctions between facts, values, and theories. Only with this move, James thought, could moral philosophy address the urgent challenges accompanying the rise of science and the diminution of traditional human values in America. By acknowledging the complex interactions between ambitions and values, extant circumstances, human psychological capabilities, and modes (or "styles") of moral decision-making, ethics can critique simplistic recommendations arising from science's materialistic bias on the one hand and religion's supernatural speculations on the other, as well as provide meaningful normative guidance. But James's approach requires a sound and complementary philosophy of the very conditions of lived reality, for only if he can account for how facts, values, and theories interact and assume meaning in individual lives is it reasonable to adopt the explanations and recommendations that he provides subsequently.

Throughout his corpus, James highlights "the contrast between the richness of life and the poverty of all possible formulas," arguing that theorization of the conditions of lived reality ought to forefront the characteristics of that reality *as they are experienced* rather than by way of philosophical abstraction (*ECR*, 489). The problem is not that philosophy's concepts and categories (or, indeed, those of science and other fields of inquiry) originate from outside experience—there are no transpersonal alternative origins—but rather that, in making them more widely applicable, there is inevitably too much generalization. For example, a monistic worldview might have originated from a personal sense of harmonious unity among aspects of nature; however, as an explanatory concept, James rejected monism as a sterile and ill-defined metaphysical effort to unify the whole variety of experience so as to simplify our relationship to the world and obviate the need for further investigations (*P*, 63–79). Such concepts and conceptual analysis "prevent us from maintaining a reflective confrontation with those areas of our conscious experience not given to systematic definition" and diminish the diversity of experience itself, rendering it "repetitive, even trite."[1]

Such detraction from life's intricate particulars indicates that no concept-dependent philosophy "can ever be anything but a summary sketch, a picture of the world in abridgement, a foreshortened birds-eye view of the perspective of events" (*PU*, 9). In ethics, use of conceptual abstraction to ground or guide moral judgments subordinates the complexity of experience and human responses to a generalizable definition of the good. Such an approach, Marchetti suggests, "prevents us from appreciating the essentially perspectival source of our attribution of value, since it describes our capacity to make moral distinctions and take moral decisions as deriving from a superior axiological dimension in which such distinctions and decisions are grounded, rather than as a genuine expression of our point of view on things."[2] James's hortatory alternative aims to reveal and guide the complex realities of moral life as it is lived rather than as it is neatly theorized.

To surmount the problems with traditional philosophy, James upends the whole approach on which it rests. Rather than emphasizing theory, authoritative concepts, disinterested reasoning and certainty, James focuses on practice, effort, speculative experimentation, and variability. Such emphases are part and parcel of his preoccupation with "concreteness"; that is, with providing a philosophy adequate to the perplexing circumstances that often confront and confound us. James means to engage as directly as possible with real-world circumstances and our actual hopes and needs in "the world of concrete personal experiences to which the street belongs," "multitudinous beyond imagination, tangled, muddy, painful and perplexed," and evidencing "the contradictions of real life" (*P*, 17–18), rather than providing "principles and general views" that serve as mere "abstract outlines" (*P*, 23–24). For him, "the whole originality of pragmatism, the whole point in it, is its use of the concrete way of seeing. It begins with concreteness and returns and ends with it" (*MT*, 115–16).

James's declared commitment to practical outcomes and real-life deci-sions in problematic circumstances means to engage such a lay audience as his psychically troubled peers. He realizes that "knowledge about life is one thing; effective occupation of a place in life, with its dynamic currents passing through your being, is another" (*VRE*, 386). His familiarity with a range of academic and professional disciplines encouraged fresh perspectives that bypassed some of philosophy's stultifying debates and oversimplifications, which sometimes meant ignoring or downplaying its most elevated questions and best-established responses.[3]

Referring to normative principles of morality, James wonders, "Shall we . . . simply proclaim our own ideals as the law-giving ones?" before replying, "no; for if we are true philosophers we must throw our own spontaneous ideals, even the dearest, impartially in with that total mass of ideals which are fairly to be judged" (*WB*, 151). For James, "the role of the moral philosopher is . . . at once descriptive and exhortative," returning us to the "rough ground of our practices" and to melioristic experimentation.[4] James aims to investigate the concrete conditions of moral life without intellectualizing them, and to provide normative ethical guidance without suggesting that it arose naturally or obviously from those conditions (or could be "read off" them). The burden of exploring and experimenting with consequent possibilities is one's own.

James believed that theorization of the concrete conditions of living, including moral decision-making and action, ought to proceed from the perspective of individuals rather than groups, communities, or schools of thought, a view that chimed with his overarching ontology. Whether one conceives of the world principally in terms of unity or disjunction, monism or pluralism, is, he thinks, "the classification with the maximum number of consequences," and "the most central of all philosophical problems" (*P*, 64). James argues in "The One and the Many" that while there is empirical and philosophical evidence on both sides, only pluralism—a commitment to conceiving of the world as a multitude of individual entities, sometimes interconnected and oftentimes not—is consistent with our experience of the world, leaving open the prospect of further empirical investigation (*P*, 72–73). Consequently, he conceived the world as "*a set of eaches, just as it seems*" (*PU*, 62), and when we use words like "experience," "being," "reality," "environment," and "world," we denote merely conceptual groupings of such elements as experiences, individual lives, objects, perspectives, and so on.

This ontological commitment, combined with James's intense interest in the human condition and human ambitions (Cornel West claims that "James is even more anthropocentric than Emerson; man truly is the measure of all things for him"),[5] focused his work much more on prospects for fulfillment in the lives of individuals rather than communities. James writes that "surely the individual, the person in the singular number, is the more fundamental phenomenon, and the social institution, of whatever grade, is but secondary and ministerial" (*ECR*, 97). For him, realization of communal and societal initiatives relies primarily on the self-determination, power, and agency of individuals and sometimes small groups ("the man more than the home, the home more than the state or the church," as Perry puts it).[6] "What are the causes that make communities change from generation to generation?" James asks. His answer? "The difference is due to the accumulated influences of individuals, of their examples, their initiatives and their decisions" (*WB*, 164).

This does not imply that James thought individuals could be understood in *isolation* from the social environment, however. He does not sidestep either the influence of social and economic circumstances on individual agency or promote an egoistic or self-centered morality (although some philosophers disagree, as we shall see). He also acknowledges ways in which the individual is dependent upon their community: "The community stagnates without the impulse of the individual. The impulse dies away without the sympathy of the community" (*WB*, 174). As Francesca Bordogna puts it, "The individualistic strain so evident in James's social philosophy was tempered by a complementary emphasis on solidarity and community," and he intended to emphasize how social meliorism rested upon the capacity of the individual to "make him/herself into a strong, competent, and effective citizen."[7] As evidenced by his involvement in social causes, James was mindful of the complex interrelationships between the individual and social realms, although political action alone would not impact the moral lives of individuals deeply enough for his liking.

Social progress for James involved combatting the large-scale economic and social forces of his day, not by means of full-scale revolution but rather small-scale activism and revolt. Combining this view with his individualism, James thought that such rebellion is best enabled by encouraging people to think more independently, to trust lessons and values born of experience, and to commit energetically to the changes most important to them. The greatest moral risk is that such capabilities are nullified by large-scale forces: "It seems to me," James writes, "that the great disease of our country now is the unwillingness of people to do anything that has no chance of succeeding. The organization of great machines for 'slick' success is the discovery of our age; and, with us, the individual, as soon as he realizes that the machine will be irresistible, acquiesces silently, instead of making an impotent row."[8] Defending one's own capacity for action is burden enough without pursuing wholesale social change: "It is enough to ask of each of us that he should be faithful to his own opportunities and make the most of his own blessings, without presuming to regulate the rest of the vast field" (TT, 149).

For a range of practical and theoretical reasons, then, James is concerned with *individual* lives rather than ethical constructs applicable to whole communities: "The facts and worths of life need many cognizers to take them in. There is no point of view absolutely public and universal . . . The practical consequence of such a philosophy is the well-known democratic respect for the sacredness of individuality" (TT, 4). As Roth defines the critical question at this juncture, "Where will the moral philosopher find the principles that are needed to help us structure our existence? James believes that they will emerge only through reflection on the structure of human experience as it is lived through."[9] Having abandoned aprioristic and metaphysical foundations for ethics, and siding with the individual perspective over the social, James's pragmatism affirms the ethical importance of first-person experience for validating and guiding the moral judgments and actions of individuals.[10]

James's focus on first-person experience is perhaps the most important characteristic of his critical and constructive philosophy, and indeed, of much classical pragmatism. Whereas philosophy is typically "dogmatic, and pretends to settle things by pure reason," substituting conceptual abstractions for "real life, . . . the only fruitful mode of getting at truth is to appeal to concrete experience" (SPP, 18–19). "So long as we deal with the cosmic and the general, we deal only with the symbols of reality," James insists, "but *as soon as we deal with private and personal phenomena as such, we deal with realities in the completest sense of the term*" (VRE, 393). Since they are first personal, such phenomena are evident just in our conscious lives and *cannot* be accurately conceptualized: "Psychologically considered, our experiences resist conceptual reduction, and our fields of consciousness, taken simply *as such*, remain just what they appear" (*SPP*, 78).

James's commitment to the "private and personal phenomena" of experience, "*psychologically considered* [emphasis added]" is crucial for defining how his ethical project deviates from the dominant tradition and justifies a holistic interpretation of his corpus. As Dewey writes, typically "philosophers have denied that common experience is capable of developing within itself methods which will secure direction for itself and . . . create inherent standards of judgment and value. . . . To the waste of time and energy, to disillusionment of life that attends every deviation from concrete experience must be added the tragic failure to discover what intelligent search would reveal and mature among the things of ordinary experience."[11] James means to correct such failures. For him, the transience of human experience emphasizes what McDermott calls "the profound inferential character of our values, decisions, and disabilities," and James's task is, "in phenomenological terms, . . . to diagnose the experience of the individual as we cast about in the flow of experience, bringing a mind-set but also getting and begetting as the press of the world filtered into our consciousness."[12] Contrary to the usual philosophical presumption, James will argue that human experience *does* create direction and establish moral standards for itself, and that the real challenge for moral philosophy is to provide appropriate normative guidance for *that* activity, rather than the ends to which it might be directed.

But it is not James's preference for personal experience over conceptual ideas and ideals that marks his approach to ethics as unique (after all, that view has its predecessors in Western thought, starting with the Greek and Roman Stoics). What *is* unique is *how* James goes about locating normative ethical guidance within experience. Having adopted an individualistic and naturalistic approach concerned above all with the inferential nature of experience "as it comes," he straddles the boundaries between philosophy and psychology. That he means to do so (rather than having been led there in error, perhaps by way of metaphysical confusion) is crucial for deciding how his various works ought to be interpreted as different aspects of the same ethical project.

One interpretation of James's studies of experience (at least those in the period between his earliest publications in the 1860s and his reworkings of themes from *Principles* in the early 1900s) is that he was pursuing a "science of consciousness," "an alternative epistemology to reductionistic positivism."[13] While there is certainly evidence for that view, we ought to remember that James was not pursuing a "science" in the experimental sense that we think of today and that his epistemological project was largely motivated by his radical reconception of philosophy.[14] Another view, also partially correct, is that he meant to conduct formal philosophical analysis of psychological constructs (something like contemporary philosophy of psychology), although this proposal rests on a sharper distinction between psychology and metaphysics than James was willing and able to sustain.[15]

A more justifiable interpretation is that James was conducting "philosophical psychology" in the sense of making observations about, and recommendations for, conscious life that were "at once empirically informed and yet infused by a distinctive philosophical vision."[16] More specifically, "The normative moral descriptions of our subjectivity sketched in *Principles* express a precise philosophical line conveying James's understanding of human nature as something to be ascertained *and* crafted at the same time," so that "James's work in and on psychology is at the same time philosophical—that is, utterly explanatory and conceptual—*and* scientific—that is, descriptive and empirically grounded."[17] On this view, James transgresses the divide between philosophy and psychology in his method, descriptions, and recommendations.

There are several reasons to favor this interpretation. First, it is sensitive to the historical fact that only during James's lifetime (and in some part due to his influence) was the discipline of psychology distinguished from philosophical speculation by establishing itself as an empirical social science. Like Wundt in Europe, James was a "transitional figure at the margin between the new, experimental psychology and the older, philosophical psychology," although he "even more than Wundt, was unable to let go of philosophy and devote himself entirely to the psychology of the laboratory."[18] Second, James's whole corpus mixes philosophical interpretations with psychological observations presented as empirical facts, necessitating difficult decisions about how to interpret introspectively attained insights into the dynamics of consciousness.

Third—and most important—James decided after his early forays into psychology that it was impossible to hold psychology apart from metaphysics, telling a meeting of the American Psychological Association that "no conventional restrictions *can* keep metaphysical and so-called epistemological inquiries out of the psychology-books" (*EPh*, 88).[19] On the one hand, psychology is usually understood as providing factual descriptions of human conscious life, free from both philosophical concerns about the nature of interactions with the world of objects and other people, and such normative considerations as duties, obligations, and principles. Yet for pragmatists, individuals are not mere spectators to events in the world but also participants in them; it is impossible to describe human conscious life properly without including interactions with objects, motivations, and so on. On the other hand, philosophy is concerned (in the main) with generalizable claims, using conceptualization to surmount the vagaries of particular lives and moments. More specifically, ethics, informed by a supposed gap between what is the case and what ought to be, is assumed to provide normative principles underivable from human nature. Yet as we have seen, James accepts neither philosophical conceptualization per se, nor a sharp is/ought distinction in ethics, and his naturalistic approach leads him straight back to experience, the subject matter for psychology. In short, for James, the two fields cannot be kept apart because "our own free, subjective inquiries . . . produce whatever conjunctions we experience, whether in the realm of physics, metaphysics, or morals. Philosophical pragmatism simply articulates this fact in a way that helps us to our advantage."[20]

James's approach to philosophical psychology was relevant for his ethics in several ways. First, it "invites us to pay attention to the way we portray the various aspects of our interiority *as* morally important," emphasizing the influence of interests, attention, will, and habits on our momentary decisions and deliberate pursuit of long-term goals.[21] Second, by rejecting the schism between philosophy and psychology, James also rejects descriptions of the self as always already morally relevant. By conceiving of ethics in terms of experimental self-transformation, he highlights the forward-looking orientation of moral decisions—that is, what one might make of one's life and self—rather than preserving an already-instantiated, morally valuable self. "From such a perspective we can uncover a space for subjectivity that is the outcome of work on ourselves, which seeks to cultivate one's sensibility and attentiveness to the richness and thickness of experience toward which we had previously been morally blind and unreflective," as Marchetti puts it.[22] Third, James's philosophical psychology allows him to mediate between aspects of conscious life that are particular to the individual and those that seem consistent across all (or at least most) people, and propose ways to test their applicability and usefulness.

Perhaps naively given its various roles and meanings in the history of philosophy, James intended the notion of experience to be philosophically uncontroversial. After all, he writes, "Experience in its immediacy seems perfectly fluent. The active sense of living which we all enjoy, before reflection shatters our instinctive world for us, is self-luminous and suggests no paradoxes. Its difficulties are disappointments and uncertainties. They are not intellectual contradictions" (*ERE*, 45). Moreover, "the more primitive flux of the sensational life" and the "concrete pulse of experience appear pent in by no such definite limits as our conceptual substitutes for them are confined by" (*PU*, 127). On the one hand, we generally go through our daily lives untroubled by theoretical questions regarding the nature of experience, even though *what* we experience can be deeply troubling; on the other, we accept that our experiences are limited by our senses and intellect rather than such logical constraints as determine our explanatory concepts.

James defines experience in such a way as to try and maintain its characteristic fluency and continuity: "By an experience, I mean . . . any thing that can be regarded as a concrete and integral moment in a conscious life. The word is exactly equivalent to the word 'phenomenon'" (*MEN*, 221). As "the entire process of phenomena," experience is the most basic fact of human existence: one's life just *is* experiential, defined in terms of the world as it is taken, consciously considered, and responded to (*ML*, 95). It includes not just sense experience (although as McDermott points out, James emphasized the perceptual "in an effort to condemn as potentially dangerous a conceptual order not rooted in our actual experiencing"),[23] but also moral, aesthetic, and religious experiences, enjoyment and pain, anger and fear, desire and repulsion, effort and ease, deduction and creation, matters of interest and indifference, dependencies and independences, and so on. Experience includes memories, needs, passions, desires, dreams, and even delusions just as much, and in the same way, as cause-effect relations and perceptual observations. That some aspects of experience are considered "subjective" and first-personal makes them for James no less real or meaningful than anything known by science.[24]

One challenge arising from James's habit of approaching an idea from several different directions is terminological and theoretical confusion. For example, at some points in his writing, "experience and reality come to the same thing," as Donald Crosby and Wayne Viney point out, so that "experience is James's metaphysical ultimate. Everything real is an aspect and manifestation of this ultimate. Instead of focusing on experience of reality, as most empiricists tended to do, James focused on the reality of experience. Instead of talking about experience of the world, he talked about the world of experience."[25] Without significant qualification and explanation, such a position is fraught, for if reality is an aspect of experience, and "experience" refers to mental life, then solipsism and even full-blown idealism are but a step away, even though James states frequently that such positions are precisely what he aims to avoid.

Some such interpretative difficulties arise from careless terminology. James uses the word "experience" to refer to both the ordinary conscious life of an individual and a kind of abstract metaphysical field, "an aboriginal form of being, embracing consciousness, together with non-conscious or non-mental forms of being, such as bodies."[26] James seems to say that onto this ontological field can be traced such dualistic distinctions as physical and psychical, subject and object, and thought and matter. Although he was aware of his conflation between meanings, and tried repeatedly to address it, his use of the term "*pure* experience" in various of the *Essays in Radical Empiricism* to refer to an ontological category and in *The Varieties of Religious Experience* and *A Pluralistic Universe* to characterize the realm of the Divine, confused matters further.[27] Worse still, he also employed "pure experience" in a sense quite close to ordinary conscious existence, as when he defines it as "the immediate flux of life which furnishes the material to our later reflection" (*ERE*, 46). In this version, experience is "pure" in the very instant of experiencing, prior to reflection and conceptual analysis: "The instant field of the present is at all times what I call 'pure' experience" (*ERE*, 13). We will see shortly that James's definitional prevarication leads him into metaphysical and methodological confusion and was partly to blame for a lasting rift among pragmatist philosophers, but at the same time it opens new ways for conceiving one's own relationship with the world of objects and other people. For now, we ought simply to note the various meanings and distinctions that James attributes to the term.

Having adopted experience as the appropriate subject for phenomenological inquiry, theorizing it presented James with a twofold methodological challenge. First, he must account for experience's incomplete and ever-changing nature, avoiding a purely hypothetical approach (with which he charges Descartes), underlying ontological structures (as in Plato and Kant), and final positions and teleological paths (like Hegel). Such "logics" exemplify the concept-laden, abstract, and timeless approaches that have blighted philosophy, whereas lived experience means "the here and now of decision and action requiring that we seek to determine which particular thoughts, beliefs and items of knowledge 'count' with respect to dealing with the life situation at hand."[28] Second, he must find a way to preserve or evoke the psychological concreteness and particularity of individual experiences, while also providing generalizable, normative moral guidance.[29] James is aware that no matter how sophisticated, any account of experience will distort the fact under description. As Henri Bergson points out (quoting Emile Boutroux), the infinitive form of the verb "experience" means "to undergo, to feel within oneself, to live oneself this or that manner of being."[30] Although theories are important for making sense of one's life, they inevitably lack this felt character.

Yet as James familiarized himself with the latest British psychological research and French studies of the subconscious, he became convinced that psychology, too—even the philosophical version to which he was committed—was flawed because it substituted broad and abstract explanatory concepts for the intricate dynamism of lived experience; its continuity, unity, diversity, relatedness, temporality, order and chaos, and novelty. Inevitably, existing theories illuminated some aspects of experience by casting others into darkness, risking abstraction that "denies us the riches of immediate experience in favor of an ever more vacuous conceptual tradition."[31]

Theorizing Experience: Radical Empiricism

For want of an existing philosophical method adequate to these challenges, James "constructed his own," as Henry Commager puts it, "and the originality and audacity of pragmatism were not the least American characteristics associated with his name."[32] While acknowledging the limits of theorization, James locates a way forward: descriptive "fulness [sic] is elusive," he admits, but "the human intellect" locates "spots, or blazes" that "give you a direction and a place to reach," "formulas" and "conceptions" that enable us to find our way through "the trackless forest of human experience" (P, 258). It *is* possible to theorize rich, ever-changing, and ever-present first-personal experience while avoiding the necessarily abstracting notion of "experience-in-general" or its supposed conditions, but never perfectly—and only if one begins with a sufficiently thorough and careful examination of the *contents* of human experience.

To this end, James aligns himself with the empiricist tradition in the form of a self-declared *radical* empiricism, commencing his investigations with human experiences as they are felt and lived, rather than as they are understood in terms of a preconceived framework or theory. Radical empiricism (James's "most important philosophical contention," according to McDermott)[33] is proposed as a way of theorizing experience *on its own terms*; that is, without presupposing *anything* external to experience itself. If there is no "getting behind" experience, as it were, then James felt that we must agree with traditional empiricists like Hume and Mill and their Darwinian successors that philosophy ought to begin with experience just as we find it.

James's clearest (though nonetheless complicated) definition of radical empiricism comes in *The Meaning of Truth*:

> Radical empiricism consists first of a postulate, next of a statement of fact, and finally of a generalized conclusion.
>
> The postulate is that the only things that shall be debatable among philosophers shall be things definable in terms drawn from experience. (Things of an unexperienceable nature may exist *ad libitum*, but they form no part of the material for philosophic debate.)
>
> The statement of fact is that the relations between things, conjunctive as well as disjunctive, are just as much matters of direct particular experience, neither more so nor less so, than the things themselves.
>
> The generalized conclusion is that therefore the parts of experience hold themselves together from next to next by relations that are themselves part of experience. The directly apprehended universe needs, in short, no extraneous trans-empirical connective support, but possesses in its own right a concatenated or continuous structure. (*MT*, 6–7)

A summary explication of James's tripartite definition will distinguish radical empiricism from concept-laden rationalist and idealist approaches on the one hand and, on the other, the traditional empiricism that provides what he takes to be a promising but ultimately inadequate alternative.

James intends the postulate as a rejection of the tendency in Kantian and Hegelian rationalism in particular to analyze the products of a conceptual analysis, and as affirmation that the relationship between percepts and concepts is defined *within* experience, thereby opening philosophy to the full range of experiential complexity.[34] Rather than exalting concepts as independent of and superior to percepts, as the rationalists tended to do, James holds that concepts are significant just as means for dealing more appropriately with the perceptual realm. The statement of fact addresses the tendency (in Kant's deductions, for instance) to posit a transcendent or transcendental construct by which things are "held together" in conscious life, rather than acknowledging that all kinds of relations between things are just as much matters of direct experience as the things are: "The great obstacle to radical empiricism . . . is the rooted rationalist belief that experience as immediately given is all disjunction and no conjunction, and that to make one world out of this separateness, a higher unifying agency must be there" (*MT*, 7). It is not the case, James thinks, that experience's unity needs to be explained in terms of some higher logical principle, construct, or Godlike agent, since experience does not exhibit any disconnection in the first place. Rather, "Parts of experience do indeed hold together by relations within the flow [of experience] and the 'trans-empirical' supporting principle of the idealists becomes offensively superfluous."[35] Experience is inherently unified, and even though we can discern parts in it, to separate them means necessarily to change their nature.

The generalized conclusion follows from the previous two parts of the definition, and, together with the statement of fact, points toward James's critique of traditional empiricism generally and Humean associationism specifically. Although James praises the empiricists for countering idealism, he contends that they made a mistake by reducing experience to atomic sensations and impressions. In *Principles,* he writes that most studies of the mind "start with sensations, as the simplest mental facts, and proceed synthetically, constructing each higher stage from those below it. But this is abandoning the empirical method of investigation. No one ever had a simple sensation by itself. Consciousness, from our natal day, is of a teeming multiplicity of objects and relations" (*PP*, 219). Classical empiricists were "not empirical enough" (Dewey's words) because they failed to include conjunctive relations in their conception of experience. Even Hume made the "intellectualist error" of departing from the nature of experience as it is experienced and focusing instead on particular ideas and their origin in sense impressions. Had the classical empiricists compiled a more thorough descriptive inventory of the contents of experience, they would have noticed that "*the relations that connect experiences must themselves be experienced relations, and any kind of relation experienced must be accounted as 'real' as anything else in the system*" (*ERE*, 22). Indeed, James argues, the feeling of experience as continuous, dynamic, and distinctively one's own confirms the "fact" of conscious relations, and so the "feeling of relation" has been "the major omission of introspective psychology" (*EPs*, 142–67).[36]

For James, the problems resulting from this error are significant: fundamentally separate units of experience are left "juxtaposed like dominoes in a game" (*PP*, 237) such that "events rattle against their neighbours as drily as if they were dice in a box" (*SPP*, 100).[37] Such experiential realities as the self, free will, material objects, and causation all became "fictions" according to the empiricist analysis because they cannot be traced directly to particular sense impressions.[38] To realign their theory with the dynamism and commonsense realities of *actual* experience, empiricists were forced to introduce extra-experiential conjunctive, unifying elements. Consequently, we find in Hume's work such theoretical concepts as "custom," "general rules," and so on, none of them drawn directly from experience.[39] For James, such theoretical constructions were yet more abstraction, such that "atomistic association" became "empiricism's family malady" (*ERE*, 22).

In contrast to traditional empiricism, a more rigorous version would attend to *all* that we experience *as we experience it*, without logical reduction: "To be radical," James writes, "an empiricism must neither admit into its constructions any element that is not directly experienced, nor exclude from them any element that is directly experienced" (*ERE*, 22). Consequently, James's own radical empiricism refuses to leave out anything that occurs in experience, "including subjective states, properties, and qualities of mind that had typically been overlooked and often devalued in the past" by rationalists, empiricists, and scientific positivists.[40]

Such a holistic conception leads the philosopher to focus on the many disparate ways in which experience "hangs together": "Every examiner of the sensible life *in concreto* must see that relations of every sort, of time, space, difference, likeness, change, rate, cause, or what not, are just as integral members of the sensational flux as terms are, and that conjunctive relations are just as true members of the flux as disjunctive relations are" (*PU*, 126).[41] Abandoning the ultimate priority accorded to sense data, the radical empiricist focuses on relations and not just ideas, changing commitments rather than settled beliefs, and self-sustaining criteria for the validity of claims rather than epistemological or moral foundations. No aspect of experience can be disaggregated from the "relations that unroll themselves in time," and so a complete account of experience is not in James's view a matter of *reconstructing* the complexity of conscious life from simple atomic components but of describing how relations comprise the flow of experience that defines it, or what Smith describes as "the substance of a person's life and being, a biography that is the ongoing record of what we have encountered, undergone and done, . . . a far cry from a succession or even a combination of sense data appearing on the private screen of an individual mind."[42]

James's focus upon the "transitions and tendencies" in experience, evident in the first-person as "conjunctive relations of various grades of intimacy and externality," is the essence of radical empiricism and fundamental to his consequent philosophy of self-transformation. As Mark Uffelman explains, "when applied to the individual, if the parts or portions of experience are related and continuous then the opportunity exists for the individual to develop a meaningful, purposeful existence. Our efforts today have a genuine relation with our future experience and the opportunity exists for the individual to create purposeful long-term existential meaning."[43] By making philosophy a study of these relations, James orientates it toward the future-directed purposefulness of human lives without abstracting from first-person experience: "To be a radical empiricist means to hold fast to this conjunctive relation [i.e., 'continuous transition'] of all others, for this is the strategic point, the position through which, if a hole be made, all the corruptions of dialectics and all the metaphysical fictions pour into our philosophy" (*ERE*, 25).

Adopting radical empiricism as a general philosophical approach does not by itself ensure an adequate conception of the first-personal immediacy of experience or discovery of its possibilities: intending to theorize the "feltness" of experience is one thing, but finding a way to study and make observations about it without first conceptualizing it in the manner of traditional philosophy is quite another (and, of course, expressing it in writing, another yet). James considered three options for pursuing such access: "experimental" method, "comparative" method, and introspection.[44] (He ignored the possibility of physiological study, presumably on the basis that while physiology might explain psychological mechanisms, it can never be identified with them, as he noted in *Principles*.) Detailed review of the reasons for James's decision would lead us too far afield. Suffice to say that although his training in laboratory-based observational psychology led him to propose comparative and experimental methods as more reliable means for locating causal laws and explaining population-wide patterns of thought, he dismissed them as inappropriate for the task of theorizing immediate, first-person thinking.

Instead, since the extant phenomena are mental, he thought it necessary to base his account upon conclusions drawn from psychology, and as they involved first-personal aspects of mental life, "*Introspective Observation is what we have to rely on first and foremost and always*" (*PP*, 185). Only introspection ("the subjective method") made it possible to describe experience *as it is lived*, complete with the character and import of situational circumstances and tendencies in one's thinking over time. It would be impossible to use resources other than one's own to try and record the immediacy and accuracy of subsequent observations and conclusions because, James believed, "the way an individual's life comes home to *him*, his intimate needs, ideals, desolations, consolations, failures, successes, always exceed the formulas by which [the] common sense of others subsumes them" (*ML*, 93). Others might know me well, or study me carefully, but they cannot grasp or describe just what it is like to have my experiences or feel my emotions or describe in detail the intricate patterns of thought developed over years of self-reflection and self-doubt. The only valid "observational" approach is "the looking into our own minds and reporting what we there discover," paying careful heed to the states and circumstances of one's own conscious-ness (*PP*, 185). (It is hardly a surprise, then, that "at its core, *Principles of Psychology* is an extended essay on what it is like to be human—based largely on what it was like to be William James. Everything we know about James the person—his rootlessness, his depression, his absorption in literature and the arts, his personal warmth, the influence of Renouvier, Emerson, Goethe, Mill, and his father—can be found there.")[45]

Despite his apparently clear definition of the term, James sometimes equivocates about precisely what introspection entails. Sometimes he suggests that the "looking inside" and "reporting" are unproblematic, even though the efficacy and completeness of the reports rely upon a simultaneous "looking into" the contents of consciousness and "noticing" what they comprise. But at others, he suggests that he is really proposing "retrospection," in which one pays careful heed to one's thoughts but only *subsequently* draws inferential relationships between whatever was noticed and its context and meaning. The latter seems more reasonable: not only does the rapidity with which conscious states change seem to preclude the possibility of simultaneous "looking" and "noticing"—opening a temporal gap, however brief—but the intensity of some mental states would seem to disallow a careful-enough "noticing" at all. For example, one might be well aware of one's own anger in a moment of confrontation and yet be so absorbed by it that only later does it become possible to reflect upon, name, describe, and make sense of the feeling.

Any "gap" between the phases of introspective reflection seems problem-atic. After all, "inasmuch as there is a temporal gap between the subjective state that is known and the state that knows it via sizing it up, reporting it, and so forth, the retrospective findings are inevitably risky and susceptible to error."[46] But some commentators believe that it is this temporal gap that enables James (and others) to generate superior analyses and conclusions about psychological tendencies. Amedeo Giorgi, for instance, notices that

James begins several of his most insightful philosophical arguments by first describing what seem to be prereflective, pretheoretical introspective observations before going on to conduct a rigorous psychological review.[47] On the evidence of Giorgi's examples, not only is the gap between James's initial "looking" and "noticing" often quite wide, but the "noticing" takes various forms, occurs at different times in different circumstances, and is conducted for a variety of purposes, yet retains nonetheless a vivid first-personal character. In this sense, Giorgi contends, the validity and objectivity of retrospective analyses of introspective observation does not rely upon "the translation of the personal into the impersonal" but rather "a faithful rendering of the personal as lived," based on "concrete, prereflective, pretheoretical experience or behavior."[48] We shall see when reviewing James's account of the experience of selfhood that he uses his introspective insights in just this way.

As a method, introspection has been consistently criticized. Problems of self-misrepresentation, incorrect reporting, uncertainty about the aspect of consciousness being reported upon (is it thought itself, thought's "object," or thoughts about thought?), the nature of the "feltness" of introspective evidence (and the claim that introspection is a kind of perception at all), the role of the unconscious, and differences in peoples' capacity to conduct, maintain, and describe introspective awareness, are some of the difficulties raised. It is always possible that even the most scrupulous introspection will result in a narrative that replaces rather than describes the experiences under review. In terms of James's legacy, the rise of behaviorist science meant that much of the work in *Principles* was rejected because consciousness, will, feelings, motives, desires, purposes, and plans were all deemed unobservable and therefore inadmissible according to the objective standards of modern science.[49]

James considered carefully the myriad methodological problems posed by introspection and was cognizant of the standard objections. Finally, though, he insisted on its fallible utility, finding no alternative way to access experience without prior conceptualization. As Myers writes, defending James, "a psychology that is pragmatic (rather than, say, rationalistic) uses introspection as an investigative tool just because it is practically valuable," and

> once fallibility and privileged access limitations are conceded, defending the role of introspection . . . in gaining self-knowledge becomes important and achievable. When I ask, "Why?" "What does it mean?" "Does it resemble anything in my previous experience?" "Am I really sincere about it?" "Have I been

denying (self-deceiving) all along?" "What conception fits this experience best?" and so forth—where what is at issue is a feeling, emotion, mood, attitude, impulse, impression, thought, altered consciousness, and so on—introspection both as observation and retrospection . . . is more often than not an essential part of the process of delivering responsible answers to such questions that we put to ourselves.[50]

By adopting a reflective, first-personal description of the various aspects of subjectivity—and only in that way—it becomes possible to compile a view of the psychological phenomena relevant to ethics. While the fallibility of introspective findings must be conceded in the face of its many challenges, the fact remains that there seems to be no alternative way of accessing first-person experience, and so it is hardly surprising that self-reporting remains a principal diagnostic tool in psychoanalysis, medicine, and psychology. Furthermore, how without employing or at least understanding introspection "can one comprehend Descartes, Leibniz, Locke, Hume, Bain, Spencer, Wundt, Titchener, and James? Or Dewey, Peirce, Watson, Ryle, Wittgenstein, Russell, Freud, Jung, and Skinner?"[51]

Although "*introspection is difficult and fallible,*" James writes, "*the difficulty is simply that of all observation of whatever kind*": accurate observation and reporting of everyday sense perception or experimental tests are as difficult as introspection (*PP*, 191). But like experimental science, introspection, too, can rely upon "the final *consensus* of our farther knowledge about the thing in question, later views correcting earlier ones, until at last the harmony of a consistent system is reached" (*PP*, 191). In other words, since introspective conclusions are subject to lifelong revision and related by way of practice to the verifiable world of actions and nonmental events, they are open to self-adjustment over time.

Despite his commitment to introspection, James remained cautious about the claims that he makes for his observations of experience. For example, he avoids drawing any universal conclusions about human existence, "argues for the fallibility of the findings obtained through introspection, and on occasion . . . refuses to conclude anything from his studies except that something seems to be the case to him personally."[52] Furthermore, mindful of the extent to which his philosophy relies upon his own, particular introspective observations, James implores his audience to "test out" his ideas in their own lives and check whether their introspective observations accord with his: "I propose it [i.e., pragmatism] to my readers, as something to be verified *ambulando*, or by the way in which its consequences may confirm it" (*MT*, 114 n.6). He consistently acknowledges the fallibility of both introspective reports and the descriptions and conclusions that he develops from them, whether or not the introspective nature of his experiential material is flagged in the text.

Although James moved routinely between various disciplines of inquiry, "He never totally transcended their orientation": each field helped him to get a better grasp of some aspect of human life, but none could "duplicate the contributions of philosophy in helping us to see things whole."[53] As a psychologist, James insists upon the veracity of introspectively reported data and emphasizes the complexity of first-person experience, and as a philosopher, he provides a thorough account of first-person reality beginning with that data and never resorting for the sake of explanatory power to generalized philosophical constructions for which there is no experiential evidence. His proposals for realizing more of life's potential by way of deliberate, carefully directed effort rely on the confluence between the two, realized in his conceptions of experience and the self.

Experience Conceived Relationally

James began *Principles* keen to avoid philosophical speculations in his descriptive account of psychological activity, deliberately setting aside epistemological and metaphysical questions in pursuit of a distinctively "scientific" psychology (*PP*, 6). But even as he developed his famous account of the continuity of thought in terms of a "stream of consciousness," he found himself unable to keep such concerns at bay. Consider his most succinct description of the stream: "Consciousness . . . does not appear to itself chopped up in bits. Such words as 'chain' or 'train' do not describe it fitly as it presents itself in the first instance. It is nothing jointed; it flows. A 'river' or a 'stream' are the metaphors by which it is most naturally described. In talking of it hereafter let us call it the stream of thought, of consciousness, or of subjective life" (*PP*, 233). The very mention of subjective life begs acknowledgment of the objective realm, and it is by no means self-evident that conscious continuity rests just on subjective characteristics, as James himself points out: "The world we practically live in is one in which it is impossible (except by theoretic retrospection) to disentangle the contributions of intellect from those of sense. They are wrapt and rolled together as a gunshot in the mountains is wrapt and rolled pinfold on fold of echo and reverberative clamour' " (*SPP*, 58–59).

Similarly, James courts metaphysical and epistemological controversy when he describes five characteristics of experience in terms of psychological observations: every thought is part of just a single stream of consciousness and exists for only a short time; each thought also carries a feeling of belonging together with other thoughts in the same stream, always seems to be about something independent of the thought itself, and can seem to influence the thoughts that follow it (*PP*, 220–78). While each of these seems defensible phenomenologically, the first, for instance, is suggestive of dualism (the conception of conscious life in terms of a problematic representational transaction between inner mental states and a nonmental world), and the fourth begs the question of just what, precisely, is the nature of "aboutness"? Given such challenges, James suggests that "*the psychologist's attitude toward cognition . . . is a thorough-going dualism.* It supposes two elements, mind knowing and thing known, and treats them as irreducible" (*PP*, 214).

In fact, James's commitment to the avoidance of philosophical conjecture wavers over the course of *Principles*, and he spent much of his career trying to untangle the implications of "the psychologists' natural dualism" (which of course was also his own). He struggled to explain the relationship between the first-personal world of felt relations and the physical world of objects that stimulates attentive focus, limits the range of possible bodily responses, and reflects actions in terms of their consequences. His early attempts (beginning in *Psychology: Briefer Course*, published in 1892, just two years after *Principles*) added little. In several of the *Essays in Radical Empiricism*, he claims that there is an ontological unity between the two fields but that rather than being linked by an epistemological connection called "knowing," subject and object are merely functional designations drawn from "one primal stuff or material in the world" called "pure experience" (*ERE*, 4). Although he quickly resiles from this position (writing in another of the *Essays* that "there is no *general* stuff of which experience at large is made" (*ERE*, 14)), James maintained that "*experience . . . has no such inner duplicity,*" and that subject and object are "the same thing" from two different perspectives: "As 'subjective' we say that the experience represents; as 'objective' it is represented. What represents and what is represented is here numerically the same; but we must remember that no dualism of being represented and representing resides in experience *per se*" (*ERE*, 6, 13). Only in lectures from very late in his career (about the time of *Some Problems in Philosophy*) does he give up dualism altogether in favor of a neutral metaphysical field comprising "phenomena," "data," and "pure experiences" (in the plural).[54]

James's shifting stance has puzzled commentators, leading to disparate interpretations of it as: a kind of phenomenalism (with Alfred Ayer, the view that one's "conception of the physical world is a theory with respect to our experiences");[55] neutral monism (Bertrand Russell's interpretation, in which the mental and physical are taken as two ways of describing the same elements);[56] panpsychism (the notion that all objects are "psychical," so that the mind is a fundamental feature of the world and everything is self-experiencing); phenomenology (whereby James's focus on first-person consciousness is taken to have much in common with Edmund Husserl's and Maurice Merleau-Ponty's views); conceptualization of the limits of conscious life (as when James defines pure experience as "the immediate flux of life which furnishes the material to our later reflection with its conceptual categories" [ERE, 46]);[57] and, methodological restriction (the rather moderate position that whatever *is* experienced must itself be describable in experiential terms).

Any attempt to reconcile all of James's diverse positions seems hopeless: they are too many, too unclear, and too disparate. As Seigfried asks of James's initial psychological investigations, "How are we to interpret the concrete findings given in *Principles* once it is recognized that it is impossible to begin with a neutral description of facts as the objective basis for further claims?"[58] It is tempting to believe that "the continuity between James's natural science of psychology and his philosophy of radical empiricism was lost, at least in part, because he equivocated on the central issue of the possibility of pure description versus perspectival appropriation of the facts of experience, that is, on whether we observe or invent experienced objects."[59]

The significance of these challenges for James's practical philosophy is dissipated by focusing foremost on his investigations of first-personal experience; that is, on philosophical psychology. Read this way, James relies neither upon "the psychologists' natural dualism" *nor* philosophical neutrality. His conceptions of conscious life (and ethical decision-making and action) begin with prephilosophical, introspectively attained observations about the relationships between oneself and the surrounding objects and other people. Issues of metaphysics and epistemology are set to one side. (We might say in a manner redolent of Husserl that James "brackets them out.")[60] Although such an approach is unsatisfying for those seeking a systematic unity in James's work, and as we shall see, for those like Rorty who believe that it dooms his whole philosophical enterprise, it will prove sufficient for his ethics.

It is also consistent with much of what James writes about our experience of objects and other people and with experience's being "unproblematic" in the usual course of life. Regarding our relations with objects, James argues that dualism is a flawed theoretical abstraction. Rather than conceiving of subject and object as discrete entities, necessitating complex epistemology and metaphysics to explain their interaction, we ought instead to notice that experience includes both those aspects that we call "subjective" and those called "objective." (This is what James refers to as the "double-barrelled" nature of experience.) In the normal course of conscious life, he observes, both elements appear as aspects of the same irreducible first-person reality, distinguishable not on ontological grounds but merely functional ones: "thoughts" and "things" seem separate only reflectively, for some explanatory purpose. He writes, "Subjectivity and objectivity are affairs not of what an experience is aboriginally made of, but of its classification" and "classifications depend on our temporary purposes" (*ERE*, 71). As such, depending upon extant circumstances, a particular perceptual experience might be classified as either a physical object along with relevant physical relations or as a subjective perception defined in terms of other ideas, although only in retrospect might the nature of the process become evident.

On relations between people, James writes (evocatively, though not very helpfully), "Our lives are like islands in the sea or like trees in the forest. The maple and the pine may whisper to each other with their leaves, and Conanicut and Newport hear each other's fog-horns. But the trees also commingle their roots in the darkness underground, and the islands also hang together through the ocean's bottom" (*EPR*, 374). In other words, even apparently isolated individuals interact with and are influenced by those around them. For the sake of accuracy and completeness, philosophy ought not to consider the individual on one side of a conceptual divide and society on the other but rather the nature of the interrelations between them.

Yet some of James's interpreters have contended that his theorization of social relations is weak or even absent altogether. McDermott, James's fellow traveler and popularizer, suggests that "readers of the writings of William James are hard put to find a doctrine of community therein" and his "position on the individual was dramatically one-sided and his innocence of the social matrix by which we became single selves was most unusual for a late nineteenth-century thinker."[61] Even James's contemporaries, Peirce and Dewey, criticized him for being overly concerned with individual agency to the near exclusion of social interrelations, and he has little to say on matters of gender, race, and class.[62]

On face value, such criticism seems fair. After all, James describes himself as "a rabid individualist" and inevitably focuses his attention on "the person in the singular number" (*ECR*, 97).[63] Only in one essay, "The Moral Equivalent of War" (*ERM*, 162–73), published late in his life, did James address social relations explicitly (although his earlier "On a Certain Blindness in Human Beings" had touched on some relevant themes, particularly the experience of becoming aware of alien ideals held by other people). He writes almost nothing about how communities form and operate, provides threadbare accounts of social history and politics, and says precious little on interpersonal manners and communication. Yet he was aware that his ideas must be applicable to the range of real-world circumstances, some of which are inevitably social. If one sets aside the traditional concerns of social philosophy and focuses instead on James's theorization of the nature of social *relations*, then a different interpretation is possible. On this view, consistent with James's overarching individualism, he is less interested with how the relations "play themselves out" in political practices, communal mores, joint decision-making, and so on than with the nature of interactions as they are experienced by individuals. In short, social factors impact upon the lives of individuals in experiential terms, as with the whole range of one's circumstances.

James approaches this explanatory task from two different directions. First, he examines social relational dynamics in terms of the very conception of "community." Rather than being granted special descriptive or interpretative status, a group (or society) ought to be understood foremost as a collection of individuals with dynamic relational connections between them. To try and explain individuals in terms of the group is for James always a mistake, despite the undeniable connection between one's own experiences and various social forces. As Smith summarizes James's position, "As a person, I must attempt to actualise myself in a community of persons, considering, on the one hand, what I am able in virtue of my own constitution to contribute to the harmonious well-being of that community and, on the other, how I must conduct myself so that I shall be constantly recognizing the reality and worth of others as persons."[64] While James is indeed interested in solidarity and community (as we saw in his responses to socioeconomic and political issues), his primary focus is on how individuals balance their own interests with those of others.

Second—and most important for James's individualistic ethics—he understands the self as influenced by social interactions in very important ways. As McDermott suggests, it might be right to say that James down-played the role of the other in day-to-day living (contra Marx, Durkheim, Mead, and Dewey, for example), but it would be very wrong to suggest that he conceived of the self as *isolated* from others.[65] He doesn't just criticize theories of individual persons that assume a substantial self conducting life independently of the social world, but he champions the alternative idea of the private self as largely defined by relations with other people. Interpersonal conflicts, informal discussions, sexual relations, war, poverty, prejudice, familial expectations, social education, and so on all play roles in determining and realizing one's own interests, judgments, and actions, so that the development of an individual person is, inevitably and in large part, a social process. James did relatively little to unpack the ways in which exercise of individual freedom is guided and constrained by communal expectations and mores, but he did not dismiss them. Rather, he considered that they influence our beliefs, decisions, and actions in the same way as other kinds of experience that influence us but over which we have limited control.

This short diversion is not meant as a definitive account of James's understanding of one's relations with objects or other people but rather to show that he was committed to neither "the psychologist's natural dualism" nor philosophical neutrality. By attending to experiential relations, he pushes his claim that, although such interactions might themselves prove ethically problematic, their metaphysical and epistemological status are not. We respond to them (in the main) by making decisions, changing behaviors, avoiding situations, altering directions, making plans, and so on, rather than by constructing philosophical theories. For ethics to be founded in experience means focusing more upon how we conceive of our interactions and decide what to do about them and less on questions of metaphysics, epistemology, or ethical ideals.

James's disparate accounts of experience and his individualistic approach to social relations were to prove problematic, encouraging a significant and ongoing schism between pragmatist philosophers committed to the primacy of experience and those "neo-pragmatists" (figures such as Rorty, Robert Brandom, Huw Price, Jeffrey Stout, Bjørn Ramberg, Michael Williams, and Misak) who turned instead to a language-oriented version. Although a comprehensive account of the disagreement would lead us too far afield, a brief survey will illustrate both James's naivety in supposing that experience could serve as an uncontroversial starting point for his philosophical psychology and its appropriateness nonetheless for his project in ethics.

The main issues in the dispute were identified by Rorty, who, despite considering himself an ally of pragmatism in the style of James and Dewey, thought that their use of terms like "pure experience" and "the immediate flux of life" suggested that they had granted to experience a foundational role in pragmatist philosophy of much the same kind as "mind," "substance," "idea," and "transcendental ego" in the metaphysically oriented philosophies to which pragmatism was opposed. Although Rorty, too, believed that there is no transcendental subject or essential human nature, and that we can transform ourselves with deliberate effort and attention, he thought that James's version of experience "is simply a version of the thing-in-itself—an unknowable whose only function is paradoxically enough, to be that which all knowledge is about."[66]

Furthermore, for Rorty and other neo-pragmatists, James's account of experience inadvertently inherits two problems from empiricist predecessors like Mill and Hume, for whom the external world is passively perceived by way of atomistic sense experiences, and knowledge is a matter of consequent, accurate mental representations of the world.[67] First, it entails that there is a world outside of one's experience to which that experience refers, reopening the metaphysical dualism to which we referred in James's critique of Humean associationism. Second, it involves what Sellars termed the "Myth of the Given," the contention that there can be no basic or "pure" knowledge of the world because the production of a belief involves conceptual arrangements necessarily; in other words, to even become aware of something as experience is to utilize some concept that is not itself a product of experience.[68] Yet as we have seen, for James, pure experience (and perhaps some other versions of James's accounts of experience, too) is preconceptual. As Alan Malachowski puts it, for Rorty and his peers, "Experience is always liable to be philosophically troublesome. Construed as a psychological intermediary of epistemological significance, it paradoxically opens a chasm between the subject and his or her environment, into which wholesale scepticism is all too easily sucked. And, considered as something of an entity in its own right, it becomes an enigma: unknowable from without and thereby also effectively cut off from the world at large."[69] On this view, neither James's context-sensitive relationism nor his critique of Hume and Mill save him from the problems of traditional empiricism.

For Rorty, pragmatism ought to avoid even the merest hint of foundationalism, not just because of the interminable philosophical disputes to which it leads, but because it is contrary to the contingent and ever-changing natures of language, personal identity, and community that everyday life shows us are impossible to avoid. As he puts it, "It is . . . impossible [to] attempt to step outside our skins—the traditions, linguistic and other, within which we do our thinking and self-criticism—and compare ourselves to something absolute."[70] Rorty proposed that language ought to take over the explanatory and descriptive roles served by Jamesian experience and any other "'natural starting points' of thought, starting points which are prior to and independent of the way some culture speaks or spoke."[71] By engaging with such luminaries of the mid-twentieth-century "linguistic turn" as Wittgenstein, Quine, Sellars, and Donald Davidson, Rorty meant to rid philosophy of metaphysical and epistemological pretentions and show that long-standing philosophical problems were nothing more than products of inadequate language, capable of dissolution by way of redescription.[72]

For philosophers of the linguistic turn, language "goes all the way down," such that there is no ineffable reality outside it against which to assess claims and utterances. In particular, there is no experience unaffected by language, since experience and language are always interwoven. Descriptive and normative principles are defined by the language in which they are expressed and by interpersonal conversational consensus rather than experiences to which they are supposed to refer. James's reliance on experience is considered to be a kind of "backsliding" into traditional metaphysical disputes that he meant to avoid and that encouraged his downplaying the social aspects of our lives. On their view, although James could not have been privy to concepts and tools developed as part of the new philosophical emphasis on language, he ought to have been more careful about the implications of using first-person experience as his starting point, particularly given that he had acknowledged some of the associated metaphysical problems in *Principles*.

That the dispute between experience- and language-oriented pragmatists remains alive indicates that there is an alternative to Rorty's view. There are numerous ways to defend James's commitment to experience, but two are especially relevant to his ethics. First is the argument that language is in fact just one aspect of experience and not one that ought to be metaphysically privileged, as neo-pragmatists suppose. As Mark Johnson writes, "It is a mistake to set language over against experience, for all linguistic practices are forms of experience" and

> there is no such thing as "language" in itself—no language without our experience of language, and no language experience without an enactment of meaning that involves more than

just linguistic structures. Consequently, we cannot pretend to escape the depths of experience by focusing only on language and linguistic practices of validation and justification, for there are no such practices that are not themselves experiences embedded within a context of perceiving, meaning-making, appraisal, and acting that is not itself all or only a matter of language.[73]

While there are self-evident and important differences between our experiences of language and such other experiences as learning, shopping, and playing, it is not clear that they are philosophically significant in terms of the *nature* of first-person experience. As such, there is no reason to suppose that we face disparate philosophical problems in two discrete domains, language and experience, rather than just the one problem of how to form appropriate habits and belief in both domains.[74] Furthermore, as Koopman has pointed out, it is not obvious why we should be more concerned with questions arising from experiences of language than, say, such practical engagements as building a home for shelter or buying groceries to feed ourselves.[75] Language might be considered as just one practical device or tool among very many others for navigating our way through life.

A second defense of James's reliance on experience is that language is inadequate for describing the range of phenomena with which his philosophical psychology is concerned. For linguistic pragmatists, "All thought is linguiform—linguistically expressible as a set of concepts, propositions, and their relations."[76] Yet James's conception of experience involves partially formed intuitions, reactions that are barely conscious (if at all), inexpressible meanings, unique feelings, and so on; the whole array of mental phenomena, some of which are inexpressible (or even inconceivable) in linguistic form. In such cases, the inherently context-sensitive and first-personal experience to which James is wedded seems wholly appropriate.

Furthermore, although it is possible to consider language as "grounded in our practical engagements in our shared social communities," thus lending it a pragmatist orientation, a focus on propositional content means that "we have already slipped almost imperceptibly into an extremely narrow conception of experience that limits it to matters of belief, judgment, appraisal, and reason-giving" with a focus on "assertion, reasoning, justification, and appraisal."[77] Clearly such a focus is inadequate to James's concern for disparate interests, habits, and beliefs, all of which can be profoundly meaningful and normatively significant without being linguistically expressible. Epistemological certainties have no special place in James's philosophical psychology relative to first-personal "meanings" and "seemings," and his conception of the self is very much more than a knowing self.

James's few discussions of language (he offered no complete theory of it) highlight what he considered to be the inadequacy of language relative to the dynamics of consciousness. On the one hand, "We name our thoughts simply, each after its thing, as if each knew its own thing and nothing else" whereas "what each really knows is clearly the thing it is name for, with dimly perhaps a thousand other things" (*PP*, 234). On the other hand, language is incapable of describing adequately the transitive parts of consciousness, tending either to ignore them or describe them in substantive terms. Although James came to acknowledge later in his career that the meanings of words and sentences can vary with their context, be performative rather than merely descriptive, and work as focal points for concentrated attention at the complex nexus between self, language, and world, he did not ever consider language adequate to the multifarious dynamism of consciousness.

In the words of Christopher Hookway, it might be that efforts by recent, language-oriented pragmatists "to retain the insights of pragmatism while abandoning what was taken to be a flawed conception of the given" have "thrown away the baby with the bathwater, losing track of deep insights that are contained in the earlier pragmatist views of experience."[78] While James's reliance on experience and his diverse positions on its metaphysical implications are problematic—a point that he acknowledged and attended to in later works, as we have seen—they do not undermine his ethics. As James explains in chapter 9 of *Principles*, our thoughts are necessarily private, and our experiences can only ever be one's own, so that some separation of self and world in psychological study is inevitable—and an individualistic focus on first-personal experience is imperative if pragmatism is to do justice to our interests, meanings, and habits. The debate between proponents of pragmatism's two sides will continue to rage (despite their proclaimed abhorrence for dualisms!), but it need not derail our consideration of James's ethics.

In terms of deciding among the various interpretations of James's account of experience (at least as he employs it in his ethics), his descriptions of our engagements with objects and people in terms of first-person conscious life point us toward the phenomenological view. As Wilshire writes, "The pragmatists maintain the primacy of *description*: the description of what actually presents itself in our immediate experiencing. The description is of something holistic and encompassing—with a vengeance. In refusing to substitute abstractions and unwitting reflective analysis for descriptions of what is presented concretely and immediately as a surrounding and sustaining presence, . . . pragmatists are also phenomenologists."[79] At issue is not how or why our engagements "hang together" philosophically speaking but how they are always experienced *as* relational, and how we discriminate between moments, things, ideas, people, and so on in order to make sense of the world and alter our behaviors accordingly. Although James does not dwell on the question of *how* consciousness comes to know the world or engage with other consciousnesses (as do Husserl and Merleau-Ponty, phenomenology's main progenitors), his emphasis on describing the conscious appearance of the world—the way in which it seems to the experiencer to be, including the attitudes and intentions correlated with it—and the intentionality of each conscious moment (that is, its "directedness" or experiential focus) marks his approach as decidedly phenomenological, at least implicitly.[80]

Several philosophers, such as Sami Pihlström, believe that it is easy to overstate the similarities between phenomenology and pragmatism because "the worldly—natural and practical—embeddedness of subjectivity is not sufficiently emphasized in phenomenological studies of experience."[81] Yet some of James's most distinguished interpreters locate thematic continuities between his philosophy and phenomenology, arguing either that James was a "proto-phenomenologist," presaging phenomenology in various ways, or that various aspects of his oeuvre were best understood through a phenomenological lens.[82] Works by William Barrett, Edie, Charles Hobbs, McDermott, Wild, and Wilshire, in particular, are instructive in this regard, with the latter naming James alongside Peirce as "the fathers of distinctly American phenomenology," and it is noteworthy that James shared with Husserl a desire to avoid nihilism, skepticism, and the failures of speculative metaphysics by focusing upon the verifiable reality of human experience.[83]

Keeping phenomenology in mind helps to explain James's introspective method, preoccupation with describing phenomena (rather than "sense data"), focus on habit, and detailed accounts of how experience seems to the experiencer to be. Although James's use of first-person experience as the starting point for his naturalistic ethics comes laden with metaphysical complexities, his critique of traditional empiricism suggests that such issues can be deferred (perhaps even bypassed altogether) by approaching experience "on its own terms" rather than *via* conceptual abstraction, using a phenomenological version of philosophical psychology to analyze the "full fact" of experience: "a conscious field *plus* its object as felt or thought *plus* an attitude towards the object *plus* a sense of self to which the attitude belongs—such a concrete bit of personal experience may be a small bit but it is a solid bit as long as it lasts" (*VRE*, 393). Thus conceived, experience is concretely relational rather than abstract, creative and anticipatory rather than passively received, and imbued with the whole of a person's biography to that point rather than appearing as an atomistic thought or moment.

Whereas traditional empiricism had oversimplified this dynamic complexity, James's radical version focuses on it almost exclusively. His philosophical psychology is a descriptive study of the ever-changing relations within and between *all* aspects of experience, irrespective of their metaphysical standing. Applied to ethics, it emphasizes the importance of context and novelty for ethical theories and decisions, representing "an opening of horizons so that experience no longer meant merely a *content* passively received but many *contexts* in which that content could be taken and its full meaning developed."[84] We experience an open-ended world of relational possibilities, our options defined by circumstances and our decisions defining which of them might be realized and which ignored or deliberately shut off.

At this point, the various threads of James's philosophical psychology weave tightly together. Philosophy makes its best contribution to real-world ethics by drawing upon the evidence of experience rather than generalizing or ordering it in terms of abstract concepts and ideals. Radical empiricism reveals the "fact" of felt relations, the dynamic flux constituting conscious life and reflecting our ever-changing circumstances and mental states. The ethical import of relations is a product of their being responses to, and anticipations of, the push and pull of everyday events involving other people and things, personal ideals, hopes, memories, life lessons, and psychological habits and capabilities. It is hardly surprising that James is less interested in the merit of particular ethical decisions than theorizing self-transformation in terms of relational thought: each person has the opportunity to improve their life, and the moral challenge is to realize that opportunity by navigating life's complexity in the best possible way.

The Field of Consciousness

Although James did not announce himself as a pragmatist until 1898, his preoccupation with the action orientation of thinking is evident even in *Principles*, where he wrote, "My thinking is first and last and always for the sake of doing, and I can only do one thing at a time" (*PP*, 960). By the time he published his clearest rejections of subject-object dualism, in "Does

'Consciousness' Exist?" and "A World of Pure Experience," his relational model of consciousness had assumed mature form, emphasizing mutually transformative engagements between a person and the world of objects and other people. In "The Sentiment of Rationality," for example, he says that "it is far too little recognized how entirely the intellect is built up of practical interests" and "cognition . . . is incomplete until discharged in act," and, in a more overtly Darwinian moment in "Reflex Action and Theism," he writes that "perception and thinking are only there for behavior's sake" (*WB*, 72, 92). In other words, consistent with much scientific psychology, James understood thinking to be inherently goal-oriented, deciding upon practical actions appropriate to the circumstances ("What am I to do?") rather than a series of engagements with theoretical questions such as "What is that?" or "What can I know?" Even abstract theoretical contemplations must finally be realized in some "practical action," broadly conceived. Put pragmatically, thinking is used to "intelligently structure experience," first by determining which ends are achievable and which desirable and then "integrating thought and action, theory and practice" by understanding, controlling, and adapting to the world in pursuit of those ends.[85]

James's best-known model of thinking and self-presence is his "stream of consciousness" (or of "thought"), which emphasized the continuous, free-flowing nature of conscious life. First presented in *Principles*, it was one element of his argument against traditional empiricism: rather than a relatively stable succession of "ideas," consciousness on James's account is more like a flowing stream of relational connections, incorporating all the disparate aspects of mental life. Ideas, memories, and feelings merge and blend together such that they are "steeped and dyed" in the thinking that surrounds them. Such a flow exhibits various rhythms of anticipation and reflection, focus and distraction, ever present in and as one's conscious reality. Turning attention "inwards," as it were (say, in a moment of introspective self-reflection), one might become more aware of consciousness's dynamism or the lingering aura of a bad dream; turning "outwards," we think instead about the flow of traffic, other peoples' expectations of us, and the series of tasks that will comprise the day, each thought mingling with others: "The rush of our thought forward through its fringes is the everlasting peculiarity of its life. We realize this life as something always off its balance, something in transition" (*PU*, 128).

While the "stream" model is justly famous for its original interpretative insights, it is not James's most sophisticated version. About 1895, he introduced a new metaphorical model to enable more concrete descriptions of the processes of experience. Rather than describing the continuity and complexity of the world of relations in terms of a river's flow, he considers them as transactions between series of points laid out on a two-dimensional plane or "field." James writes:

> The world it represents as a collection, some parts of which are conjunctively and others disjunctively related. Two parts, themselves disjoined, may nevertheless hang together by intermediaries with which they are severally connected, and the whole world eventually may hang together similarly, inasmuch as *some* path of conjunctive transition by which to pass from one of its parts to another may always be discernible. Such determinately various hanging-together may be called *concatenated* union, to distinguish it from the 'through-and-through' type of union, 'each in all and all in each' . . . which monistic systems hold to obtain. . . . In a concatenated world a partial conflux often is experienced. . . . Where the experience is not of conflux, it may be of conterminousness (things with but one thing between); or of contiguousness (nothing between); or of likeness; or of nearness; or of simultaneousness; or of in-ness; or of on-ness; of or for-ness; or of simple with-ness or even of mere and-ness. (*ERE*, 52–53)[86]

Conscious life is not on this account either a series of discrete items or actions, or a readily identifiable, unidirectional stream. Rather, one's thoughts and actions are all at once potentially present, to be realized and attended to in some sequence or relationship respondent to one's circumstances. As such, consciousness is fundamentally relational and contextual. Phenomenal relations assume various, constantly changing combinations and permutations; are more or less temporary; are related together immediately or at a remove (such that a thought might "feel itself *as related* to previous thoughts" even though separated from them by a period of sleep or unconsciousness); assume simple or complex configurations (James discusses such complex phenomena as the taste of a drink, where the compound flavor is "known together" rather than seeming like an amalgam of simpler states); and so on (*EPh*, 71, 78, 87). A chance physical interaction might call to mind a memory that would otherwise lie dormant, as when an accidental encounter with a friend prompts the recall of events from long ago, or one might be prompted to try this or that action in an attempt to light a dimmed bulb, not as a consequence of understanding how electrical circuitry works or even a memory of a previous successful attempt but just because such actions sometimes work in "cases like this."

Without referring to the specific circumstances from which they arise, such relational connections can seem inexplicable. As James writes,

> Neither an outside observer nor the Subject who undergoes the process can explain fully how particular experiences are able to change one's centre of energy so decisively, or why they so often have to bide their hour to do so. We have a thought, or we perform an act, repeatedly, but on a certain day the real meaning of the thought peals through us for the first time, or the act has suddenly turned into a moral impossibility. All we know is that there are dead feelings, dead ideas, and cold beliefs, and there are hot and live ones; and when one grows hot and alive within us, everything has to re-crystallize about it. (*VRE*, 163)

It is not that the feelings, ideas, or beliefs have themselves changed but that they have attained new significance or relevance in the light of circumstantial context.

Furthermore, although fundamentally continuous, the field of consciousness exhibits *dis*continuities, too; discrete occurrences come and go amid the conscious flow. It might be that at 4:59 p.m., one has in mind all of those "work-related" items and people and tasks, but then, when the clock ticks over, these are moved "to the back of mind" as it were, replaced by whatever thoughts are needed to drive home and prepare to read a children's book, accompanied all at once by the love for a new daughter and dutiful intentions to set tables and wash dishes. Each item and task is not simply "present" either more or less obviously, but it is also in some contextualized relationship with all the others. As such, when describing the first-person immediacy of consciousness, James believes that "we ought to say a feeling of *and*, a feeling of *if*, a feeling of *but*, and a feeling of *by*, quite as readily as we say a feeling of *blue* or a feeling of *cold*" (*PP*, 238).

The fact that consciousness can be conceived as a whole field of relational connections is not meant to imply a *closed* system, however. The open-ended and uncertain nature of conscious life means that the field of experience "can grow by its edges," each moment merging into the next "by transitions which, whether conjunctive or disjunctive, continue the experiential tissue" (*ERE*, 42). Finality and closure seem to James to "violate the character with which life concretely comes," failing to accommodate "an 'ever not quite' to all our formulas, and novelty and possibility forever leaking in."[87] Consciousness is always "on the move," so to speak, an open-ended engagement with the next stimulus involving so many thoughts and relations between thoughts that our grasp of conscious life must remain forever incomplete.

To describe the open-ended character of experience, James describes each conscious moment as having indeterminate "fringes" at the periphery of one's awareness, which foreshadow or anticipate possible connections with ideas beyond what is noticed and focused upon. Attention structures consciousness into those phenomena that are more central and those more peripheral, not in terms of how the world appears but as one's own perspective on all of conscious reality.[88] At one moment a particular idea is the center or focus of attention, the one of which I am most conscious and actively aware, while the next it might be at the "fringe," such that I am only dimly aware of it. In phenomenological terms, "Anyone with self-awareness knows that thoughts and impulses flit through the margins of consciousness that we are lucky to register at all. Moreover, they are never found alone, as discrete mental contents or elements, but always in a whole flowing experiencing-experienced context, which is the presence in some way of the world around us. Our moment-by-moment life is pre-reflective: we are immediately involved in what presents itself as a whole world, even though most of it is blurred at any particular moment."[89]

Because of the interrelated nature of conscious phenomena, any alteration to the field's configuration invokes dynamic effects that spread across a portion of the field rather than remaining local to the point of disturbance. Such changes in relations "are not complete annihilations followed by complete creations of something absolutely novel. There is partial decay and partial growth," so that "without being one throughout, such a universe is continuous. Its members interdigitate with their next neighbours in manifold directions, and there are not clean cuts between them anywhere," as James puts it (*PU*, 115). "Our earlier lines, having grown irrelevant, are then dropped," leaving relational patterns to follow "a zigzag; and to keep it straight, one must do violence to its spontaneous development" (*PU*, 152). We can imagine, then, why a death in the family might bring us to think differently about a range of other matters: the "ripple" effects of this single incident radiate "outwards," to be felt as immediate sadness, maudlin, or joyful memories months later, and in deeper reflections years on, perhaps on one's own deathbed. The single event might be evidenced in reflections upon one's own mortality, the need to leave a valid will, and motivation toward exercise and good diet.

If we try to imagine the arrangement of the conscious field at some instant, we might derive a (necessarily inadequate) conception of the number and range of thoughts and the relationships between them. If instead we attempt to trace the patterns of the experiential field "playing out" over time in response to a disturbance, then the shifting dynamics of relations would become more evident.[90] In either case, conceiving of experience in terms of such intricate relational dynamism "results in an almost maddening restlessness," to use James's words.[91] Not only might one more relationship emerge at any moment between one's ideas or emotions or interests, and not only is the range of experiences always growing, but the focus of one's attention is shifting constantly, whether as a product of philosophical reflection or, more likely, a prereflective response to changed circumstances. For a philosopher to focus for even a short time on the complexity of experienced relations brings a reflective awareness of the extreme—even unfathomable—diversity and dynamism of consciousness, and the realization that "reality, life, experience, concreteness, immediacy, use what word you will, exceeds your logic, overflows and surrounds it" (*PU*, 96).

For James, the mind "is at every stage a theatre of simultaneous possibilities" from which the mind selects "by the reinforcing and inhibiting agency of attention" (*PP*, 277). The ability to pay attention to some phenomenon and then shift attention to another one in response to a new stimulus is the critical counterpoint to consciousness's dynamism. Attention is "the focalisation of consciousness" and "implies withdrawal from some things in order to deal effectively with others, and is a condition which has a real opposite in the confused, dazed, scatterbrained state which . . . is called distraction" (*PP*, 382). Since we have limited cognitive resources, it is only possible to draw relevant connections and avoid being overwhelmed by the myriad relational possibilities and "maddening" complexity of conscious experience by focusing on *relevant* ideas, thoughts, or feelings. "Consciousness, from our natal day, is of a teeming multiplicity of objects and relations," James writes (*PP*, 219). "Millions of items of the outward order are present to my senses which never properly enter into my experience. Why? Because they have no *interest* for me. *My experience is what I agree to attend to.* Only those items which I *notice* shake my mind—without selective interest, experience is an utter chaos. Interest alone gives accent and emphasis, light and shade, background and foreground—intelligible perspective, in a word" (*PP*, 380–81).

To the extent that consciousness commits scarce resources to the fulfillment of interests, it is a *"fighter for ends"* and *"a selecting agency"* (*PP*, 144, 142). All the various aspects of mental activity, from sensation and perception to conception and memory, exhibit this same dynamic of selective attention in the cause of one's purposes, projects, and interests: "Consciousness is always interested more in one part of its object than in another, and welcomes and rejects, or chooses, all the while it thinks. . . . But few of us are aware how incessantly it is at work in operations not ordinarily called by these names" (*PB*, 154–55).

On James's field model of consciousness, the central or "focal" point is whatever phenomenon is most important in that moment—the one of which we are most actively aware—and the rest of the conscious field is oriented around it such that at the margin (forming a "penumbra" or "halo") are matters of which we are less aware, or perhaps unaware altogether. But with a momentary refocusing of attention in response to some new interest, those marginal matters might move to the very center. For James, "Consciousness consists in the comparison of these [various possible loci of thought] with each other, the selection of some, and the suppression of the rest by the reinforcing and inhibiting agency of attention" and "as life goes on, there is a constant change of our interests, and a consequent change of place in our system of ideas, from more central to more peripheral, and from more peripheral to more central parts of consciousness" (*PP*, 277; *VRE*,161).

James is not proposing a series of neat, sequential mental movements from one configuration of consciousness to another. His description of each moment as having a "fringe" and a "focus" indicates the exploratory nature of our shifting attention. At any instant, we are vaguely aware in a "penumbral nascent way of a 'fringe' of inarticulated affinities" surrounding whatever idea is at the center of attention and which of these is pursued and which not is a result of tentatively exploring these fringes in response to one's interests (*PP*, 250). The activity of consciousness is an ongoing mediation between those vaguer elements at the fringes of consciousness and those of which we are most fully aware:

> One may admit that a good third of our psychic life consists in these rapid premonitory perspective views of schemes of thought not yet articulate. . . . "Tendencies" are not only descriptions from without, but . . . are among the objects of the stream, which is aware of them from within, and must be described as in a very large measure constituted of *feelings of tendency*, often so

vague that we are unable to name them at all. It is, in short, the re-instatement of the vague to its proper place in our mental life which I am so anxious to press on the attention. (*PP*, 245–46)

Crucially, in terms of the philosophical psychology that frames James's forward-looking, melioristic ethics, the richness of individual experience is not so much a matter of the myriad ideas and relations of which one is already aware but rather of the possibilities that they carry for adjusting to new circumstances and interests. As James Albrecht puts it, "If moral selfhood entails the ability to recognize the ideal possibilities of a given situation, this requires cultivating a salutary openness to the vague aspects of experience that point beyond the practical focus of any given moment."[92]

On James's account, then, all aspects of thought's dynamism can be understood in terms of the interplay between the multitudinous relational possibilities of experience and our ability to focus attention—however fleetingly—on one thing at a time. In this example from McDermott, the evocative nature of memory is described in Jamesian terms:

> Growing by its edges, the rivulets from our stream of consciousness are pregnant with connections that do not show their hand until subsequent, even allegedly alien, experiences occur. Say I come across my childhood toys. . . . My consciousness is jarred, and I can barely rein in the flood of memories, relations now bathed in the affairs of the present. The toys are old, and I am old, and the experience is profoundly new. The transition at work is thick and revelatory. The routinised edges of my present way come alive, sparking in many directions. The old has bequeathed the new in a manner that the new alone cannot achieve.[93]

Albeit drafted in terms of James's older image of the stream,[94] there is no need for McDermott to invoke a faculty of memory or a theory of time to make his point. The field of experience makes sense not just of the importance of recall or the shift in one's immediate focus in response to a chance encounter but of one's capacity to "move" between the instants of a life, each imbued with a meaning that is felt rather than cognized. Instead of dwelling on mechanism, it calls to mind the poignancy and significance of such events in terms of the whole course of a life. To the extent that James accords philosophical priority to first-person experience *as it is experienced*, the example validates his model and approach, and in so far as it makes sense of the way that memories of past events might sway one's contemporary decisions and commitments by means of their emotional power, the field of experience seems a potent tool for his ethics, too.

It is not entirely clear from James's accounts of his model just what he conceives its limits to be. His interest in how to delimit the field of consciousness and what lay "beyond its margins" is clearest in his proposal in *The Varieties of Religious Experience* that

> the most important step forward that has occurred in psychology since I have been a student of that science is the discovery . . . that, in certain subjects at least, there is not only the consciousness of the ordinary field, with its usual centre and margin, but an addition thereto in the shape of a set of memories, thoughts, and feelings, which are extra-marginal and outside of the primary consciousness altogether, but yet must be classed as conscious facts of some sort, able to reveal their presence by unmistakable signs. (*VRE*, 190)

Some philosophers have proposed that James's theory of relations provides a helpful way to understand the sub- and unconscious realms without resorting to complicated or mechanistic psychological theories. Ford, for instance, writes, "Given his notion that conscious awareness is fringed with vague feelings of relations that constitute the mood or the emotional tone of a thought, James might easily have accepted the idea that the fringe is itself fringed with feelings that are wholly unconscious."[95] Others have suggested that the fringe is best understood *in terms of* unconsciousness or semiconsciousness.[96]

Yet despite James's praise for the work of psychologists such as Joseph Breur, Sigmund Freud, and Pierre Janet, and his acknowledgment that the subconscious meant that "there is actually and literally more life in our total soul than we are at any time aware of," he steered clear of such a path in his less speculative works because "the distinction. . . . *between the unconscious and the conscious being of the mental state*" is "the sovereign means for believing what one likes in psychology, and of turning what might become a science into a tumbling-ground for whimsies" (*VRE*, 402; *PP*,166). Not until *The Varieties of Religious Experience* did the subconscious assume a significant place in James's published work. Although he considered "the problem of the subliminal" to be "possibly . . . the greatest problem of psychology," and despite his field theory seeming to presage a model of the nonconscious realm, he provides insufficient commentary to fill out the proposal.[97]

So long as James is read sympathetically—as providing a descriptive phenomenological account of experience, testable in our practices and introspected realities rather than in philosophy's more rarefied (conceptual) air—then his theory provides a sound basis for naturalistic ethics. (Whether or not his metaphysical musings are equally acceptable is another matter altogether.) Methodologically, introspective self-review accounts for feelings and meanings as much as knowings, relations as much as particular ideas, and long-established behavioral tendencies as much as momentary ethical judgments. His theory engages with thought's dynamism rather than seeking after some static or foundational aspect of consciousness, true to the shifting contexts and uncertainties associated with "real world" moral judgments. It recognizes that our relations with objects and other people frame our assessments and acknowledges that no moral judgment is isolated from the lessons that we have learned in the past or the hopes that we have for the future. In James's words, the pulse of inner life contains "a little past, a little future, a little awareness of our own body, of each other's persons, of these sublimities we are trying to talk about, . . . of truth and error, of good and bad, and of who knows how much more?" (*PU*, 129). In short, James's theory of experience fills the holes into which he thinks that previous ethical theories have fallen.

Furthermore, James's model of the relational field of consciousness represents not only the range and open-endedness of experiential phenomena and relational possibilities but also the means by which selective attention configures experience so that we act appropriately in response to our circumstances and in pursuit of our interests. On this model, "Human experience is not only a process; it is also creative. The ability of thoughts to control actions, and . . . incorporate aspects of previous thoughts without being completely predetermined by them, provide human beings with free will."[98] James's account makes sense of the lived reality of memory, anticipation, changes of focus, planning and executing courses of action, and (perhaps to some extent) the interplay of the conscious with un- and subconscious realms. However, whether it is adequate for a whole ethics of self-transformation is quite another thing and will depend on whether (and how) it can make sense of, first, one's capacity to change one's self, and second, the very nature of selfhood. Can it explain not just the dynamic aspects of consciousness but the self that seems to outlast any moment and to be intimately tied to all of the moments comprising a life? And can it do so without resorting to the kind of static, foundational model of selfhood to which James is fundamentally opposed?

Chapter 3

Defining Life's Potential

The Self-Transforming Self

Self as Relational Product

James's therapeutic ethics aims to articulate ways for making one's life richer and resisting the simplistic temptations of worldviews that are too limited in scope, such as materialism and religion. Two questions remain, though: Who is this "one" or self? And how is one able to direct attentive focus in pursuit of these ends from "inside" (so to speak) the dynamic field of consciousness? James's response rests on an innovative conception of the self as both a dynamic, self-interested entity conceived from one perspective as "I" and from another as "me," introspectively discriminable from the fullness of one's experience just on the basis of interests. Consistent with the pragmatist emphasis on practice, this description is situated in the world of decisions and actions, and real successes and failures, rather than conceptual abstraction and generalization. After all, as Dewey points out, "The more one is convinced that the pressing need of the day, in order to make headway against hedonistic ethics on one side and theological ethics on the other, is an ethics rooted and grounded in the self, the greater is the demand that that self be conceived as a working, practical self."[1]

As with his account of experience, James's model of self is largely a product of his methodological choices. In as early a text as *Principles*, he identifies two different ways in which philosophers might study conscious life in terms of experiential continuity: either by seeking after the "conditions of its production, and its connection with other facts" or as "analysis: What does it consist in? What is its inner nature?" (*PP*, 913). For philosophers inclined to the first approach and unwilling to content themselves with a phenomenological account, James's work on selfhood is entirely unsatisfactory: his inconsistencies are too much to bear, and it is impossible to locate the necessary and sufficient conditions of selfhood in "one of his free-floating 'Thoughts' in the mother-sea of consciousness."[2] But philosophers empathetic with the second approach—phenomenologists such as James Edie and Aron Gurwitsch, and those like McDermott and Smith who emphasize the existential implications of James's model of consciousness—are more likely to indulge such shortcomings as the inevitable consequence of having "taken so much of the meaning of personal identity out of the clouds and made of the Self an empirical and verifiable thing" (*PP*, 319).[3] For this latter cohort, James's phenomenological approach, using just the first-person experience of how selfhood *seems*, makes it unnecessary to speculate about underlying causes and structures, as more traditional metaphysical accounts of selfhood have tended to do.

As with the discussions of experience and dualism, inconsistency between metaphysical and phenomenological approaches is evident in James's corpus, making it difficult to determine just what he meant by "self" and how he intended to explain it. Richard Stevens notes "a certain methodological ambiguity" in James's work on selfhood, swinging between "a purely descriptive method without concern for the discovery of necessary structures" and a search "for the basic structures of consciousness."[4] In earlier essays, James adopted a model of unified consciousness as spontaneous, selective, and possessing causal efficacy and posits an "I" that can stand apart from its own states of consciousness and analyze them. In *Principles*, an organizing subject remains but now in more metaphysical form. In *Essays in Radical Empiricism*, the self seems almost to disappear, but in *A Pluralistic Universe* it is back, assuming substantive form.[5] As with his explorations of experience, these various descriptions evidence not linear development of (nor subtle variations in) James's views but his preoccupation with and equivocation on the philosophical problems that he is seeking to solve or avoid. Whenever he strays into metaphysical speculation, the self takes on a form at once more substantive and self-aware; however, whenever he pursues philosophical psychology, he reverts to descriptive accounts of selfhood on the basis of evidence attained introspectively.

James's commitment to studying selfhood as it is revealed experientially is especially evident in his critique of conceptions of the self as a unifying principle or structure of consciousness that enables, underlies, or orders the inherent dynamism of experience. Dewey insists that James was in fact always dubious about the existence of a subject or soul, even in his more metaphysical moments.[6] Whereas the preeminent theories of his day (the "mind-stuff," spiritualist, and transcendentalist views) all posited some form of generalized, substantial self to undergird phenomenal life, James rejected such approaches on three grounds. First, they compromised psychology's scientific credentials. "All attempts to *explain* our phenomenally given thoughts as products of deeper-lying entities . . . are metaphysical," he writes, unwarranted experientially (*PP*, 6). Second, they begged the question of the relationship between mental states and the substantial posit. Third, they were unsupported by introspective evidence.[7] As Sing-Nan Fen puts it, "To James, the fact that an I is an I is just a fact, directly perceivable," and so "it is absolutely unnecessary to have an intellectual power such as that demonstrated in Kant's transcendental apperception."[8] Direct experience of our own selfhood, whether in the usual course of life or when we pay deliberate attention to the phenomenon referred to as "I," makes it unnecessary to reconstruct that same phenomenon by way of a logical derivation, as Kant had done.[9] To go beyond the evidence of introspection is needlessly speculative and "contradict[s] the fundamental assumption of *every* philosophical school" that admits "a continual direct perception of the thinking activity in the concrete" (*PP*, 291). As such, the substantial self in whatever form is, for James, "the name of a nonentity" with "no right to a place among first principles" (*ERE*, 3).

Although James sometimes acknowledged the *possibility* that phenomenal life might rely upon a substantial subject, he remained firmly of the view that the conscious self, "*as a psychologic fact*, can be fully described without supposing any other agent than a succession of perishing thoughts, endowed with the functions of appropriation and rejection [emphasis added]" (*PP*, 323–24). Human consciousness contains all the relations and content required to explain the phenomenological reality of selfhood as complex, continuous, and felt immediately as one's own, the three characteristics that frame his theory of self.[10] As James writes, "*The states of consciousness are all that psychology needs to do her work with. Metaphysics or theology may prove the Soul to exist; but for psychology the hypothesis of such a substantial principle of unity is superfluous*" (PB 181).

In his phenomenological mood, James acknowledges the introspective revelation that "*every 'thought' is a part of a personal consciousness*" (*PP*, 220) and stakes out the primacy of selfhood for understanding human consciousness at all: "It seems as if the elementary psychic fact were not *thought* or *this thought* or *that thought*, but *my thought*, every thought being owned. . . . On these terms the personal self rather than the thought might be treated as the immediate datum in psychology. The universal conscious fact is not "feelings and thoughts exist," but "I think" and "I feel." No psychology, at any rate, can question the *existence* of personal selves" (*PP*, 221). On this (Cartesian-sounding) account, all of consciousness exhibits the mark of unified selfhood, so that experience 'belongs' in some sense to one's self. James will need to describe the evident unity and personal identity of consciousness if he is to furnish a complete phenomenology of selfhood.

As with experience generally, James's version of introspection is suitable for the study of those aspects pertaining specifically to selfhood, as Myers points out: "Convinced that experiences are richly textured and multiply veneered, perhaps superficially clear to the casual inner eye but increasingly murky to the searching eye, James recognized how introspective the task is of giving or finding the cash-value of terms such as 'I,' 'will,' 'consciousness,' 'sense,' 'attention,' 'remember,' 'imagine,' and so forth. Experiences are to explore introspectively, partly for the experimental discoveries enjoyed, but also for revealing the pragmatic value of notions like, for instance, *oneself*."[11] A complete phenomenological account requires James not just to define the terms that we use in our accounts of selfhood but also to describe the various ways that selfhood seems to us and how such phenomena relate to our self-descriptive terminologies and their ongoing interplay. Thus, for example, James writes that "*the words* ME, *then, and* SELF, *so far as they arouse feeling and connote emotional worth, are* OBJECTIVE *designations, meaning* ALL THE THINGS *which have the power to produce in a stream* [or field] *of consciousness excitement of a certain peculiar sort*" (*PP*, 304). Having eschewed a metaphysical account, he is not about to list "all the things" but rather to describe how they seem to us.

Three key themes emerge in James's early studies of the self and are retained throughout his oeuvre: first, experience and selfhood implicate one another (in the sense that the presence of one is always indicative of the other); second, experience is essentially a matter of activity (rather than, say, the product of a substantive mind); and third, this activity involves mutually transformative, interest-guided engagements between self and environment. These claims are crucial to James's contention that selfhood is an empirically verifiable psychological fact and so require careful review.

James's philosophical-psychological account of self is developed most explicitly in chapter 10 of *Principles*, where he explores both the experiential dynamics of selfhood and how these are described in language. James points out that whatever we refer to as "self" (and "me" and "I") is vague and always changing, and as such is only clearly conceivable once "fixed" before the mind as "thought's object." In other words, it is impossible to provide a descriptive account of selfhood just as it emerges in the course of thinking, and so (redolent of his approach to the descriptive study of experience generally) we have no choice but to instead group together various kinds and patterns of mental activity that we most associate with our "self" and describe them *after* they have been experienced. As such, the conceptual terminology that he employs to make the self intelligible—successive thinkers, "me," "I," material, social and spiritual "me's," and so on—must also be thought of in terms of dynamic consciousness rather than as discrete entities or components of some ontological structure.

Understood in these terms, and having discounted alternatives, James contends that the self emerges as a *product* of conscious activity. Whenever we "attend to" conscious life, we are initially aware just that there is thinking going on, even though our thoughts seem to be indisputably our own (*PP*, 221). Only with deliberate and careful introspective effort do we become aware of two principal classes into which fall our experiences of the self: on the one hand, as an object known and identifiable as separate from other objects of thought, an empirical self that we call "me"; on the other, as a self that seems to sort and arrange our experiences into those that are personal and those that are not, a "pure ego," which we refer to as "I." Once again, although James's terminology *seems* to invoke a metaphysical account of self, he is actually describing it phenomenologically, as

> a stream of thought, each part of which as "I" can remember those which went before, know the things they knew, and care paramountly for certain ones among them as "*Me*," and *appropriate to these* the rest. This Me is an empirical aggregate of things objectively known. The *I* which knows them cannot itself be an aggregate; neither for psychological purposes need it be an unchanging metaphysical entity like the Soul, or a principle like the transcendental Ego, viewed as "out of time." It is a *thought*, at each moment different from that of the last moment, but *appropriative* of the latter, together with all that the latter called its own. All the experiential facts find their place in this description, unencumbered with any hypothesis save that of the existence of passing thoughts or states of mind. (*PB*, 190–91)

"Me" comprises a plurality of material, social, and spiritual facts, whereas "I" is the singular self-identity of a self, and *in its widest possible sense . . . a man's Self is the sum total of all that he CAN call his* (*PP*, 279). This doesn't mean that the two perspectives on the self are separate things—there is, after all, only one field of consciousness or stream of thought—but just that it is possible to discriminate between the self as knower (I) and as known (me), both descriptively and functionally. They remain interdependent, however, and the interplay between them is very subtle.

James points out that it is always difficult on the evidence of introspection to distinguish "me" from what is merely "mine." Nonetheless, he locates three dimensions of "me," loosely defined by a typology of characteristics experienced of and by "me": material, social, and spiritual. Materially, "me" refers not just to one's own physical body but also to those aspects most closely associated with it (where "associated" is meant quite broadly), including one's clothes, immediate family, home, property, wealth, and whatever else has been derived from one's own labor (*PP*, 280–81). Socially, "me" refers to all the images that others associate with one, any recognition received from others for one's accomplishments, and all the expectations that others have of one (*PP*, 281–83).

According to James, it is the spiritual self that we conceive whenever we think about ourselves as thinkers or reflect on "who we are" (and we can *only* conceive of our innermost self reflectively). The spiritual "me" is "the most enduring and intimate" aspect of self, referring to "a man's inner or subjective being, his psychic faculties or dispositions" (*PP*, 283). It comprises our mental abilities, tendencies, and memories and enables us to discriminate between phenomena and ideas that are of interest and those that can be ignored or deliberately set aside (thus defining and orientating one's conscious field):

> Probably all men would describe it in much the same way up to a certain point. They would call it the *active* element in all consciousness; saying that whatever qualities a man's feelings may possess, or whatever content his thought may include, there is a spiritual something in him which seems to *go out* to meet these qualities and contents, whilst they seem to *come in* to be received by it. It is what welcomes or rejects. It presides over the perception of sensations, and by giving or withholding its assent it influences the movements they tend to arouse. . . . It

is the source of effort and attention, and the place from which appear to emanate the fiats of the will. (*PP*, 285)

These few sentences make clear that we refer to the spiritual me whenever we refer to our capacities to think, choose, and commit effort. Our moral freedom relies on the capacities that are most characteristic of James's spiritual "me": the ability to identify phenomena on which we ought to act (those that are of interest), the capacity to decide a response, and the commitment of effort needed to enact that response. As such, it is the form of "me" most crucial for James's ethics.

James does not mean to suggest that the various incarnations of "me" are *neatly* separable or discriminable. Experiential evidence indicates that they coalesce with each other and with other experiences, too. One's conception of self can at any moment contain thoughts of one's possessions (material "me") *and* others' judgments of them (social "me"), say, ideas that can merge quickly with an awareness of the cost of acquiring those possessions (an idea only loosely related to thoughts of "me," or even unrelated to them). It is only with careful introspective effort, if at all, that we can clearly define the various aspects of "me."

Furthermore, "me" is experientially continuous with "not-me," these two together comprising the entirety of thought's objects. What distinguishes "me" from "not-me" experientially is just a matter of "interest," those phenomena that orientate and define the focus and limits of the conscious field. James had much to say about the nature and role of interests as they pertain to self-transformation, as we shall see. For now, we need only to recall the way they operate amid the dynamism of consciousness, representing "that ongoing and interwoven sequence of preferential attention, instinctual adjustment, emotion and tendency to action which the present thought feels as a matter of fact with respect to certain objects related to survival or development."[12] All of the aspects of conscious life referred to by James's material, social, and spiritual "me's" entail such interest, whether evidenced in instinctive reactions, emotions, or deliberate actions.

By contrast, with "me" James takes the "I" as that present and passing thought that does the selecting and balancing of competing interests. He could be charged here with "smuggling in" just the kind of underlying (perhaps transcendentally derived) soul, subject, structure, or capacity that he overtly rejects as introspectively undiscoverable. Such a reading would avoid the difficult matter of how the plurality of relational experience can be organized or subsumed into a simple unity. But James so consistently uses radical empiricism to undercut such theories as Kant's transcendentalism that such a rendition would be disingenuous. As we have seen, for James, the use of "trans-experiential agents of unification, substances, intellectual categories and powers, or selves" to deal with thought's discontinuities and inconsistencies is the "hole" through which "all the corruptions of dialectics and all the metaphysical fictions pour into our philosophy," contrary to his commitment to the veracity of experience (*ERE*, 23, 25).

James's "I" is best understood in terms of the dynamism inherent in consciousness understood as an ever-changing field or stream, in which each thought is related to those that have gone before. Reminiscent of Locke and Hume, James describes the "I" as "the real, present onlooking, remembering, 'judging thought,'" the present assessment of whether some moment of experience is related appropriately to the past to be conceived as part of "me" (*PP*, 321). Rather than a substance, it is a "principle of self-unity" ensuring that each present thought is "aware of the same past in the same way," even though every such determination differs in time and context from all the others (*PB*, 181). No characteristic of experience persists beyond the present instant, and the "I" is constituted in the moment of assessing whether each present thought is related appropriately to those preceding ones to be one's own. In other words (words remarkably like Hume's), "a past time with past thought or selves contained therein" is compared against "the present self . . . in its various forms," and whether a thought is one's own "is a conclusion grounded either on the resemblance in essential respects, or on the continuity of the phenomena compared" (*PP*, 316; *PB*, 180).

James is careful to describe this process in temporal terms appropriate to the felt continuity of experience, the feeling that we "own" or "possess" an ever-growing range of experience:

> Each pulse of cognitive consciousness, each Thought, dies away and is replaced by another. The other, among the things it knows, knows its predecessor, and finding it 'warm,' . . . greets it, saying "Thou art *mine*, and part of the same self with me." Each later Thought, knowing and including thus the Thoughts which went before, is the final receptacle—and appropriating them is the final owner—of all they contain and own. Each Thought is thus born an owner, and dies owned, transmitting whatever it realized as its Self to its own later proprietor. . . . It is this trick which the nascent thought has of immediately taking up

the expiring thought and 'adopting' it, which is the foundation of the appropriation of the remoter constituents of the self. Who owns the last self owns the self before the last, for what possesses the possessor possesses the possessed. (*PP*, 322)

The strong sense of personal identity inherent in the experience of selfhood is, for James, "exactly like any one of our other perceptions of sameness among phenomena. It's a conclusion grounded either on the resemblance in a fundamental respect, or on the continuity before the mind, of the phenomena compared" (*PP*, 319). Each of one's own thoughts seems unified with other thoughts within the flow of consciousness by way of their "warmth," "intimacy," and inherent interest (*PP*, 232–33), and "whatever past feelings appear with those qualities must be admitted to receive the greeting of the present mental state, to be owned by it, and accepted as belonging together with it in a common self" (*PP*, 232).

Although these qualities are impossible to describe precisely, James nonetheless believes them to be decisive for defining where the self begins and ends:

> One great splitting of the whole universe into two halves [self and other] is made by each of us; and for each of us almost all of the interest attaches to one of the halves; but we all draw the line of division between them in a different place. . . . The altogether unique kind of interest which each human mind feels in those parts of creation which it can call me or mine may be a moral riddle, but it is a fundamental psychological fact. No mind can take the same interest in his neighbor's me as in his own. (*PP*, 278)

Since one's self is defined by thoughts that are of interest, expressions of selfhood go beyond overt descriptions of self-consciousness and self-unity to straightforward declarations of one's views and preferences. Whenever we conceive of such thoughts in terms of their transience, we tend to relate them to "I" (as in "I think that" or "I believe"); when conceiving them in terms of the felt continuity of experiential flow over time, we relate them to "me" ("my view is" and "that theory is mine").

Whether or not James's account of self in terms of "me" and "I" is philosophically defensible (and the nature of his mistake if it is not) is open to debate. Is he right to assume that a unified, self-identifiable self can be properly understood on just empirical grounds, introspectively observed? Scholars such as Yumiko Inukai contend that his phenomenological studies are sufficiently careful and faithful to the first-person reality of selfhood as to avoid the problem of how multitudinous experiences are unified. In short (and contra Hume), experience generally, and selfhood particularly, come to us as a continuous reality, such that there are no discrete elements that need to be unified, and so there is no problem to solve.[13] As James writes, atomistic analyses of experience such as Hume's are products of "confusion . . . between the thoughts themselves, taken as subjective facts, and the things of which they are aware. It is natural to make this confusion, but easy to avoid it when once put on one's guard. The things are discrete and discontinuous; they do pass before us in a train or chain, making often explosive appearances and rending each other in twain. But their comings and goings and contrasts no more break the flow of the thought that thinks them than they break the time and the space in which they lie" (*PP*, 233). Provided that one avoids atomistic analysis, the continuity of experience is preserved, and the problem of unification doesn't get off the ground.

Such approaches as Inukai's have not satisfied all of James's readers, however. Myers, for example, criticizes James for distinguishing consciousness itself from the contents of consciousness when he claims that "the sense of our own personal identity . . . is exactly like any one of our other perceptions of sameness among phenomena" (*PP*, 318). When James conceives of the "I" in terms of the assessment of particular thoughts to decide whether or not they belong to "me," he seems to Myers to introduce a discontinuity that is inconsistent with first-personal experience of the self.[14] (On a somewhat similar note, Dewey claims that James's discrimination of "I" from "me" represents "an extraordinary compromise" that reopens the question of James's dualism.)[15]

Surely Myers is mistaken, and as with James's account of experience, assessments of his theory of the self must be referred to his method to clarify his arguments and meanings. So long as we understand James's account in terms of his introspective method and field (or stream) theory of experience, there can be no separation of thought from contents of thought; they are one and the same necessarily. Thought's object is inevitably complex and dynamic, containing a penumbra of relational possibilities. The process of thinking resolves such possibilities, synthesizing past and present, observations and feelings, activities and perceptions, objects and selves, and so on. James's point is not that we somehow literally separate thought's object (self) from thought in order to comprehend it but that we must turn our attention toward the experience of selfhood if we are to provide an adequate descriptive account of it. In other words, he is proposing a psychological maneuver rather than an ontological or epistemological one. It is not that James has separated consciousness from the contents of consciousness but that he identifies more than one perspective on the same field of consciousness.

There remains one further crucial issue regarding interactions between "me" and "I": how they pertain to the physical body, which, it will be recalled, was designated by James as an aspect of the material "me." That the body is crucial to James's conception of selfhood is clear. For him as for all the pragmatists, the self ought not to be understood as a mere psychical presence but also as a physical object (one that includes the brain) located in the world of objects and other people, with "we ourselves and our living bodies . . . at the centre . . . and the objects in which we are really interested" around us.[16] James writes: "The individualized self, which I believe to be the only thing properly called self, is a part of the content of the world experienced. The world experienced (otherwise called the "field of consciousness") comes at all times with our body as its centre, centre of vision, centre of action, centre of interest. Where the body is is 'here'; when the body acts is 'now'; what the body touches is 'this'; all other things are 'there' and 'then' and 'that'" (ERE, 86 n.8). James is making a bi-fold observation. On the one hand, the body seems in the conscious field to be "the origin of co-ordinates," the physical place that one occupies and around which "everything circles." Here, James's focus is on physical position such that "the word 'I' . . . is primarily a noun of position" (ERE, 86 n. 8). The self extends outward into the world of objects and other people from a central point focused upon the physical body. On the other hand, the self "lives through" the body in relation to other people, objects, and beings. The emphasis is on physical actions and interests, so "the word 'my' designates the kind of emphasis" by which, "so far as 'thoughts' and 'feelings' can be active, their activity terminates in the activity of the body" (ERE, 86 n. 8). We conceive of the world of objects and other people from a perspective defined by our physical presence but attributed to our psychical self. As Edie puts it, capturing both points, "The various 'selves' which I cognize at different times, the ones with which I identify myself and whose side I take, are not all reducible to my material position or physical drives, but they all have this in common[:] that all these selves carry as part of their meaning a reference to my body."[17] Again, we find James sidestepping metaphysical speculation by favoring a descriptive interpretation of experience. In this case, rather than suggesting some mysterious connection between consciousness and body, he records and describes various ways in which we experience the bodily self.[18]

Bearing in mind the introspectively evident characteristics of the two facets of James's description of selfhood—self-conception borne of the unity of consciousness evident in the relationship between "I" and "me," and self-identity borne of the intimacy of one's thoughts—it becomes possible to explain the self in terms of the field theory of consciousness. Like all that we experience, the self is "a process, a passing parade of bits and pieces exhibiting various kinds of connections and disconnections, characteristics and capacities."[19] Despite the fact that one's self can seem stable and continuous, it is in fact inherently dynamic, as James describes:

> My present field of consciousness is a centre surrounded by a fringe that shades insensibly into a subconscious more. I use three separate terms here to describe this fact; but I might as well use three hundred, for the fact is all shades and no boundaries. Which part of it properly is in my consciousness, which out? If I name what is out, it already has come in. The centre works in one way while the margins work in another, and presently overpower the centre and are central themselves. What we conceptually identity ourselves with and say we are thinking of at any time is the centre; but our *full* self is the whole field, with all those indefinitely radiating subconscious possibilities of increase that we can only feel without conceiving, and hardly begin to analyze. The collective and the distributive ways of being coexist here, for each part functions distinctly, makes connection with its own peculiar region in the still wider rest of experience and tends to draw us into that line, and yet the whole is somehow felt as one pulse of our life—not conceived so, but felt so. (*PU*, 130)

On the field at every moment are the current thought, new relational connections that may or may not be realized, and, at the fringe, other ideas that may or may not be brought to full conscious awareness. New relations are realized continuously, with every change of circumstance and each new stimulus. Among these, we locate the transactions between "I" and "me" and the unification of those "warm" thoughts that together constitute a self, "an altogether other dimension of existence from the sensible and merely 'understandable' world" (*VRE*, 406). As a *felt* reality, the nature of this self, the center of our whole consciousness, seems perfectly clear: it is "the home of interest," "the source of effort and attention," and "the place from which appear to emanate the fiats of the will" (*PP*, 285). But as a *philosophical* reality, it is complex beyond belief, ever-changing, and impossible to derive adequately from a structure or logic.

As Andrew Bailey summarizes James's account of self, "We are, more or less, just the unbroken flow of our experiences" on the field, felt as "the phenomenological data of our continuity."[20] While James professes an imperfect understanding of the complex psychological dynamics involved, he furnishes an extraordinarily rich descriptive account of them, among which are those aspects most relevant to his ethics. It is not the case that my self is "bestowed upon me in advance," requiring for its full realization just exposure to some set of external conditions over which I have little or no control, as might have been suggested by a more metaphysically oriented approach. Rather, as McDermott points out, our relational experience reveals that "the self . . . is more of a permeable membrane than a spectating redoubt," such that "relational changes do not happen 'around us'" so much as "penetrate the very fabric of our being and, optimally at least, demand that we reshape, reassess, reconnoitre, rework, and revisit each of our previous relations undergone."[21] To the extent that we can control the constitution of the field of experience by pursuing certain relations and leaving others unrealized, we have some say over what becomes of our self. But how and to what extent are we able to realize this control, and how ought we to do so?

The Self-Transformative Project

For James, consciousness is the whole field of our experience, expanding and changing in every moment of a lifetime. But that part of the field discriminable as one's self is not a wholly passive product of this dynamism, lurching this way or that in response to chance circumstances. It is not only *possible* to take an active role in constituting one's self but an unavoidable aspect of human life, and the extent to which it is embraced determines the intensity and rewards of one's whole existence. If "experience is what I agree to attend to," as James claims, and if the relational thoughts and patterns of experience that are of most interest to me define the self (as both "me" and "I"), then my self-transformation rests squarely on deciding what to focus upon and what to exclude from consideration. In other words, to the extent that my interests guide my attentive focus, they are crucial for defining what (or who) "I" become, and it is by way of changing my interests and focus that James thinks I have some control over this lifelong project. James's ethics is a guide for, and justification of, decisions meant to best realize that task. As Smith writes,

> The hallmark of James's pragmatism is its uncompromising belief in each person's right, and even duty, to take his own experience seriously and to use it as a touchstone for thought and action. James's thought has often been characterized as "voluntarism"—the doctrine that effort, activity, and will have primacy over the acquisition of theoretical knowledge—and this judgment can stand if it is properly qualified. While it would be an error to attempt a reduction of James's philosophy to a neat system or to the proportions of a single idea, it is surely possible to describe the *heart* of his thought as a consistent voluntarism. Human intentions, purposes, plans, and goals are the dominant powers in his universe.[22]

James is undoubtedly a kind of voluntarist in the sense that he considers human intentions and will among the basic factors determining the future course of events,[23] and Smith's emphasis on the place of experience and theoretical knowledge as pursuant to action accords with our reading of James to this point.

But there is something troublingly one-sided about the suggestion that James holds human purposes and goals to be *dominant* forces in the experienced world. In his diagnosis of the socioeconomic circumstances to which he was responding, James is clear that people are constrained by their physical and social circumstances. Furthermore, his philosophical psychology is concerned with both the nature *and limits* of human psychological apparatus. Against Smith, it seems right to agree that James considers the possibility of creative growth to rely upon satisfaction of two conditions: "Human existence must be such that there is a genuine possibility for meaningful action" *and* "the world must be such that it is receptive to the effects of human action."[24] To the extent that both conditions are implicated in enabling and limiting free decision-making, they also define the scope for self-transformation. While at first blush this suggests an unfeasibly broad scope, we will see that James's analysis reveals significant constraints upon it.

Granted that the field of consciousness is oriented from moment-to-moment by selective attention, and that our attention is directed by our interests in the face of the circumstances that we encounter, it would seem that selfhood is to a great extent a mere *product* of whatever the world "throws our way," as it were. My responses transform some dormant possibility into fact according to what I experience, my interests serving just to mediate between stimulus and response. Such a direct, seemingly passive, relationship suggests that human behavior is predictable in the same way that experimental science has shown to be the case for the material world, explicable in terms of inviolable laws of nature. As James puts it, "In the physical world one can exhaustively deduce the resultant if one knows the elements. There is no real novelty—all is repetition, for the configuration doesn't count as a separate fact" (*ML*, 233). Perhaps this is the case for human responses, too.

Yet James's mature theory of self is an extension of his early repudiation of Herbert Spencer's theory of consciousness, which described human thought and action in terms of just such passive responses to external stimuli. In his critique, James argues that Spencer had ignored human powers of "active originality and spontaneous productivity," or "free will" (*ML*, 136). There is no denying that sensations borne of chance circumstances are "beyond our control; but *which* we attend to, note, and make emphatic in our conclusions" depends on the perspective that we adopt (*P*, 118). James writes, "What we say about reality . . . depends on the perspective into which we throw it. The *that* of it is its own; but *what* depends on the *which*; and the which depends on *us*. . . . By our inclusions and omissions we trace the field's extent; by our emphasis we mark its foreground and background; by our order we read it in this direction or in that. We receive in short the block of marble, but we carve a statue ourselves" (*P*, 118–19). In other words, even though we cannot control the range of phenomena that we encounter, the field of consciousness is defined and configured by our efforts and interests.

In contrast to the material world, where the arrangement of particular plants and animals (usually) makes little difference to the environment as a whole, the configuration of the field of consciousness according to momentary circumstances, interests, and memories matters very much and indicates the unceasing prospect of relational novelty: "In the mental world [the configuration of ideas] does so count; so there is always something really new . . . and not given in the mere sum of the elements. This new as such becomes one of the determinant conditions of further action, as is especially evident wherever it takes the form of *feeling*. For the reception of new experience is not simple addition, feeling and conation are simultaneously aroused, and the farther additions proceed along lines of attention and desire, thereby set in motion" (*ML*, 233). In our engagements with the world of objects and other people, for instance, our actions are not always simple products of a stimulus triggering some "automatic" response (although, as we shall see in his account of habit, James is aware that *most* human activity is of this kind: "We think the act, and it is done" (*PP*, 1131). We are experientially aware—sometimes only dimly, sometimes more clearly—of both causal regularities *and* uncertainties in experience, and so we believe in our prospects for making decisions and taking actions that change it, sometimes in significant ways.

Although this is a misleadingly simple summary of an extraordinarily complex dynamic (more of the detail will be drawn subsequently), it illustrates the space that James locates for "the genuine possibility for meaningful action" in self-transformation. He separates the chance configuration of circumstances that we encounter from the decision about whether and how to respond to them, a decision guided by such other aspects of experience as deep-seated beliefs, feelings and desires, life-lessons and other memories, self-conceptions, identification of options, and so on. Here, the instrumental value of consciousness is most evident, deciding the nature of, and means for, the adjustment of the human organism to its environment, directed toward the attainment of preferred ends.

For James, this gap between stimulus and response is the moment of "indeterminism" in which we influence what our experience will become, countering mechanistic theories like Spencer's by "giv[ing] back to the mind the free motion which has been blocked in the purely contemplative [theoretical] path" and "mak[ing] the world seem rational again" (*WB*, 66):

> Indeterminism . . . says that the parts have a certain amount of loose play on one another, so that the laying down of one of them does not necessarily determine what the others shall be. It admits that possibilities may be in excess of actualities, and that things not yet revealed to our knowledge may really in themselves be ambiguous. Of two alternative futures which we conceive, both may now be really possible; and the one become impossible only at the very moment when the other excludes it by becoming real itself. (*WB*, 118)

Although there is no way to *prove* that that we are not determined just by the circumstances that we encounter (because once an act has been performed, it is impossible to repeat it to determine whether it might have been altered), we *feel* that the future is undetermined and that we have a part to play in deciding its course. Every momentary encounter leads to a choice by which one preferences "one possibility and transforms an equivocal ambiguous *future* into an unalterable and simple *past*."[25] As such, the moment of indeterminism is the moment that defines each configuration of consciousness, and the feeling that we play a part in it is all the evidence that James requires to sustain his theory of human freedom: "That we ourselves may be authors of genuine novelty is the thesis of the doctrine of free will" (*SPP*, 75).

Although James's belief in the existence of free will relies by-and-large on experiential evidence, he finds another reason for committing to it, too: "I believe more and more that free will . . . must be accepted as a postulate in justification of our moral judgment that certain things already done might have been better done."[26] He means that the possibility of moral judgment *demands* postulation of free will in order that the decision-maker carry some responsibility for her decision, and the practical need to believe in free will trumps any justification on merely philosophical grounds.

The freedom exhibited in the moment of indeterminism derives from the human capacity to pay attention to (or "concentrate on") some things and ignore others; in other words, to configure the field of experience according to interests. The capacity for selective attention is, for James, "the very keel on which our mental ship is built," such that "each of us literally *chooses*, by his ways of attending to things, what sort of a universe he shall appear to himself to inhabit" (*PP*, 640, 401).

Without qualification, this claim seems problematic, implying that we literally (perhaps deliberately) choose a focus for our attention in every moment. But this is not what James is suggesting. He acknowledges that "granting consent" can be more or less habituated ("unconscious" or "automatic"), deliberate, or careful, and so the moment of indeterminism will not always end with deliberate attentive effort. There will be innumerable instances in one's life when one does not *deliberately* acknowledge, reject, or exercise the option of turning attention in this direction rather than that, instances including straightforward motor responses, deeply habituated patterns of thought or action, moments of distraction and boredom, or cases where circumstances demand an immediate physical response (as with perceived threats to one's safety). But so long as we do sometimes pay attention or ascribe meaning to a particular stimulus over others in the moment of indeterminism, "I" play a role in determining how I think and, so, who I become.

Let us turn to James's account of self-transformation in the moment of indeterminism, and how it relates to the configuration of consciousness. Because he located no introspective evidence for the presence of a substantial self, but only momentary configurations of mental phenomena felt to be one's own, his account of self-transformation rests upon a description of how relations between ideas are decided *in the process of their being formed*—that is, in the exercise of selective attention, just as we experience them. As such, the freedom exhibited in resolving the moment of indeterminism is less akin to "Kantian sovereign self-control" and more a matter of "self-transformation, or self-experimentation, or self-education, or even (if we can hear the label without certain contemporary connotations) self-improvement."[27] James explains how the self is created in each moment by honing his account of the selective processes that define both the limits of the field of consciousness (that is, those processes that determine which stimuli are of relatively greater importance than others) and relations on the field (those of special interest and warmth, in terms of which I organize my thoughts, thus defining "me").

Regarding the limits of the field, we notice certain stimuli because they represent a danger, the prospect of pleasure, evidence supporting a deeply held belief, or because they are aligned in some other way with our goals or desires. James's point is clearest in reference to sense data. He writes, "Millions of items of the outward order are present to my senses which never properly enter into my experience. Why? Because they have no *interest* for me. *My experience is what I agree to attend to.* Only those items which I *notice* shape my mind—without selective interest, experience is an utter chaos" (*PP*, xxxii). Unless we were able to discriminate some stimuli from the whole range, our mind "loses its way altogether," its "strength . . . dispersed" by being overwhelmed and distracted (*WB*, 165). Regarding the configuration of relations on the field, we find some ideas that are relatively "warm" and recognizable as "mine," *and* a range of alternatives that could at any moment become more or less "warm," more or less immediate to "me," depending upon momentary circumstances, needs, and interests.

In such cases, "The human mind is essentially partial. It can be efficient at all only by *picking out* what to attend to, and ignoring everything else—by narrowing its point of view" (*WB*, 165). As Sandra Rosenthal puts it, "Consciousness is a selecting agency, and from the most rudimentary perceptions of sense experience to the most abstract realms of thought, the selection is guided by interest or intent. At all levels of activity, our purposes and attention . . . direct our way of cutting into the flux of experience. . . . Our interpretive, organizing activity unifies, but in a plurality of ways. An element of novelty enters through the diversity of possible ways of contouring that within experience upon which we focus."[28] The freedom that we feel and exercise in the moment of indeterminism *just is* the capacity to discriminate between ideas and relations based on the interest that they hold and so to define and orientate the field of experience. The same general principle of selective attention applies whether we are attending to the danger posed by an onrushing car, the notion that some abstract philosophical concept might be worth pursuing, or wondering if one's friends will admire a new purchase.

To fully understand the implications of the moment of indeterminism for self-transformation requires an awareness of its limits. After all, it is a selective moment of *response* to circumstances, defined in most cases by characteristics either wholly or partly beyond our control, such as the physics of materiality, the social arrangements of one's community, the family into which one is born, inherited genetic traits, the larger social histories of which one is a part, chance events, and so on. Unless we bear in mind the contingent characteristics of experience as James described them in establishing his field model, we might be tempted to take the moment of indeterminism as a doorway to a much less constrained philosophy of self-transformation than he intends, perhaps even as a moment of relatively unconstrained or even wholesale reconfiguration of consciousness. Such a view would be inconsistent not only with James's model of selfhood in terms of a relatively stable "me" but with the theory of habit that underpins that model, too, as we shall see.

One interpretation has it that James considers our freedom to be very great indeed. Some commentators, mindful of his admiration for Emerson and the other Transcendentalists, suggest that he shared Emerson's extravagant faith in human potential, "the infinitude of the private man."[29] West describes James's "romantic veneration of the creative powers and combative energies of individuals" as promoting "a moral heroism, martial in form," and Bacon contends that James's pragmatism is straightforwardly a "successor to romanticism through its combination of the romantic sense of the importance of self-transformation with an awareness of public commitment."[30]

But although James's "self is Promethean: making, constructing, reconstructing, and bold in its effort to transcend the accepted conceptual frames of human experience," James is no Pollyannaish Romantic, at least not with regard to the freedom offered by selective attention.[31] The moment of indeterminism does not provide an opportunity to surmount one's personal history, enculturation, genetic inheritance, and chance circumstances but rather to reconcile such factors with one's passing interests and most passionately held goals. In the moment that I decide whether to commit time to practicing football or guitar, I cannot simply choose a path toward inevitable sporting or musical greatness, but I can decide to commit more time to practicing one or the other, to decide which one will serve me best into old age, and to balance up the enjoyment that I foresee from each. Such considerations point me in one direction or the other (or to some way of balancing them), and my whole understanding of the situation, together with my commitment to act, will be decided in consequence.

The limited but significant extent to which any individual self is "a power unto itself" is evident in the dynamics of selective attention. It is simply impossible to ignore with impunity an imminent danger, terrible physical pain, or the rule of law but equally impossible to ignore one's own freedom. It is always a necessary ingredient for navigating the limited range of options available at any moment. As Gay Wilson Allen points out, "James did not argue . . . that man has a wide freedom of choice. His choice of action may, in fact, be quite limited, but so long as events—some at least—hang in a delicate balance of uncertainty, so that a human action may tip the scales one way or another, there is *possibility*, hope, a chance to improve one's life and possibly the world."[32] James's melioristic ambitions rely upon his establishing the 'space' in conscious life for freely attending and acting. That such a moment exists seems clear enough to James on the evidence of experience:

> Our acts, our turning-places, where we seem to ourselves to make ourselves and grow, are the parts of the world to which we are closest, the parts of which our knowledge is the most intimate and complete. Why should we not take them at their face-value? Why may they not be the actual turning-places and growing places which they seem to be, of the world—why not the workshop of being, where we catch facts in the making, so that nowhere may the world grow in any other way than this? (*P*, 138)

Experience reveals a world that accommodates and responds to our decisions to some limited extent. In the moment of indeterminism, we decide what ideas to attend to from a range of alternatives, only some of which we control. Of the thoughts and actions that follow, any (or none) might prove significant or decisive for life's future course. The two conditions for the possibility of self-transformation—the possibility of meaningful human action, and the world's being (at least somewhat) receptive to the effects of such action—are satisfied.

Interests and Self-Transformation

Perry might be right when he says that "the essentially active and interested character of the human mind" is the "one germinal idea from which [James's] whole thought grew."[33] But whether or not we are prepared to go quite that far, it is crucial to an understanding of James's actionable proposals for self-transformation that we grasp the role of interests in defining the extraordinarily many experiential arrangements that together comprise a life.

The term "interest" is difficult to define with precision, and James devoted little time to the attempt. In one sense we simply chance across circumstances in our daily lives and either they are of interest to some degree or not at all, and that is that. Yet as James points out, our lives are replete with aims, purposes, ideals, goals, and ambitions arising not just from reflective activity or as reflexive responses to physical stimuli, but through interactions with the whole range of our social and physical circumstances. As Suckiel summarizes James's position, "His picture of the human being is that of a project-laden, desiring, goal-oriented, purposive, active, interested, value-affirming, interpretive individual, with whatever activity he engages in having as its ultimate aim the fulfillment of his diverse projected ends. It is difficult to find one single term to refer to these goals, desires, purposes, ideas, preferences, wants, and needs. As a general term . . . he calls them 'interests.' "[34] So for James, "interests" is shorthand for the entire range of ways in which we organize our lives, desires, and decisions around future outcomes that we value in the present, realized in subjective focusing of evaluations and attention.[35] The human capacity for pursuing deliberately chosen goals by means of planned actions is the ultimate mark of human intelligence, he believes, distinguishing persons from "the fatal automaton which a *merely* instinctive animal would be" (*PP*, 1013). We are distinctively purposeful beings whose self-affirmation is framed in terms of our desires, or "wants."[36]

Of the various kinds of interests, one in particular—ideals—is especially important for James's therapeutic ethics. We can exert greater control over our life and environment by pursuing paths of thought and action directed deliberately toward an ideal. However, for James, ideals are not universal or absolute behavioral goals, as in traditional ethics, but particular and personal ones that are historically contingent and often short-lived: "There is nothing absolutely ideal: ideals are relative to the lives that entertain them" (*TT*, 163), he writes. But in even the most fleeting and tenuous cases, ideals are products of a person's interest: "An ideal is a possibility which has made connexion already with some portion of reality. It is *somebody's* possibility: 'Hurrah!' for it!' " (*MEN*, 220).

As with interests generally, James invests little effort in defining and theorizing ideals, but he does make clear that two distinguishing characteristics mark them as a special type of interest.[37] He writes, "An ideal . . . must be something intellectually conceived, something of which we are not unconscious, if we have it; and it must carry with it that sort of outlook, uplift, and brightness that go with all intellectual facts. Secondly, there must be *novelty* in an ideal—novelty at least for him who the ideal grasps. Sodden routine is incompatible with ideality, although what is sodden routine for one person may be ideal novelty for another" (*TT*, 163). In other words, first, whereas other kinds of interests are often at the fringes of consciousness, we are *always* conscious of our ideals; and second, our ideals have a compelling "novelty" that James thinks attributes them a special motivational power, reflecting a relatively greater attractiveness and significance. The greater the motivation that we feel for realizing an ideal, the more likely is our progress toward it (although the relationship between these two is mediated by the effort that we summon, as will become clear), and conscious adoption (and readoption) of an ideal is both an expression of commitment to a desired outcome and a test of the strength of that commitment. Whereas unthinking patterns of habitual thought and action have their uses, their very unconsciousness leaves them unable to rouse such deliberate, effortful commitment.

It is worth noting the extent to which James's conception of persons as dynamic centers of interests and goals betrays a strong teleological leaning and hints of a kind of vitalism.[38] "Taking a purely naturalistic view of the matter," he writes, "it seems reasonable to suppose that, unless consciousness served some useful purpose, it would not have been superadded to life" (*ECR*, 302). James believes this purpose to be the attainment of ends, holding that "mental life is primarily teleological," "*pursuance of future ends and the choice of means for their attainment*" is a sign of the "*presence of mentality*," "*classification and conception are purely teleological weapons of the mind,"* and "the organism of thought . . . is teleological through and through" (*PB*, 11; *PP*, 21; *PP*, 961; *EPh*, 18). Moreover, consciousness is *always* directed toward advancing one's own current or future welfare, such that "the most natively interesting object to a man is his own personal self and its fortunes" (*TT*, 63). Indeed, the extent and intensity of commitment to our own interests tends to handicap our ability to empathize with the goals of others, "blinding us" to what it would be like to live according to their projects and meanings.[39]

Taking his teleological presumption still further, James holds that "the conceiving or theorizing faculty . . . functions *exclusively for the sake of ends* that . . . are set by our emotional and practical subjectivity altogether" (*WB*, 94–95). He describes interests—whether practical, aesthetic, ethical, religious, or bodily—as selective principles by which we direct our attentive resources. We tend to focus conscious effort upon matters that attract our attention *because* they are aligned with our plans, ambitions, goals, and desires. As Suckiel explains, "Human cognitive activities—concept formation, belief acquisition, theory construction, and the like—function like tools which are limited and moulded by the individual's preferences, desires, goals, and interests" where "the individual's goals themselves have the status of posits on James's view—they themselves neither require nor receive justification."[40] There will be instances where dominant interests will emerge in an instant, perhaps from a physical stimulus; James gives the example of schoolchildren whose interest can be drawn in a heartbeat to "the spitballs that Tommy is ready to throw" (*TT*, 61–62). Others will evolve over a lifetime, perhaps as the product of occasional reflections on one's ambitions, successes, and failures; for example, "the objects of professional interests are most of them, in their original nature, repulsive; but by their connection with such natively exciting objects as one's personal fortune . . . they grow to be the only things for which in middle life a man profoundly cares" (*TT*, 65). But in every case, attentive interest is guided and focused by one's interests.

Indeed, for James, our interests are "behind every distinction we draw, every selection we make, and every response we exhibit in coming to terms with ourselves and the world about us. Purposes may be broad or narrow, trivial or momentous, but they are always there."[41] For example, regarding memory, events of the past are drawn upon to the extent that they relate to some present interest, that interest pertaining to a preferred goal or outcome. (Recall McDermott's example of the old man chancing across his childhood toys.) Regarding sense data, where attending to the most relevant portion of a vast range of physiological intake can be a matter of survival, interests determine which sensations will be dealt with, which ignored, the conceptual means for determining and responding to their relevance, and, finally, what action to take.

Critically for James's melioristic intent, our interests are never finalized: "Experience is remoulding us every moment, and our mental reaction on every given thing is really a resultant of our experience of the whole world up to that date" (*PP*, 228). Our interests are always up for revision in light of a new experience, stimulus, or item of knowledge. But this is not to suggest that we lurch unpredictably from aim to aim and belief to belief, our life projects mere flotsam on an ocean of chance stimuli. We are naturally "conservative" creatures, epistemologically speaking, meaning that there is a bias toward maintaining our desires, commitments, and world views (*P*, 97). Our beliefs and intentions are relatively and generally stable, although each moment entails the prospect of seeing them in a new light, imbuing them with different meaning, or indicating new means for achieving them. In other words, every experience has the *potential* to change even a previously treasured goal unexpectedly and altogether, even though the strength of one's interest in the earlier goal is impossible to compare objectively against that of a later one. The change in focus is not a matter of rationally "weighing" one goal against the other but a moment of genuine experiential novelty.

The role of interests in deciding successive focal points for conscious attention is crucial for James's thesis that human lives can be deliberately changed and developed. Informed by knowledge, beliefs, and memories, a change in interests means that future configurations of experience will differ from those that would have followed otherwise. New relational connections will be forged to enable achievement of the new goal, and new ideas might be brought to consciousness, perhaps even some that had been far removed from the here and now on the wider fringes of the field of consciousness.

For instance, developing James's own example regarding professional goals, one might have commenced a career in business, convinced that it held the key to financial riches crucial for one's happiness. Yet years later, disillusioned with managerial life, financial advantage is thrown over in favor of intellectual succor, and one's resources are marshalled anew and with as much vigor as they were committed to the original enterprise. In this case, the dynamic interplay between goals, interests, circumstances, and attentive focus follows the same general pattern as with the initial one, years before, and yet the consequent actions are entirely new. There might be no final (or perhaps even detectable) moment when the goal has changed, no "weighing up" of one path against the other, and no apparent scale of contentment or wish-fulfillment against which a comparison is made. Instead, there is either a gradual accretion of realization, a flash of inspiration, or careful consideration of options (or all three) consequent to one's experiences taken together and focused on the issue of employment. As McDermott writes, "Experience is pedagogical," and the key to a richer, more fulfilling life "is not in objects, names, and definitions" but "in relations and symbols. Not by the obvious, alone, doth man live."[42]

We are in position now to enunciate more clearly the relationship between James's model of the self (in terms of those thoughts that are "warmest" and of most intense interest) with his theory of selective attention (where interests focus attention). Those more intensely interesting ideas in consciousness we designate by the word "my" and take to be part of "me" (*PP*, 309). To the extent that the "I" reflects the relative warmth of such thoughts in determining what is mine and what is not, "the self discovers itself as an agent of selection, of interest, and of critical judgment; the self becomes manifest through the experiences of *responding* to what is encountered. The self as a reality with limits and boundaries, with a place and a date, comes before us when we encounter our own *interest* both in the world and in that limited being that responds to what is encountered."[43] Literally, the self as James conceives it is the self-evident mechanism of consciousness configured in response to circumstances and in accordance with interests. To change one's interests—as we do over time, as we have more and different experiences—is necessarily to select differently, to change the configuration of consciousness, and so to change one's self.

Some of these changes to one's interests will be imperceptible, while others will involve deliberate adoption, amendment, or development. In any case, the effects on "me" can be difficult to predict. On occasion, a single experiential stimulus will "play itself out" in a whole raft of changes to one's interests, some unnoticed and others carefully thought through. For example, the sudden death of a sibling might significantly change my conception of my own mortality, alert me to the need for urgent lifestyle changes, bring me to rethink my roles within the family, cause me to reflect more carefully on shared childhood experiences, and perhaps become self-consciously maudlin in the process of each of these responses: realizing changes to all three aspects of "me," the material, social, and spiritual. But none of this is *necessarily* the case. It is also possible that my interests are such that the event might be ignored (the family having grown apart years ago, or a long-established antipathy resurfacing on mention of the death) or its importance downplayed in the light of other, more urgent and consuming worries, or even be taken as a reflection of my own status ("I was always the stronger, healthier one"). In short, the nature and effects of changes to one's interests cannot be predicted with certainty. Even quite dramatic events might change "me" very little, whereas relatively trivial ones might trigger a wholesale reassessment of my ideals, self-understanding, and character.

The ethical significance of paying careful attention to changes in our interests and selves, even though they are not always predictable or controllable, is well made by Konstantin Kolenda, when he writes:

> Contingent relations, impinging on one's psyche from within or from without, are candidates for inclusion in one's self-image as at least a web, not an inchoate concatenation of unregistered and undigested happenings, without any significant relation to a person's beliefs and desires . . . As independent nonhuman events, contingent occurrences cannot be appropriated and transformed. But our *awareness* of them . . . can amount to a sort of power over the world. So while we cannot affect the occurrence of contingencies, we can hope to face them, at least up to a point, on our terms. Coming to terms with contingencies is taking them up into the purview of one's beliefs, desires, hopes, and expectations, thus putting them into relation with something which in time becomes a person's more or less stable character which tries to deal with contingencies in terms of its own self-image.[44]

Subject to my interests, all the stimuli, ideas, and relations that I experience have the potential to be appropriated into the complex, structured conscious field that defines "me." I might not be able to influence very much of what happens to or around me, but I do in some cases have a say over how I respond. If things are of interest to me, I am more likely to reflect on them, plan a deliberate response, and adopt them as aspects of conscious life, whereas if they are of no interest, they might barely register in consciousness, if at all.

To discriminate between, and arrange, experiences according to interests is crucial for an orderly life and a stable sense of self. By successive acts of attending to or withholding attention from stimuli, we establish patterns of consciousness that make "me" a more or less reliable, more or less predictable, and more or less exploratory self. Consequently, "paying attention and thinking are moral acts. To pay attention or to think is to focus on particular interests and features of the world and at the same time to exclude other possible topics from consideration. What one attends to and how one attends are forms of action and uses of freedom that are massive in their ethical implications."[45] By such activity, "the result of unknown forces within the nervous system" expressed as our interests, we come to establish and exhibit our own "personal uniqueness," which is "the personal tone of each mind, which makes it more alive to certain classes of experience than others, more attentive to certain impressions, more open to certain reasons" (*WB*, 186).

For some philosophers, James's phenomenologically descriptive account of self-transformation will seem incomplete because it is unable to explain precisely *how* the self can focus, decide, and act on interests: "How do the act and effort of analysing and interpreting take place from within or as a deliberate act of the self, viewed as a stream of consciousness? How can a mere stream of consciousness be understood to have the capacity of functioning as an active agent?"[46] Even when James's account is framed in terms of his field theory rather than as a stream, providing an image of the limits and dynamics of consciousness, we seem no closer to a solution because a field is no more capable of acting than a stream.[47]

To have tried to explain these matters by invoking a mental structure or transcendentally derived capacity would have been inconsistent with James's broader philosophical views and methods. His naturalism precludes structural solutions from beyond the bounds of introspective evidence, and there is no introspectively attainable justification for hypothesizing structures to underlie our abilities to interpret, decide, and act upon our interests. For a pragmatist committed to the primacy of experience, it is enough to identify that we have such capacities and draw out the implications of that fact for making the best of one's life and self.

At this point, the two conditions identified earlier in the chapter as essential for meaningful moral action have been satisfied by James's account of conscious life. On the one hand, selfhood is experienced relationally, lessons from the past informing the thoughts and actions that decide one's future, with consciousness operating as a selective mechanism based on interests. On the other, we experience a world of real change and novelty, where freely made decisions and freely taken actions alter the course of events, indicating that "the inmost nature of the reality is congenial to *powers* which you possess" (*PP*, 942).

However, contrary to Smith's suggestion in the opening quote of this section, it is not the case that our goals are *dominant*: the materiality of the world and the chance circumstances of our lives see to that. Rather, our goals and ideals are decisive *relative to our psychological capacities and material and social constraints*. Although our "higher, more penetrating" moral ideals are "probable causes of future experience, factors to which the environment and the lessons it has so far taught us must learn to bend," it remains up to us to decide which of these imperatives we pursue (*WB*, 144). To this extent, at least, James is indeed a voluntarist. Putting it (perhaps too) simply, humans experience what they are *interested* in experiencing, and "without selective interest, experience is an utter chaos" (*PP*, 381).

With specification of the active role that each of us has in the process of self-transformation, the full meaning of James's ethics of self-transformation becomes evident. Precisely because the self is not metaphysically fixed, conscious life is a process of repeatedly making and remaking the self.[48] We each have responsibility for that task, such that "amidst the porous and leaky contours of the self one may paradoxically find the strongest sense of self and form of agency. In this ongoing quest for unification, the recurrent need to re-establish and maintain the self brings a unique sense of 'self-directedness and self-determination.' "[49] To the extent that one can decide one's responses to chance circumstances in pursuit of such goals, self-transformation is an active rather than passive affair.

As such, James's descriptive theory of relations sustains his proposals for how to replace dogmatic and universal ethical prescriptions with more constructive, creative, and individualized alternatives. As McDermott writes, "Everything we perceive teems with relational leads, many of them novel, and therefore often blocked from our experience by the narrowness and self-defining, circular character of our inherited conceptual scheme. The human task is to let our experiences speak to us in all of their manifold vagueness."[50]

Chapter 4

Realizing Life's Potential

An Ethics of Habit and Creative Willing

I will posit life (the real, the good) in the self-governing resistance of the ego of the world. Life shall [be built in] doing and suffering and creating.

—William James, *Letters*

The Habitual Self

James understood the key challenge for his ethics was to encourage people to become more receptive to the rich potential of human experience rather than limiting themselves to interpretations and options established through a single lens, such as the deterministic theories of scientific materialism or moral dogma derived from religious supernaturalism. As McDermott puts it, using imagery from James's field theory of consciousness, "for the most part we live our lives focally, that is, within a familiar range of experiences rendered clear to us by our conceptual systems or simply accepted by habituation. Ideally this focus opens outwards, reaching toward a fringe of experiences, often vague and inarticulate, but subtly continuous and profoundly meaningful."[1] Since James defines consciousness in terms of relational engagements across and between various aspects of experience, to live "focally" implies leading a narrower, less rich, and less exploratory existence than might be the case if one remained open to a wider range of new or revised relational possibilities. To take the latter course would require becoming (and remaining) more alert to the rewards that might arise from pursuing new causes, new interests, fresh perspectives, and new places, people, loves, achievements, forgiveness, skills, perspectives, and so on, and taking seriously their influence upon the kind of person that one becomes.

James's ethics is forward-looking in that it conceives of moral progress as involving changes to the ways that one thinks based on ongoing experimentation. Unlike scientific experiments, "Moral experiments involve an exercise of the self on the self. . . . Moral progress has thus the form of a personal transformation of the way in which we portray and live with our moral principles, which we can question in the measure to which they frustrate or augment our dearest ideals."[2] Not only are our experiential relations changing from each moment to the next, but one's self is changing with them as new relational connections form and old ones fade away:

> Life is in the transitions as much as in the terms connected; often, indeed, it seems to be there more emphatically, as if our spurts and sallies forward were the real firing-line of the battle, were like the thin line of flame advancing across the dry autumnal field which the farmer proceeds to burn. In this line we live prospectively as much as retrospectively. It is 'of' the past, inasmuch as it comes expressly as the past's continuation; it is 'of' the future in so far as the future, when it comes, will have continued *it*. (*ERE*, 42)

The key questions for the *practice* of James's melioristic ethics are how and to what extent one adopts an experimental, inventive attitude, making the most of life's relational possibilities rather than relying unthinkingly on established patterns of thought and action.

Specifically, in the socioeconomic context with which James was most immediately concerned, how might religious folk come to conceive of the world in modern, scientific terms, and how can the scientifically minded person become capable of locating spiritual dimensions to her experiences, as well as material ones? "Abstract rules indeed can help," he writes, "but they help the less in proportion as our intuitions are more piercing, and our vocation is the stronger for the moral life"; the more we understand the dynamics of free consciousness, the more acute our moral intuitions become, and the more we are willing to commit to a life of active experimentation (*WB*, 158).

For James, the capacity to realize new configurations of experience relies upon the free selective powers of consciousness. Roth summarizes James's position as follows:

> To say that we are free means that in the present moment we can control our concentration of attention on feelings, ideas, and objects in the world. Moreover, in James's view, acts of attending and thinking are choices that lead naturally to other actions in the world. Thus, moving from an original capacity to focus attention, which can be developed . . . through time, freedom is extended into all human life and into the world as a whole. Novel purposes, values, and actions are introduced, and they shape the world in a plurality of ways.[3]

> Man's life is permeated by freedom, and this freedom produces ambiguity in the self. This is revealed in the fact that a man can find out who he is only as he acts and chooses, and yet as long as he exists, his tasks of choosing and acting remain unfinished. Real clarity begins to emerge only as one's freedom orders itself and as one tries to achieve a consistent pattern of meaning through time. The stance toward existence that is urged by James's philosophy gives us a goal that can help to provide a person with clarity about who he is and where he is headed.[4]

James saw that the capacity for shifting conscious attention was essential for enabling thought and actions appropriate to the imperatives of each moment, allowing us to anticipate the future, identify and evaluate alternatives, and act appropriately. Patterns of attentive focus over time, and the effort committed to realizing them, define the person that one becomes. Consequently, ethics for James is "an essentially reflexive enterprise in which an agent reflexively works on itself in order to transform itself," and so "morality to James describes the relation between self and itself, not herself and a rule outside of the self."[5]

This view leads James to propose very different moral guidance from the kind that prescribes or proscribes certain actions based on authority (as with Divine Command Theory), universal rules for action (utilitarianism and deontology), or traits to instantiate or live up to (virtue ethics). In fact, on James's view, it is not free *actions* that need to be directed or constrained but free *thinking*. Neither is it the case that particular *actions* define moral character but rather *patterns of thinking* that emerge over the course of a lifetime: drunkards become drunkards and saints become saints "by so many separate acts and hours of work" (*PP*, 130–31). "If selfhood is a process or history, then 'character'—the capacities and dispositions that constitute a self at any given moment in its history—can be described as a composite of habits," as Albrecht puts it.[6] James believes that whenever one chooses some idea or action over another, the choice "really lies between one of several equally possible future Characters. What he shall *become* is fixed by the conduct of this moment," and so, "the problem with the man is less what act he shall now choose to do, than what being he shall now resolve to become" (*PP*, 276–77). We create ourselves through successive moments of free selective attention in accordance with our interests, in the context of extant circumstances, limited just by the emotional energy that we are willing and able to commit. James means to provide practical guidance on the first and last of these, making recommendations for how best to conceive of and influence the moral path of one's life, and so, the direction of one's self-transformation.

James's account of habit is crucial for his therapeutic ethics, as his "entire approach to ethics—from his most specific pedagogical suggestions to his broadest vision of individual vocation in a pluralistic universe—reflect this dynamic by which our actions in and on the world around us recast our habits and so remake our characters."[7] The "*ethical implications of the law of habit*," James claims, are "numerous and momentous" (*PP*, 124). Indeed, according to James at his more extravagant, even the social order is a product of habit: "Habit is the enormous fly-wheel of society, its most precious conservative agent," he writes, and "it alone is what keeps us all within the bounds of ordinance, and saves the children of fortune from the envious uprisings of the poor. It alone prevents the hardest and most repulsive walks of life from being deserted by those brought up to tread therein" (*PP*, 125). Habit is also behind our persistence through hardship, as it "keeps the fisherman and the deck-hand at sea through the winter; it holds the miner in his darkness, and nails the countryman to his log-cabin and his lonely farm through all the months of snow" (*PP*, 125). In short, habit in one form or another guides and constrains every aspect of human life.

According to James's philosophical psychology, the crucial role of habits in moral life is a product of our being "mere walking bundles of habits" (*PP*, 130): "Our virtues are habits as much as our vices. All our life, so far as it has definite form, is but a mass of habits,—practical, emotional, and intellectual,—systematically organized for our weal or woe, and bearing us irresistibly toward our destiny, whatever the latter may be" (*TT*, 47). We are, quite literally, a web of entrenched patterns of thought and behavior, and to the extent that each of us is definable by our consistent thoughts and actions, habit is "an invisible law, as strong as gravitation" that "keeps [each person] within his orbit, arrayed this year as he was the last," with a particular and definite character (*PP*, 126). Whereas selfhood is a process of ever-changing configurations of consciousness, the dispositions, capabilities, and histories that constitute the self at any moment is a collection of habits, such that "character is an aggregate of tendencies to act in a firm and prompt and definite way upon all the principal emergencies of life" (*PP*, 129). Habits or patterns of attentive focus are, then, real forces in one's life, and the moral challenge is to utilize and develop them correctly.

So precisely what is habit for James, psychologically speaking, and how does it relate to the patterning of thought and action that define self and character? On the one hand, aspects of James's version can seem familiar, with predecessors from the history of philosophy acknowledged in his texts. He draws heavily (via Peirce) from Scottish physiological psychologist Alexander Bain and the English physiologist William Carpenter, both of whom published studies of habit in the decades just prior to *Principles*.[8] Even some of James's most distinctive imagery has its precursors. The logician Bishop Richard Whately characterized habit in similar physiological terms, as "like a continued stream of water, which wears for itself a channel that it will not easily be turned from. The bed which the current had gradually scooped at first, afterwards confines it."[9] Similarly, John Locke wrote that "*custom* settles habits of thinking in the understanding, as well as . . . the will, and of motion in the body: all of which seems to be but trains of motions in the animal spirits, which, once set a going, continue in the same steps they have been used to; which, by often treading, are worn into a smooth path, and the motion in it becomes easy, and as it were natural."[10]

Yet on the other hand, James's account can seem highly enigmatic. While he would agree with Dewey that, straightforwardly, "The essence of habit is an acquired predisposition to *ways* or modes of response," he expands upon that notion with a narrative that veers between physiology, philosophical and scientific psychology, and epistemology: involving the relationships between body and mind, and choice and action.[11] McGranahan proposes that this approach was James's way of "thickening up a broadly naturalistic discussion about organisms and their capacities," enabling "a full-blooded interdisciplinary study of the human being as a concrete purposive organism," although it is also possible to see it more simply as a product of his underlying Darwinism, expressed in the fields of study with which he was most familiar.[12]

James's initial description of habit comes in the section of *Principles* concerned with physiology and derives from his biological conception of consciousness as the intermediary between the environment's multitudinous stimuli and bodily motor responses to them, structured by patterns of thought and mediated by free will. He claims there that "the moment one tries to define what habit is, one is led to the fundamental properties of matter" (*PP*, 109). But rather than leading to a deterministic account of human action, this physicalism emphasizes how thought processes enable us to be creative and adaptable in deciding our responses. He locates this flexibility in the "*plasticity of the organic materials of which* [our] *bodies are composed*" which allows the formation of relatively consistent yet changeable pathways of neural discharge in the brain: "*An acquired habit, from the physiological point of view, is nothing but a new pathway of discharge formed in the brain, by which certain incoming currents ever after tend to escape*" (*PP*, 110; *PB*, 125).

For James, plasticity means "the possession of a structure weak enough to yield to an influence, but strong enough not to yield all at once," and habits are possible because the brain is "plastic enough to maintain its integrity, and be not disrupted when its structure yields" (*PP*, 110). Every interaction with the environment reconfigures pliant brain tissue either by deepening existing neural pathways or forging new ones; and with repetition some of them are "carved into" brain tissue deeply enough to become habitual. As James describes the process, "The mind . . . works on data it receives very much as a sculptor works on his block of stone," and although "we receive in short the block of marble, . . . we carve the statue" (*P*, 119). Initially, when one is young or a stimulus new, the structure is malleable, but it becomes more rigid over time, as when "India-rubber becomes friable, or plaster 'sets' " (*PP*, 110).

That James describes habit in physical terms does not mean that habits are realized just in physical actions, however. As "the enormous fly-wheel of society," habits are not restricted to such tendencies as buttoning a shirt from top to bottom, patting the dog's head, and swinging a bat just so. Pragmatists have tended to emphasize the extent to which human mental adaptation invokes physical actions to alter those circumstances, as when Dewey asserts that habit "is quite as much adaptation *of* the environment to our own activities as of our activities *to* the environment."[13] But some commentators on James's theory have *over*emphasized the physical aspects of habit (in terms of the eventual expression of habits in bodily movements or alterations made to the physical environment) relative to the psychological mechanisms from which they derive. Robert Talisse and Micah Hester, for example, provide an initially bald definition of habit for James as "a function of life wherein physical bodies respond to given conditions, adjusting as required by those conditions."[14] Without extensive qualification (which Talisse and Hester only partly provide), such a characterization is misleading, a consequence perhaps of James's own extensive use of physiological imagery and his early work on reflex-arc theory, or as a way of emphasizing pragmatism's distinctive focus upon action.[15] In any case, it draws attention toward James's account of instinct and "sensori-motor mechanisms" and away from his accounts of more complicated versions of mental and behavioral adaptability, alluded to when he writes that "experience is remoulding us every moment" and "brain redistributions are in infinite variety" (*PP*, 228–29). Although it *is* true for James that the body serves as "the centre of one's interests," and that thinking ought always to be understood in the context of eventual physical action, it is *not* the case that physical reactions are *unmediated* expressions of one's interests except in the very simplest cases nor that they are without a nonphysical context (including past experiences). As we have seen, James understands mental life in terms of relational events on the field of experience, and "interests" extend far beyond the physical realm to include, for instance, social and spiritual circumstances.

While our everyday conception of habit typically pertains to actions of minor import, James recognizes that the tendency to establish and maintain habits ranges from primitive animal instincts (or "innate tendencies") to the most sophisticated aspects of human behavior (those involved in "acts of reason"). The case of "a simple habit" (James mentions snuffling, nail-biting, and putting our hands in our pockets) is "nothing but a reflex discharge," whereas (recalling his account of the field of experience) "the most complex habits" are "*concatenated* discharges in the nerve-centres, due to the presence there of systems of reflex paths, so organized as to wake each other up successively" (*PP*, 112–13). Simple bodily habits of the former kind are mere activations of "ready-made arrangements" in the nerve centers, whereas complex cases like learning a new language, striking a moving ball, learning to forgive, or placing a memory in a new context initially require careful, conscious effort and repetitive training in pursuit of habituation that "*diminishes the conscious attention with which our acts are performed,*" thereby enabling efficient and reliable implementation, time after time (*PP*, 119).

Habit encourages more efficient repetition because "a path once traversed by a nerve-current might be expected to follow the law of most of the paths we know, and to be scooped out and made more permeable than before," and "nothing is easier than to imagine how, when a current once has traversed a path, it should traverse it more readily still a second time" (*PP*, 113).[16] Habituated relational connections, physiologically described, are pathways of least resistance, requiring less energy and effort than those less familiar ones demanding greater concentration and rehearsal. "A strictly voluntary act has to be guided by idea, perception, and volition, throughout its whole course," he says, whereas for "an habitual action, mere sensation is a sufficient guide, and the upper regions of brain and mind are set comparatively free" (*PP*, 120). Not only is this a matter of practical convenience (for "we would all go mad if every part of our daily routine—buttoning and unbuttoning—had to be thought about and decided on")[17] but also "the more of the details of our daily life we can hand over to the effortless custody of automatism, the more our higher powers of mind will be set free for their own proper work," including the cultivation of other good habits (*PP*, 126). In other words, as more of our thinking and responses are dealt with habitually, greater conscious capacity is available for dealing with more interesting, perplexing, and unformed situations, so that "the great thing is to form habits which then leave [the] hemis[pheres] free for higher flights and in forming habits, to keep them unbroken" (*ML*, 37).

Although James uses the image of brain pathways as "a mechanistic metaphor for processes of electrochemical rearrangement" in terms of "then-current accounts of neurology," his description recalls the basic efficacy of today's theories of neuroplasticity and neural connectivity.[18] Once a particular neural connection has been established or a previous one reactivated, a human adaptive response results in the tendency to follow it again and again until some stronger force—a newly successful action, for example, or a change in one's environment that renders a previous habit unsuccessful—induces a new one.[19] Consequently, as Menand puts it, "Our reaction to stimulus will—on average, for habit is a statistical concept—be predictable, repeatable, habitual," whether the stimulus leads to a basketball jump shot or believing in God: if the tendency has, in a sense acceptable in the circumstances, "worked" as a response to past stimuli, then it is more likely to be repeated.[20]

The economizing advantages of habituation can also be expressed in terms of attentive focus and the field of consciousness. James explains that "habits depend on sensations not attended to," and habit *"diminishes the conscious attention with which our acts are performed"* (*PB*, 131; *PP*, 119). Habits enable mental energy to be allocated to more difficult and problematic circumstances: those that require greater concentrative attention. As Marchetti writes:

> Attention, . . . when it is directed to objects and situations with which we are confident and familiar, is not particularly mentally burdensome, but it can become so when we turn our attention to previously unexplored regions of experience. Then, James writes, its effects on our overall mental attitude are particularly significant. Attention in fact sharpens our perception, helps our memory and improves our ability to form and criticize concepts. However, its most important consequences are of a practical and moral kind, since attention characterizes us as *agents* and not mere spectators of the life of the mind.[21]

By freeing attentive capacity, habits enable active consideration of new problems and ideas, including such demanding matters as one's own moral well-being, so that "the practical and theoretical life of whole species, as well as of individual beings, results from the selection which the habitual direction of their attention involves" (*PP*, 401).

The advantages conferred by habit are accompanied by risks associated with becoming less consciously aware of patterns that define one's thinking and behavior. Although one's habits are expressions of past experiences, deliberate practice, and so on, they form tendencies that can go unquestioned, overly simple perspectives, behaviors engrained long ago but no longer appropriate, or even laziness and passivity. In terms of James's theory of self-transformation, four aspects are of particular concern.

First, the natural human tendency to make habits unconsciously, essential for day-to-day living, means that the self is to some uncertain degree a product of tendencies of which one might remain unaware. In terms of the relational field, one will tend to repeat and reinforce the same connections time and again: using the same words to describe oneself, telling the same stories about formative events in one's life, traveling a particular route to work each day, pursuing favored pastimes, living in accordance with invariant values, and so on. As such, one's character is a product and mark of both efficient thinking *and* failure to amend habits adopted previously, whether or not they remain efficacious. Regarding James's ambition to reform patterns of thinking among his contemporaries, those who conceived of the world simply in terms of the new scientific materialism tended to emphasize without question physical phenomena and mechanistic accounts of reality to the detriment of human cares and traditional values, whereas those prone to religious irrationalism emphasized prayer and baseless hope over practical, active interventions, and simplistic creeds of ancient origin over modern scientific proofs. Only by keeping up the "ongoing exercise of self-criticism" might we avoid "dissipat[ing] our energies and jeopardis[ing] our potentialities."[22]

Second, "the range of an individual's habits is not only wide but also randomly multifarious, not to mention whimsical. Humans build habits out of almost anything, from head scratching up to writing philosophical essays. Although James gives us a sense of what habits do, . . . he is not implying that any particular habit is thereby self-evidently justified."[23] James's theory seems incapable of justifying any habitual response over others, consistent with his very general conception of the good life in terms of experiential richness. Final arbitration relies upon one's own experiences, forever revisable but never justifiable "in principle" or forever.

Third, there is a risk of creating habits that are disadvantageous or lead to unfavorable outcomes evident only after the habit is engrained (and perhaps not even then). James writes that "the hell to be endured hereafter, of which theology tells, is no worse than the hell we make for ourselves in this world by habitually fashioning our characters in the wrong way. . . . We are spinning our own fates, good or evil, and never to be undone. Every smallest stroke of virtue or of vice leaves its never-so-little scar" (*TT*, 53). It will always take greater effort and commitment to counter an entrenched neural pathway than to continue with it. But even if we can leave our worst habits behind, so to speak, they will always remain to some extent a part of our self: not only must addicts commit great energy to battling addiction, but their regrets, self-reproach, and continuing need for vigilance will forever define them to some extent.

Fourth, habits can engrain a kind of "conservative inertia," a matter with which James was deeply concerned: "Most of us feel as if we lived habitually with a sort of cloud weighing on us, below our highest notch of clearness in discernment, sureness in reasoning, or firmness in deciding. Compared with what we ought to be, we are only half-awake. Our fires are damped, our drafts are checked. We are making use of only a small part of our possible mental and physical resources" (*ERM*, 131). The consequent tendency is to "sleepwalk through life," whether that means failing to appreciate new stimuli or reconceptualize experience to date: "Disinterested curiosity is past, the mental grooves and channels set, the power of assimilation gone" (*PP*, 1021). Only by invoking "some unusual stimulus," new "*excitements, ideas, and efforts*," might we overcome this tendency, carrying us "over the usually effective dam" and freeing "reservoirs of energy that habitually are not tapped" (*ERM*, 132).

Whenever James refers to realizing life's richness, or broadening our focus, he is encouraging us to counter this fourth risk and reminding us of the need to retain a capacity for recognizing and pursuing new relational possibilities. The person whose thinking is so deeply habituated that relational alternatives remain hidden (that is, on the more distant fringes of the field of experience), or the one who, having noticed such opportunities, rejects them in favor of the comfortable familiarity of sameness, will remain a product of engrained relations to a greater extent than someone who keeps a lookout for opportunities to think and act differently and commits to realizing at least some of them. "Most of us grow more and more enslaved to the stock conceptions with which we have once become familiar," he says, "and less and less capable of assimilating impressions in any but the old ways. Old fogyism, in short, is the inevitable terminus to which life sweeps us on" (*PP*, 754).

The risks of such a fate extend to all aspects of life: habits pertaining to self-conception (thinking about oneself into adulthood as still an awkward youth, for example), guiding principles for one's activities and life projects (always favoring efficient travel over rambling exploration), tendencies in one's personal life (the aging single time and again pursuing partners of a particular appearance), habits of task execution (always washing the cutlery last), approaches to career development ("working your way up" in a single organization or profession), habits of ethical judgment (following religious edicts for fear of damnation), and even the broadest tendencies of thought (the analyst's habit of thinking about thinking just in terms of epistemic criteria). In every case, conceiving of one's self and life in wholly habitual terms means closing one's mind to new relational possibilities on the field of experience, and to those new interests, activities, and forms of flourishing "at the fringe."

The risk of becoming an "old fogy" sounds insignificant—perhaps even a caricature of the inevitability of middle and old age—but in the context of James's theory of self, the implications of deep habituation are significant and not limited to the elderly. Using the imagery of optics consistent with James's description of successive foci on the field of experience, McDermott describes them in detail:

> Speaking diagnostically . . . about human well-being, James's philosophy offers the following cautions and suggestions. First, if our focus is concave, we tend to duplicate our experiences or at a minimum, no matter their actual differences, they are slotted in an already articulated and accepted conceptual scheme . . . This attitude becomes increasingly defensive, even shrill in overestimating the importance and reach of our focus and in time develops a hostility to experiences not already included within our range. In effect, we tend to identify and evaluate experiences only in terms already familiar to us and sanctioned by us.
>
> Self-encapsulating, this approach results in relation-starvation and in an increasing narrowness of person. What is to be lamented is not the decrease in the quantity of relations formulated, although that is often, if not necessarily, a factor, but in the absence of novelty, differentia, and, in short, the developing inability to be open to experience. In this pillbox mentality, novelty is ever a threat so we burn out the relational ground around us. Little comes to our consciousness which is not duplicative or replicative. . . .
>
> By contrast, if our focus is convex, we have the advantage of reaching out and thereby reconstituting our frame of reference, flooding us with enormous possibilities, for, as James tells us, anything that makes a difference anywhere, makes a difference elsewhere.[24]

Although framed in terms of the risks of a particular mindset, this quote effectively summarizes James's whole ethical project. The ways that we think decide in large part the person that we become—the self that one creates, one's character—and the kind of life that we lead, and in McDermott's words again, "to accept a derivative ethics or an a priori meaning of the self, as in the classical doctrine of the soul, is to abort the making of relations" and alienate one's self from the rich possibilities evident in experience more carefully attended to.[25] To interpret and respond to disparate experiences primarily or solely in terms of their similarity to others, to respond to them according to habits relevant in one case but not another, to become less willing or able to experience events afresh or locate new possibilities, to narrow unnecessarily one's conception of what life might become: all of these are at odds with the enrichment and betterment promoted by James's ethical meliorism. Consequently, as Unger puts it, "The vitality of the individual . . . depends on his success in fashioning a character resistant to the narrowing of experience, to the rigidity of response, and to the consequent constriction of possibility that surrender to a hardened version of what the self implies."[26]

But is "old fogyism" strictly *inevitable*, as James suggests? Is it the case that there is something about human nature and habit making that makes "relation-starvation" or a "concave focus" unavoidable? At various points, James seems ambivalent about whether and to what extent melioristic reform of the self is possible. In the chapter on habit in *Principles*, for instance, while insisting that individuals are responsible for the habits that define them, he writes that "could the young but realize how soon they will become mere walking bundles of habits, they would give more heed to their conduct while in the plastic state" and claims that "in most of us, by the age of thirty, the character has set like plaster, and will never soften again" (*PP*, 130, 126). Our early formed dependence upon certain habits of thought and action "dooms us all to fight out the battle of life upon the lines of our nurture or our early choice, and to make the best of a pursuit that disagrees, because there is no other for which we are fitted, and it is too late to begin again" (*PP*, 125). Although consideration of empirical evidence for James's claims is beyond our scope, we can make sense of them by considering such phenomena as the rate at which young children learn, the tendency for youths to copy the behaviors of their peers, parental influences that only become evident in choices made decades later, and those occasions when an ill-advised tendency from one's teen years comes back to haunt.[27]

But it seems just as reasonable to agree with the more positive James that some people can—and do, albeit perhaps infrequently—change significant aspects of their thinking and actions later in life, sometimes as the result of a deliberate project and sometimes in ways that seem almost inevitable. "I have been accused . . . of making old habits appear so strong that the acquiring of new ones, and particularly anything like a sudden reform or conversion, would be made impossible by my doctrine," James writes, and yet "new habits *can* be launched . . . on condition of there being new stimuli and new excitements. Now life abounds in these, and sometimes they are such critical and revolutionary experiences that they change a man's whole scale of values and system of ideas" (*TT*, 53), while on other occasions, changes to character are the products of a gradual accumulation of actions, thoughts, and feelings.[28]

Rather than trying to reconcile these two positions, it seems best to take James's assertion that we cannot readily change habits formed in youth as his way of emphasizing the significant extent of character development in early life and the *relative* difficulty of changing our most stable and rehearsed habits later. The former is empirically verifiable; the latter is a consequence of the strength of neural pathways forged by long periods of repetition. We all tend to live "within a familiar range of experiences rendered clear to us by our conceptual systems or simply accepted by habituation," but some more than others: some people do indeed live life largely based on habits left unreviewed and unquestioned, without perhaps recognizing or being much interested in alternatives, comfortable in or tolerant of established patterns and thereby avoiding much risk.[29]

Nonetheless, as we have seen, learning, adapting, and enlarging one's life means constructing new habits—that is, realizing new relational patterns and opportunities—and such activity is a precondition for adapting to one's environment. As Albrecht points out, "If individuality exists only through interactions with environing conditions, it is not therefore fatally determined by them, for . . . objective conditions provide the opportunities for the new interactions through which the self grows and changes."[30] Furthermore, while relying on old habits is ordinarily safe, it is important to keep in mind that experience contains a whole range of other possibilities that might entail wonderful opportunities or prove crucial for a good life. Although with James we might puzzle over the scale and frequency of changes that we are capable of conceiving and implementing successfully, especially later in life, the potential and need for doing so are inherent in the human condition (even in responding to processes of physical aging). This more optimistic position, developed in James's writings to a greater extent than the pessimistic one, accords better with his general buoyancy, relational pluralism, and several proposals for just how such changes might—and ought to—be achieved.

Although James's own descriptions of the "wider sea" of new stimuli and specific possibilities "at the fringe" tend toward the exotic (religious revelations, peculiar psychic experiences, drug-induced episodes, psychophysical experiences such as with yoga, and so on), and his concrete examples of new relational connections are relatively few, he considered his physiological account of habit "the most powerful ally of hortatory ethics" because it reveals and describes the means by which to alter one's habits. Whenever

James emphasizes the world's malleability and the extent to which it waits "to receive its final touches at our hand," when he lays out his constructivist epistemology and emphasizes the malleability of the field of experience and the plasticity of the brain, when he deploys radical empiricism to uncover the relational potential "between things, conjunctive as well as disjunctive," and when he emphasizes life's "flights" as well as the "perchings," he is highlighting prospects for enriching conscious life and overturning conservative habits. To the extent that habits are changeable, so too are one's dispositional tendencies and thus one's self; for if one's thinking and responses are "plastic," then we are educable, even if the process of amending our habits can prove demanding.

As Dewey puts it, summarizing James's disparate approaches to the matter, "Everywhere there is an opportunity and a need to go beyond what one has been, beyond . . . the body of desires, actions, and habits which has been potent in the past. . . . The good person is precisely the one who is . . . the most concerned to find openings of the newly forming or growing self."[31] The self-transformative challenge is to counter those deeply imbued reactions and tendencies that have become stale, irrelevant, or overly restrictive and instead to engage with the world in ways that expand our thinking and enrich our actions; or, as McDermott so colorfully expresses the imperative, we ought to "make relations! Build, relate, and then reflect. Reflect, relate, and then build. Seek novelty, leave no stone unturned. Fasten on colours, shapes, textures, sounds, odours, sights. Above all, never close down until the fat person sings. The only acceptable denouement is death. Until then all signs are go—that is, make relations until the maker is unmade."[32]

Habituating Destiny: Self-Transformation and Willing

There is a tension in James's philosophical psychology between his phenomenological account of experience (and the experiential field) and his physiological version. Regarding self-transformation, the latter implies that simply committing to change one's habits will be inadequate for the task, for "moral resolve and moral exhortation cannot, in themselves, directly influence habit, since habit has a structural basis in the nervous system."[33] Consequently, James's explanation of deliberate self-transformation, and his practical proposals for achieving it, need to be more rigorous and complex than the kinds of admonition found in self-help books championing "the power of positive thinking" (although there are elements of such an approach in James, too). James's approach is built on his intricate and complex analyses of consciousness, together with his phenomenological account of the relationship between mind and body. It rests heavily on principles established early in his career, in *Principles*, developed subsequently in *The Will to Believe* (which Koopman has argued is really a *case study* in James's ethics of self-transformation),[34] and given practical bearing in *Talks to Teachers*, and elsewhere.

To alter the habits comprising one's self, one must first be aware of them. In philosophical terms, we must be able to reconcile habit's "passivity" (the tendency to follow established lines of thought or "privileged paths of inertia" of which we are less consciously aware) with the active intervention required to recognize and overturn them and establish new habits in their stead. Although habits enable us to conduct many aspects of life without deliberate attention, it only requires an unexpected outcome, a slightly changed circumstance, or a moment's reflection for a previously habitual thought or action to come to consciousness, demanding attention.

However, to rely on a habit's proving inadequate for coping with some new stimulus or unanticipated result is not a reliable means for activating habit's productive potential in pursuit of self-transformation. Indeed, to rely on such an approach would mean that self-transformation was not, strictly speaking, "active" at all, as the awareness of one's habits would be initiated as a *response* to problematic circumstances over which one has no (or limited) control. James's voluntarism indicates a different path, relying instead on our capacity for active intervention in habit formation, sometimes with a view to self-improvement, as Michael Eldridge and Sami Pihlström have pointed out:

> One of our most important habits is the meta-level habit of critically reflecting on, revising, and transforming our habits. Thus, our habits are not simply given to us once and for all; we are responsible for continuously self-critically examining whether they enable us to achieve our purposes (which are themselves in view only through the habitual actions we engage in) or not. . . . We are fallible beings, and a key element of our acknowledging that fallibility is the recognition that in many cases we have to revise our habits of action (including obviously any beliefs we might hold about the world). This is, indeed, what inquiry ultimately amounts to in pragmatism: as our habitual actions in some cases may lead to unexpected consequences, we may start

to doubt the beliefs (i.e., habits) that led to those actions; it is this doubt that then launches an inquiry into the matter, aiming at new—revised—beliefs and thus to a smooth continuation of the interrupted habitual actions.[35]

The authors draw attention to two points of great importance for James's ethics of self-transformation: the need for self-reflective review of one's habits, and the extent to which even habitual physical reactions are consequences of beliefs that are forms of habituated thinking. They are describing the complex experiential nexus between perceptions of the world, interests, and habits, and the need for ongoing review of the appropriateness or otherwise of our responses. It *might* be that such self-reflection is prompted by the failure of an existing habit (a dropped catch indicating a flaw in technique, a partner's reminder that routine grumpiness is inconsistent with a happy household, or the weight-scale alerting us that habitual late-night eating is a bad practice), but it might instead be a product of *practiced* self-reflection (as with deliberately entertaining a new route to work each week, more careful review of the weekend routine, or even paying careful attention to the words and opinions of other people). Critical self-reflection means remaining alert to tendencies of thought and action, bringing those habits to the center of attention as often as circumstances allow, considering them carefully, and keeping in mind that they are always open to review and change, however entrenched they might have become. In these ways, "Our acts of voluntary attention, brief and fitful as they are, are nevertheless momentous and critical, determining us, as they do, to higher or lower destinies" (*TT*, 111).

To reconfigure a settled, heavily habituated consciousness by attending deliberately to habits means following the same course as any other shift of attentive focus, whether prompted by a physical stimulus, studying philosophy books, or a partner's words. The field of consciousness is either extended (by entertaining new ideas at the fringe) or relationally reconfigured, thereby disrupting established connections between ideas. As Megan Craig puts it, "What one needs is a habit of disrupting fixations—a very peculiar habit in the art of self-interruption and transformation."[36] Such a transformational habit involves "bringing into focus" both one's existing habits and "something that usually lurks at the margins or in the 'fringes' of consciousness."[37]

The "peculiarity" to which Craig refers is that the habit of deliberately reviewing one's constitutive habits seems to be different than the habits under review, requiring both a deliberate and repeated engagement and relatively more effort. We will see shortly that James's conception of habits is very broad indeed and accommodates such diversity in a manner consistent with recent developments in psychology. For the moment, it is sufficient to realize that, for James, attending to one's own habits of thought brings a new, reflective perspective, making it feasible to transform one's self by countenancing new ideas (not least, the idea that it is possible to change one's self in important ways) and new relations between ideas (in particular, thinking about what changes to pursue, and how to go about them).

James usually conceives of these transformative processes, not in terms of sudden or revelatory changes to one's whole consciousness, made once and for all (such "sudden reform and conversion" is exceedingly rare) but in terms of moral education.[38] Whereas James thinks that education generally involves "getting orderly habits of thought," *moral* education means cultivating habits of thinking that encourage a richer life, including the habit of critically reviewing and amending other habits to avoid inappropriate fixation and habituation.[39] In the absence of an urgent moral crisis, it is best to "nibble away" at established habits of thought, gradually habituating self-reflective review. James reminds us that "only when habits of order are formed can we advance to really interesting fields of action—and consequently accumulate grain on grain of willful choice like a very miser; never forgetting how one link dropped undoes an indefinite number."[40] Misers can be more or less effective accumulators, and James's practical recommendations for good moral education are concerned more with effective, long-term acquisition than tempting, short-term speculation.

Because so many aspects of James's philosophy and psychology coalesce in his account of deliberate self-transformation, there are numerous ways of approaching his practical proposals for pursuing self-reflexive review. One of these is suggested in a marginal notation to James's copy of *Psychology: The Briefer Course* that is something of a precis of his whole approach to self-transformation (and to his personal recovery from melancholy and tedium vitae, too), despite its being an appropriation of a quote from the British novelist and dramatist, Charles Reade: "Sow an action, & you reap a habit; sow a habit & you reap a character; sow a character and you reap a destiny" (*PB*, 448).[41] Our discussion will loosely follow this path.

James's voluntarism and phenomenological and physiological conceptions of experience are incorporated in his proposal that action ought to be the first step in deliberate character development. To change one's habits and introduce new ones (including the habit of critiquing previously established habits) is, subject to constraints imposed by one's circumstances, a matter of "free will"—albeit a very particular conception of will, as we shall see. Just as free will was James's own antidote to the overwhelming specter of determinism,[42] so it is also the key to self-creative salvation for his peers. Whereas our conversational references to habit and will typically emphasize an oppositional relationship (e.g., "I will improve my sleep patterns, but I am in the habit of staying up late"), James points to a positive one essential for self-transformation. To conceive of the world afresh and as conducive to a better, more meaningful life, one needs to act in ways that encourage more receptive and positive thinking. Deliberate, willed action is crucial for transforming one's own habits of thought, and so, one's conscious existence.

James's "action/habit/character/destiny" incantation is most easily understood when applied to acquiring new motor skills, where an initial act is the first step in a cycle of repetition that encourages improvement, habituation, and eventually, expertise. Although the very possibility of a deliberate act originates with instinct, "an apparently goal oriented behaviour that was never learned,"[43] as with the idea of catching a ball following an involuntary, protective parrying of a thrown projectile, it never ends there. To develop a skill means committing to action, practicing repetitively and consistently until the new neural pathways are properly established.

But although James sometimes calls on examples of physical skill (especially in his discussions of ideo-motor and reflex responses), his proposals for deliberate habituation of thought rely more usually on his psychology. "I want more than anything else to emphasize the fact that volition is primarily a relation, not between our Self and extra-mental matter (as many philosophers still maintain), but between our Self and our own states of mind," he writes (*PP*, 1172). Whether James is describing how to change a physical response, a moral judgment, or self-reflective practices, he begins with the need to *act*, as Craig describes:

> A simple example might be to attempt to laugh or smile in the midst of sadness. James's theory is that the physical act of smiling will do more to dispel a pervasive sense of sorrow than any thinking by itself could ever do. Such actions may be utterly mundane—such as commitments to waking early, exercising, or reading more poetry. They may also be more far-reaching and difficult to begin—a commitment to sobriety, for example. But even in the case of seemingly impossible actions, James reminds us that action begins with a single step. . . . James's writings are suffused with an atmosphere of the incremental and the ordinary,

coupled with a fascination with "the physical courage of common man." One of the striking features of James's vision of existence is his belief in the efficacy of even the smallest action and its potential to change the course of an entire life.[44]

Although contemplating a new thought or action must commence with a chance exposure to that alternative so that it might be conceived as possible, the crucial thing in terms of habituation is that it be acted upon subsequently, commencing the cycle of practice that, but for conflicting interests, will mark and entrench the new path in the nervous system. In the case of those habits of mind that define one's self, the relevant "act" is turning one's attention inward, paying deliberate heed to one's own habits.

This attentive focus can play either of two roles—or both. On the one hand, it can constitute a project of *critical* self-awareness. Remaining alert to the tendency to create habits counters their "unthinking" formation (to some extent) and keeping in mind the benefits of identifying and reviewing habits encourages those practices. Without such conscious attention, we tend to go on following the same relational paths, since "the determining condition of the unhesitating and resistless sequence of the act seems to be *the absence of any conflicting notion in the mind*" (*PP*, 1132). On the other hand, it can play a *constructive* role, highlighting prospects for different relational connections on the field and fringes of consciousness. As Marchetti puts it, "By deciding to pay attention to a certain idea which is to adhere to a particular aspect of reality: that choice then determines the self one becomes—the experiences we enjoy [or might enjoy], how we are able to express and account for those experiences."[45] Using language and concepts from our previous chapter, it means realizing at the moment of indeterminism and in response to one's interest in a better life, that it is always possible to think afresh, to respond to this circumstance differently than in previous, similar cases. Practically, it entails both "the ability to . . . examine the uniquely meaningful fringes" of the field of experience, and "the will to risk pursuing the possibilities that emerge once one *does* see beyond indistinguishable occurrences of the same old things, described by the same old names."[46]

For James himself, having experienced lengthy spells of helpless depression as a young man, awareness of the importance of habits and deliberate commitment to controlling them came from reading the French neo-Kantian Charles Renouvier. James recorded in his diary that he could "see no reason why [Renouvier's] definition of free will—'the sustaining of a thought *because I choose to* when I might have other thoughts'—need be the definition of an illusion," and that he intended to adhere to it in order to "voluntarily cultivate the feeling of moral freedom."[47] (Perry, James's pupil and intellectual biographer, thought Renouvier "the greatest individual influence on the development of James's thought.")[48] This meant adopting the habit of framing his decisions in terms of moral freedom and reminding himself of his ability to influence the course of events rather than lapsing into helplessness prompted by a deterministic perspective, or confusion between freedom and determinism. The first step, though—James's crucial *act*—was to pay attention to the patterns of thought that preceded his decision-making.

Since humans are "bundles of habits," and habits require relatively less attentive deliberation and energy, the great majority of our decisions and actions are straightforward: "We think the act, and it is done; and that is all that introspection tells us of the matter" (*PP*, 1131). But cases involving deliberate focus require greater attention and effort. James draws the distinction most clearly in chapter 26 of *Principles* where, starting with a contrast between ideo-motor responses and deliberate actions, he identifies five types of volitional decision on a continuum between wholly "automatic" responses and a single kind of "voluntary" decision, properly so-called.[49] At the former extreme are cases where reflex, "the mechanical principles that govern interest and association," determine our response, such that "sensible impressions . . . produce movements immediately and of themselves," without the need for a conscious *fiat* (*TT*, 101–2).[50] Here, consciousness is related so "intimately" with bodily movement that a phenomenon immediately awakens a movement-response "*whenever it is not kept from so doing by an antagonistic representation present simultaneously to the mind*": since the mind is "*in its very nature impulsive*," then "we don't bestow" the "accommodation and the resultant feeling" but rather "the object draws it from us. The object has the initiative, not the mind" (*PP*, 1134, 1134–35; *PP*, 425).[51] According to James, most human thought and action is of this general kind.

At the other end of the spectrum are those relatively rare and exceptional cases of purely voluntary decisions enabled by deliberate attentive effort:

> In the *fifth and final type* of decision, the feeling that the evidence is all in, and that reason has balanced the books, may be either present or absent. But in either case we feel, in deciding, as if ourselves by our own wilful act inclined the beam; in the former case by adding our living effort to the weight of the logical reason which taken alone, seems powerless to make the

act discharge; in the latter by a kind of creative contribution of something instead of a reason which does a reason's work. (*PP*, 1141)

James is referring here to decisions that might be considered "authentically free," where in the absence of evident, compelling reasons to favor one alternative over another, we feel the need to add "our living effort to the weight of the logical reason which, taken alone, seems powerless to make the act discharge" (*PP*, 1141). This kind of decision is distinguished from the others just by the feeling of effort rather than any other criterion.

Several factors relevant to James's proposals for self-transformation emerge from his discussion of simple and complex decisions. First, each type invokes the same psychological functions and activities. Even in the most complex cases, where a conflict between ideas requires commitment of great mental effort for resolution, there is no superior faculty "supplying the effort" or "in control," as it were, but just the regular machinations of consciousness: "*Movement is the natural immediate effect of feeling, irrespective of what the quality of the feeling may be. It is so in reflex action, it is so in emotional expression, it is so in the voluntary life,*" indicating that "ideo-motor action is thus no paradox" but rather that "it obeys the type of all conscious action, and from it one must start to explain action in which a special fiat is involved" (*PP*, 1135). Second, the *only* way to tell the various cases apart is by referring to the conscious effort committed to them: "Sometimes the bare idea is sufficient, but sometimes an additional conscious element, in the shape of a fiat, mandate, or express consent, has to intervene and precede the movement" (*PP*, 1130).[52]

Third, James's account explains how the word "habit" and its definitional characteristics can apply both to deeply entrenched, definitive, and "automatic" patterns of thinking and to such a deliberate habit as noticing and reassessing one's own settled habits (the "peculiarity" of the habit of deliberate self-reflection, mentioned previously). Not only does the latter involve relatively more attentive deliberation and energy, but it can be encouraged by deliberate use of various stimuli. For example, one might incorporate in the habitual weekly routine a casual review of one's behaviors over the past week, thereby interrupting the "flow" of more deeply engrained habits to reconsider their appropriateness and consequences. Alternatively, one might utilize the techniques of cognitive behavioral therapy designed to disrupt problematic stimulus/response relationships, perhaps using a diary to keep track of stimuli that prompt recourse to inappropriate and destructive habits.[53] Or again, one might simply practice an occasional, informal identification and interrogation of newly formed habits whenever the idea comes to mind.

Fourth, without recourse to a "special fiat," it seemed to James impossible to account for long-term, carefully planned projects of self-development or resolution of moral crises where the best response was not self-evident. Regarding the latter, and highlighting the contrast with much self-help literature, Gale writes that "these are complex cases in which we are not able to 'just do it' but instead first must work on our own minds so that we become vividly conscious in a certain manner. In the important character-determining cases we need to dramatically envision our performing the competing alternative actions and the consequences of doing so. Not only can this be the key factor in determining us to pursue one of the alternatives, it also can greatly increase the chances of our successfully pursuing it."[54]

The kind of attentive effort to which James refers in the case of ethics is no different from that involved in dealing with the world of objects. "Everyone knows what attention is," James insists, "it is the taking possession by the mind, in clear and vivid form, of one out of what seem several simultaneously possible objects or trains of thought. Focalization, concentration, of consciousness are of its essence. It implies withdrawal from some things in order to deal effectively with others" (*PP*, 382).[55] James writes, "Our moral effort, properly so called, terminates in our holding fast to the appropriate idea. If then, you are asked, '*In what does a moral act consist* when reduced to its simplest and most elementary form?' you can make only one reply. You can say that *it consists in the effort of attention by which we hold fast to an idea* which but for that effort of attention would be driven out of the mind by the other psychological tendencies that are there" (*TT*, 109–10). In other words, the feeling of effort derives from the activity of attending to one idea over others that might be attractive, deliberately reorienting the field of consciousness around the central idea and consigning the others to the fringes of awareness. In the case of moral self-reflection, effort is required to pay attention to one's own patterns of thinking, whereas the alternative of allowing habits to operate unchecked has the appeal of requiring little or no deliberate attention.

Precisely *which* alternative to pursue is decided on the basis of one's interests, but even in cases where an alternative seems "difficult to sustain or somewhat repulsive," it can still supplant an easier, habituated one provided that the foreseeable consequences motivate sufficient attentive effort. This is also true in cases of "that peculiar feeling of inward unrest known as *indecision*" (*PP*, 1136), where the effort involved in selecting one idea is matched by that involved in choosing another. James is convinced that the matter will be resolved so long as we continue to pay attention to it because, eventually, our thinking about one alternative will neutralize or silence the antagonistic one(s), and the normal flow of consciousness and action will resume.[56] James famously uses the case of climbing out of bed on a freezing morning to present "in miniature form the data for an entire psychology of volition," the conflict between a bed's warm comforts and the imperatives of the cold world outside only resolved by a "fortunate lapse of consciousness" in which the idea of staying put is momentarily displaced (*PP*, 1133).

As we have seen, James believed on the basis of introspective evidence that actions follow naturally from thought. "Consciousness is in its very nature impulsive" (*PP*, 1134), he writes, and "when an idea *stings* us in a certain way, makes as it were a certain electric connection with our Self," then we adopt a kind of "imperative" stance toward it and "say, *let it be* a reality" (*PP*, 1172, 1173). Unless we become interested in some contrary idea, "that activity . . . when once rightly located, possesses all the efficaciousness that can anywhere possible be supposed" (*ERE*, 257–58). It is *only* in cases of a clash between conflicting ideas—as with a life of habitual ease against one of active self-transformation, or continuing to rely on a single framework of understanding (such as science or religion) rather than entertaining alternatives—that attentive effort is required, and attending to one particular idea "*is* the *fiat*; and it is a mere physiological incident that . . . motor consequences should ensue" (*PP*, 1166).[57] Although the relationship between thinking, acting, and volition will vary according to the kind of habits involved, as we have seen, volition is always "a psychic or moral fact pure and simple, and is absolutely completed when the stable state of the idea is there" (*PP*, 1165). Regarding the realization of self-creative potential, it means remaining alert to both those "easier" ways of thinking that are customary but perhaps no longer beneficial and prospects for new interpretations and actions in their stead.

To this point, in the absence of a superior faculty or transcendental self, the source and nature of this psychic effort remain unexplained, and James takes a surprising turn in dealing with it. Pursuing his phenomenological approach and relying on his readers' own experience for corroborative evidence, he claims that the "*effort of attention is . . . the essential phenomenon of will*" (*PP*, 1167).[58] But whereas this might suggest that the will is a faculty that motivates the effort or provides the attention (or both), James means that the will just *is* attentive effort and that to suggest otherwise is to exceed the introspective evidence available.[59] Will is a reflexive function "between our Self and our own states of mind" (*PP*, 1172), "literally a fiat, a state of mind which consents, agrees, or is willing, that certain represented experiences shall continue to be, or should now for the first time become part of Reality" (*EPs*, 111). The *"essential achievement of the will, in short, when it is most 'voluntary,' is to ATTEND to a difficult object and hold it fast before the mind"* until that idea defines "the disposition of the man's consciousness" such that the consequent action might be affected unimpeded (*PP*, 1166, 1168).[60] Whenever mental focus drifts from one idea or train of thought toward another, or retreats to indecision, it has to be brought back to that idea deliberately, and the feeling of inner mental effort involved is what we refer to as "will." Willing is "absolutely completed when the stable state of the idea is there," orientating the field of consciousness, at which point "nature . . . 'backs' us instantaneously and follows up our inward willingness by outward changes on her own part" (*PB*, 385; *PP*, 1169).

James maintains that the effort involved in willing is "just what we feel it to be," "an original spiritual force . . . originating *ex nihilo* . . . [as though] from a fourth dimension" rather than a product of, say, universal will, Freudian primal impulse, or some other basic animating force.[61] Smith writes that James "accuses those who take our direct experience of striving and achieving to be no more than a surface illusion of being guilty of animism, and of invoking 'principles' which cannot be justified. James's contrary view credits the experience of activity as an ultimate fact," such that "genuine efficacy . . . is embedded in experience."[62] (Indeed, contra Freud, James and other classical pragmatists emphasize the brain's plasticity and the deep connections between habit and will when they hold that even our most primal and intractable tendencies can be amended or redirected by new experiences.)

This account might lead James's contemporary reader to conceive of will as something like what today we call "willpower": energetic personal commitment to delay short-term gratification in favor of long-term goals. In both cases, there is conflict among one's interests, resolution of it demands mental effort, the situational context plays a part in defining and deciding options, both the effort committed and the outcome achieved are first-personal, and so on. However, the critical distinction is that "willpower" is usually understood in terms of the imposition of some capacity (or activation of some faculty) called "will" with sufficient intensity (or "power") to delay an action, whereas James conceives of the power as originating and operating within the dynamism of consciousness rather than being imposed upon it.

Though James's account of the will (and willing) is "modest" and concerned almost as much with criticizing other conceptions as explaining his own, it "is nevertheless sufficient to give us a sense of the potency and value of our own initiative."[63] Human will is *free* will, not in the sense of a human capacity to circumvent natural laws or control one's fate regardless of circumstances and the decisions and actions of others but because it allows us *some* control over our fate and *some* attribution of meaning to our decisions.[64] James writes, "The action of the will is the reality of consent to a fact of any sort whatever, a fact in which we ourselves may play either an active or a suffering part. The fact always appears to us in an idea: and it is willed by its idea becoming victorious over inhibiting ideas, banishing negations and remaining affirmed" (*EPs*, 115). The implications for his meliorism are profound: "Free-will pragmatically means *novelties in the world*, the right to expect that in its deepest elements as well as in its surface phenomena, the future may not identically repeat and imitate the past. . . . It holds up improvement as at least possible; whereas determinism assures us that our whole notion of possibility is born of human ignorance, and that necessity and impossibility between them rule the destinies of the world" (*P*, 61, 60–61).

To the extent that attentive effort configures the field of experience, the human person is a product of willing, and the potency of one's willing will decide, at least in part, the kind of person that one will become: more active or passive, creative or habit bound, interested more in a life of energetic self-improvement or one of relative ease. As Smith puts it,

> Viewing the person as a subject marking out, in the medium of action, a dynamic biography through time and change demands that we seek the center of the self in something that can provide both unity and directionality throughout the process. . . . [The] best candidate for such a center is the willing of a dominant purpose or life plan expressing what a given person means to be. A purpose of such a nature is a living togetherness of a one in the form of the projected goal and a many in the form of that succession of deeds required for reaching it. The person in willing the plan is at the same time willing whatever needs to be done to realize the end in view.[65]

Willing is a matter of deciding one's whole personhood within constraints imposed by genetic endowments, social systems, family conditions, and so on. Such external factors define and limit our possibilities in advance of our decisions and effortful willing; however, as the exercise of attentive effort, free will enables *some* control over one's life. The scope of that control might not necessarily be very great, but it is the unique and characteristic marker of each person's life. As James puts it, "*The fons et origo of all reality, whether from the absolute or the practical point of view, is thus subjective, is ourselves. . . . [A]s thinkers with emotional reaction, we give what seems to us a still higher degree of reality to whatever things we select and turn to* WITH A WILL" (*PP*, 925–26). The significance of this for our moral lives cannot be overstated:

> In all this the power of voluntarily attending is the point of the whole procedure. Just as a balance turns on its knife-edges, so on it our moral destiny turns. You remember that, when we were talking of the subject of attention, we discovered how much more intermittent and brief our acts of voluntary attention are than is commonly supposed. If they were all summed together, the time that they occupy would cover an almost incredibly small portion of our lives. But I also said . . . that their brevity was not in proportion to their significance. . . . It is not the mere size of a thing which constitutes its importance; it is its position in the organism to which it belongs. Our acts of voluntary attention, brief and fitful as they are, are nevertheless momentous and critical, determining us, as they do, to higher or lower destinies. (*TT* 110–11)

If one is prepared to commit sufficient effort, remain sensitive to context, and take some risks in those relatively few moments when opportunity presents itself, then it is possible to deliberately fashion and refashion the field of consciousness over the course of a life and so become a different and better person. "It is in this sense," Smith writes, "that being and sustaining ourselves as persons is not [for James] to be understood as a natural endowment totally given in advance but rather as a moral achievement."[66]

Like so many of James's concepts, his accounts of the will are not always consistent. Sometimes he implies that will is, after all, a wholly physiological correlation between stimuli and bodily responses, leading Ayer to worry: "What place does this account leave for the freedom of the will? It would seem, very little. Our thoughts just come to us. The emotions that may move us to act are physiologically determined."[67] By contrast, at other times, James writes as if *all* instances of will—even the simplest motor responses—involve intentional effort. But James more often identified willing with the spontaneous activity of selection, the *fiat* of the mind itself. If consciousness is a "fighter for ends" that "loads the dice" of the mind in pursuit of one's goals, as James asserts, then "willing" is his name for the effort required for the battle.

There are other issues with James's account, too. Stevens contends that his extensive use of mechanistic language "gives the impression of an interruption of the transitive thrust of the attentive glance of consciousness," contrary to his accounts of the continuity of consciousness.[68] Flower is concerned that James's "unit of action" is "atomic" (at least sometimes, and despite his usually acute use of metaphor), making him susceptible to some of the problems that he located in traditional empiricism.[69]

These grievances are more stylistic than substantial. Of greater concern is James's inability or unwillingness to clarify the *limits* of the will's efficacy. Will the drunkard's paying deliberate attention to "the blessings of having an organism kept in lifelong possession of its full youthful elasticity by a sweet, sound, blood, to which stimulants and narcotics are unknown, and to which the morning sun and air and dew daily come as sufficiently powerful intoxicants" really be sufficient to "will away" alcohol dependency, for example? (*TT*, 114).[70] How is it possible to distinguish in advance cases that deserve very great attentive effort due to their significant long-term moral consequences from those deserving less? As Ruth Anna Putnam points out, "Some of our moral choices will change us radically, while others will do so, if at all, only slowly and in minor ways. Alternatively, some of our moral choices deliberately and dramatically reaffirm our character, while others simply reflect the being we are."[71] Can people really achieve "salvation" by way of "the stock of ideas which you furnish them; . . . the amount of voluntary attention that they can exert in holding to the right ones, however unpalatable; and . . . the several habits of acting definitely on these latter to which they have been successfully trained"? (*TT*, 110). In his more "strenuous" moments, James seems to suggest so, such that when "we say to our intemperate acquaintance 'you can be a new man, *if you will*'" the real problem is *only* that "he finds the willing impossible" (*EPs*, 102). James provides no obvious or final position on these conundrums, and so we are left to decide them based on our own experience, although we might quickly agree that the long-term effects of even limited willing can be profound, as with defeating addiction or addressing a lack of confidence.[72]

If one reads James's philosophical psychology separately from his practical advice on habit formation, he can also appear inconsistent on the question of whether it is possible to summon and sustain sufficient attentive focus for realizing significant changes to the self. James is clear that even when we have an interest in some stimulus, problem, or topic of conversation that "it is impossible to sustain the effort of voluntary attention for more than a few moments. Successive acts of voluntary attention may bring a given topic back again and again to the focus of our consideration," but "unless the topic itself is sufficiently 'congenial' and interesting to engage a passive attention, we will eventually succumb to the distraction of some more immediately stimulating topic."[73] Yet we know that James believed the ability to sustain and repeat concentrated focus (and thus to sustain and repeat orderly reconfigurations of experience) to be crucial for his melioristic ethics.

The key to resolving this apparent inconsistency is found by reading James's practical advice on habit formation in conjunction with his psychology of will. In the case of focusing one's attention on reconfiguring the experiential field, the point is to make self-reflexivity a "natural" mode of thought, thereby enabling "the harmonious complementarity of both voluntary and passive attention."[74] To pursue this approach involves moving from the first to the second part of James's summary imperative: "action, habit, character, destiny."

Living Willfully: Discipline, Effort, and Self-Transformation

James maintains that "the maximum of attention may . . . be said to be found whenever we have a systematic harmony or unification between the novel and the old. It is an odd circumstance that neither the old nor the new, by itself, is interesting: the absolutely old is insipid; the absolutely new makes no appeal at all. The old *in* the new is what claims the attention— the old with a slightly new turn" (*TT*, 70). James is referring here to the relationship between "old" or habituated ideas and relations in consciousness and "new" stimuli and relational configurations. Applied to his self-creative ethics, it indicates that attentive energy can be maximized by bringing "old," relatively passive, previously habituated patterns of thinking into relationship with new ideas on the fringes of the field of consciousness. It also suggests (though not obviously) the benefits of habituating self-reflective review of the conscious field, so that one remains alert to new relational possibilities, whether as responses to physical stimuli, plans for self-development, inter-personal interactions, or reading a philosophical argument.

As with any new habit, developing the tendency to remain alert to one's own habits is more difficult than relying on habits already in place, at least initially. Furthermore, even when the habit of self-reflection is habituated, the attentive effort required to realize a new ideational focus or configuration of relations might seem too great, leaving one to revert to "old" relations rather than realizing "new" ones. Thus, changing one's habits of thought "will not happen through a mere fiat of the so-called will [i.e. attentive focus], but only through a disciplined effort which enables the mind to pay attention to unattractive objects still on the fringes of consciousness and, therefore, still vague and confused."[75] To create one's experience afresh—and so re-create the self—requires *both* the critical habit of self-reflection *and* the constructive one of acting on (at least some of) the alternatives. One will not become a philosopher rather than a business manager merely by becoming aware of and entertaining the possibility, or by repeatedly reconsidering the possibility of alternative career paths; rather, one must be prepared to focus and act upon the idea with sufficient energy.

For James, commitment of attentive effort to developing these habits is a wise investment in one's own future, since without it, prospects for a richer life will slowly evaporate. "We forget that every good that is worth possessing must be paid for in strokes of daily effort," he tells us, yet typically "we postpone and postpone, until those smiling possibilities are dead. . . . By neglecting the necessary concrete labor, by sparing ourselves the little daily tax, we are positively digging the graves of our higher possibilities" (*TT*, 51–52). The "labor" to which James refers takes two forms. The first is deliberate, persistent adoption and reinforcement of thoughts and actions that will help to develop better, more productive habits, and diminish harmful, less productive ones. "There is no more valuable precept in moral education than this . . . if we wish to conquer undesirable emotional tendencies in ourselves, we must assiduously, and in the first instance cold-bloodedly, go through the *outward motions* of those contrary dispositions we prefer to cultivate. The reward of persistency will infallibly come, in the fading out of the sullenness or depression, and the advent of real cheerfulness and kindliness in their stead" (*EPs*, 178). The second form is to "accumulate all the possible circumstances which shall re-enforce the right motives; put yourself assiduously in conditions that encourage the new way" (*PB*, 134), ensuring that conditions work in support of developing new habits rather than against them. It would be foolish to put oneself in the company of heavy drinkers when trying to reduce alcohol intake or to discuss politics (or football) just with partisans of one side or another when seeking to become a more balanced pundit.

James writes about the commitment of such self-transformative effort as a kind of "heroism": the "pure inward willingness to face the world" in ways typical of "the masters and the lords of life" (*PP*, 1181). Although such rhetoric is excessive in reference to our more modest reflective and creative moments, it seems appropriate when applied to "daily labor" considered over the course of a lifetime, or to more significant ideals, including the melioristic one entailed by James's ethics. Attempts to amend one's own character or pursue new ideals require maintenance of strenuous effort to resist the force of old habits and a path of ease. To use James's own description, they are like muscular strength borne of regular exercise and testing, requiring deliberate focus and careful management of energy. As such, deliberate self-transformation is a "heroic" repudiation of passive existence, in both conception (adopting self-transformation as an ideal) and realization (the effort and rehearsal required to develop new habits). Let us consider these in turn.

As McDermott writes, the very ideal of self-transformation undercuts existential certainty: "Abandonment of an inherited self, while liberating, is nonetheless challenging and even dangerous. If the will is not given as meaningful and self is but our capacity to be meaningfully present, then the making of relations becomes equivalent to who we are."[76] The existential risk becomes even more apparent with the realization that one's self and welfare are guaranteed by neither God nor nature:

> The moral implications of eschewing an overbelief as to transcendence, and especially as to the doctrine of specific providence, is daunting. If I do not believe that there exists a face, a power, a force which has *me* as its focus, then I must take full responsibility for what I think, what I say, and what I do. To live a life without excuses, without a bailout, and without resorting to assessments, *sub specie aeternitatis*, is burdensome, reflectively and emotionally exhausting. To that end, I take worrying not to be a defect, but rather appropriate to being a responsible, helping, and caring human being.[77]

Adopting an ethics of deliberate self-transformation means risking the arrangement of consciousness determined by those "warm" phenomena that for James comprise the spiritual self. And yet, James believes that "it is only by risking our persons from one hour to another that we live at all," for without a commitment to change one's self by realizing new ideas and experiences, life will comprise a series of regrets over missed opportunities, and "wise men regret as little as they can" (*WB*, 215, 125).

Additionally, an ethics of deliberate self-transformation entails an awareness that, for each alternative chosen, others are forgone. To commit our limited attentive resources effectively means deciding between incommensurable alternatives, and so we inevitably suffer—and live in the shadow of—moral losses; dreams forgone, opportunities missed, and so on.[78] For anyone committed to self-transformation, "the chooser realizes," "in the very act" of "deciding on the triumphant alternative" and "murdering the vanquished possibility," just "how much in that instant he is making himself lose" (*PP*, 1141). To give up some options is the unavoidable cost of pursuing more appealing ones.

James believed that pragmatists are especially well equipped for facing up to this reality, and so for adopting successfully the self-transformative self as an ideal. Pragmatism's characteristic focus on experience, unmediated by abstraction and conceptualization, helps avoid what James calls (referring to Leibniz and his followers) a "feeble grasp of reality" typical of those philosophical idealists and religious believers who conceive "a universe already formed, or in a process of perfect formation" such that "the individual's active energies appear superfluous" (*P*, 20). Pragmatists tend to adopt a realistic assessment of life, balancing the benefits of melioristic experimentalism with the inherent risks and burdens. On the one hand, they know that things might not work out as intended. With time, happenstance, mistake, loss (including the loss of forgone alternatives) and failure will be parts of everyone's experience, and some of these characteristics make the consequences of even our most careful decisions and committed actions unforeseeable.[79] But on the other hand, such significant prizes as the restoration of self-determinative agency and recovery of human values in the face of rising materialism are profoundly valuable.

James claims that "the pragmatism or pluralism which I defend has to fall back on a certain ultimate hardihood, a certain willingness to live without assurances or guarantees" (*MT*, 124). He challenges his readers with this test: "Suppose that the world's author put the case to you before creation, saying: 'I am going to make a world not certain to be saved, a world the perfection of which shall be conditional merely, the condition being that each several agent does its own "level best." I offer you the chance of taking part in such a world. Its safety, you see, is unwarranted. It is a real adventure, with real danger, yet it may win through. . . . Will you join the procession? Will you trust yourself and trust the other agents enough to face the risk?'" (*P*, 139). The "genuine pragmatist" will, he thinks, "accept sincerely a drastic kind of universe" and be "willing to live on a scheme of uncertified possibilities which he trusts; willing to pay with his own person, if need be, for the realization of the ideals which he frames" (*P*, 142–43). James considered himself "willing to take the universe to be really dangerous and adventurous, without therefore backing out and crying 'no play'" because "when the cup is poured off, the dregs are left behind forever, but the possibility of what is poured off is sweet enough to accept" (*P*, 142). The prospect of realizing more of life's potential is enough to motivate strong willing even when the inevitable losses are accounted for.

In *Principles*, James writes, "if a brief definition of ideal or moral action were required, none could be given which would better fit the appearances than this: It is action in the line of the greatest resistance" (*PP*, 1155). For him, a person's moral standing is best judged according to the amount of effort that they can commit to difficult actions:

> We measure ourselves by many standards. Our strength and our intelligence, our wealth and even our good luck, are things which warm our heart and make us feel ourselves a match for life. But deeper than all such things, and able to suffice unto itself without them, is the sense of the amount of effort which we can put forth. Those are, after all, but effects, products, and reflections of the outer world within. But the effort seems to belong to an altogether different realm, as if it were the substantive thing which we are, and those were but externals which we carry. If the 'searching of our heart and reins' be the purpose of this human drama, then what is sought seems to be what effort we can make. He who can make none is but a shadow: he who can make much is a hero. (*PP*, 1180–81)

This is especially true, he believes, when circumstances are very dire, or the moral risks associated with a decision are very great:

> When a dreadful object is presented, or when life as a whole turns up its dark abysses to our view, then the worthless ones among us lose their hold on the situation altogether. . . . But the

heroic mind does differently. To it, too, the objects are sinister and dreadful, unwelcome, incompatible with wished-for things. But it can face them if necessary, without for that losing its hold upon the rest of life. The world thus finds in the heroic man its worthy match and mate; and the effort which he is able to put forth to hold himself erect and keep his heart unshaken is the direct measure of his worth and function in the game of human life. . . . Thus not only our morality but our religion, so far as the latter is deliberate, depend on the effort which we can make. *"Will you or won't you have it so?"* is the most probing question we are ever asked; we are asked it every hour of the day, and about the largest as well as the smallest, the most theoretical as well as the most practical, things. We answer by *consents or non-consents* and not by words. (*PP*, 1181–82)

With the risks, burdens, and inevitable sacrifices demanded by self-creative ethics fresh in our minds, the tone of these texts, so reminiscent of Nietzsche in extolling moral heroism, seems entirely appropriate. Someone able to muster attentive effort over the long term and accept that things will not always go to plan is more likely to effect real change than others who cannot.

According to James, people capable of mustering and sustaining sufficient energy for a life-changing project typically exhibit "the strenuous mood," a willingness to struggle and fight for favored ends (and sacrifice alternatives) over the long term rather than taking a more "easy-going" approach to life. He writes, "The deepest difference, practically, in the moral life of man is the difference between the easy-going and the strenuous mood when in the easy-going mood the shrinking from present ill is our ruling consideration. The strenuous mood, on the contrary, makes us quite indifferent to present ill, if only the greater ideal be obtained" (*WB*, 159–60). To adopt a long-term goal and deem it important enough to pursue even at great cost is one way of sustaining attentive energy in the face of setbacks and inevitable short-term losses without losing heart. In the case of self-transformative ethics, commitment to a richer, more fulfilling life encourages our remaining alert to and pursuing new ways of thinking and living.

James claims that the pluralistic world described by pragmatism "demands" a strenuous attitude "since it makes the world's salvation depend upon the energizing of its several parts, among which we are" (*MT*, 123). But his discussion of heroism can be read as suggesting that this path is open only to those few people with inherent mental strength and commitment.

Either a person is capable of adopting the strenuous mood, taking the challenge issued by "the world's author," and sustaining a long-term vision over short-term comforts, or not; either one is prone to take "moral holidays" or not; a person is either capable or incapable of "putting their own spiritual house in order" in pursuit of "personal salvation."[80] As John Stuhr points out, James "increasingly and insightfully recognized that pragmatism, immensely right in theory, was unlikely to be a 'definitive triumph' in life because it constituted in practice a philosophy that is insufficiently a live option or is a far too demanding and strenuous an option for many persons," being instead "a future philosophy for those few persons with pluralistic attitudes and hardy temperaments."[81] On James's assessment, few of his peers exhibited the hardihood required to realize the strenuous mood, "the 'spirit' of our age" being marked by "effeminacy and unmanliness" (*VRE*, 291).

Yet as we might expect given the scope that James envisaged for his hortatory, melioristic ethics, this is not the whole story. His valorization of the heroic self is not limited to the capabilities of a few specially endowed individuals but extends to all.[82] In "Moral Philosopher," for instance, James writes that "the capacity for the strenuous mood probably lies slumbering in every man, but it has more difficulty in some than in others in waking up" (*WB*, 160). His whole ethical project is an endorsement of the ideal of personal growth for everyone, not just those few gifted with exemplary psychological capacities, and it is built around his model of the dynamic, empirical self rather than any specific attitudinal characteristic.

It is not the case that the strenuous mood is required "all at once" for the process of self-transformation to commence. Like other psychological tendencies, it can be trained, starting with just "a still small voice which must be artificially reinforced to prevail" (*PP*, 1155). Because neither character nor temperament is fixed, "heroism" can be developed from very modest ambitions and chance events, moments that prompt a new "set" to the brain (as with a turn to healthier living after a medical scare), releasing sometimes extraordinary reserves of energy and power. Changing a single habit or adopting just one new practice might set us on the path. Alternatively, we might be inspired by others whose heroic attitude and energetic commitment to change serve as moral exemplars. So while James sometimes suggests that the strenuous mood cannot be adopted voluntarily (whether summoned by will or roused on intellectual grounds), he observes at others that people sometimes *do* "choose their attitude and know that the facing of its difficulties shall remain a permanent portion of their task" (*EPs*, 233).

James delivered numerous public lectures on ways to develop our strenuosity and ability to develop good habits and eliminate harmful ones. Many of his recommendations are presented in *Talks to Teachers*, where he records that "I have found by experience that what my hearers seem least to relish is analytical technicality, and what they most care for is concrete practical application" (*TT*, 3). This realization, coupled with a belief that moral educators will be more effective by encouraging "inhibition [of bad habits] by substitution" rather than "by repression," leads him to propose actions and exercises that promote positive ideals and strengthening of the will, rather than prohibitions on particular behaviors, ideas, or ways of thinking. They center around five themes: education, the role of ideals, managing energy, religious belief, and improving processes of habituation.

The first of these concerns the value of education for fostering character. McGranahan suggests that "James's pedagogical theory and his ethics of self-transformation are of a piece, and both build upon the moral psychology of *Principles*. The major difference is that education is principally other-directed (by teachers), whereas self-transformation is essentially self-directed. Ideally the former process sets a useful habitual structure for the latter process to build upon."[83] Self-transformation "means utilizing selective willing to mediate one's own habitual structure," and "one learns how to do this in part from one's teachers and other role models, who should inculcate the habit of willing in the service of some ideal (*sub specie boni*) rather than negatively or blindly."[84]

James thinks that effective education will foster "the kind of character that is both the means and end of [his] ethics of self-transformation: firm yet malleable; stable yet imaginative"[85] and equipped with the requisite curiosity, sensitivity, and intellectual persistence to pursue a line of thinking and action to its conclusion. Addressing teachers directly, he writes that "your task is to build up a character in your pupils; and a character . . . consists in an organized set of habits of reaction. Now of what do such habits of reaction themselves consist? They consist of tendencies to act characteristically when certain ideas possess us, and to refrain characteristically when possessed by other ideas. Our volitional habits depend, then, first, on what the stock of ideas is which we have; and, second, on the habitual coupling of the several ideas with action or inaction respectively" (*TT*, 108). Whether or not a teacher is successful will depend on a range of factors, from the subjects taught to teaching style, and from the level of a student's commitment to the competence of the teacher, but in every case the harnessing of a student's energies is crucial: "In all pedagogy the great thing is to strike the iron while hot, and to seize the wave of the pupil's interest in each successive subject"

(*PP*, 1021) so that a student's impulses and enthusiasms might be directed toward critical self-reflection and reasoned consideration of new arguments and ways of thinking.

James's support for education flows into his second theme, which relates to the deliberate adoption of personal ideals to better orientate self-development. As Koopman records, "Will involves working from where we are and launching ourselves towards an end-in-view that is not yet fully determinate (such that its attainability cannot be evaluable with full certainty)."[86] In "What Makes a Life Significant," James writes that "education, enlarging as it does our horizon and perspective, is a means of multiplying our ideals, of bringing new ones into view" (*TT*, 163). In other words, formal education widens the range of alternative personal goals from which to choose, enabling us to better identify the ideals to which we are already committed and others that might be adopted to our advantage.

But of course, to decide upon and adopt certain ideals as one's own is but one aspect of their realization. As James points out, "The solid meaning of life is always the same eternal thing—the marriage, namely, of some unhabitual ideal, however special, with some fidelity, courage, and endurance; with some man's or woman's pains.—And, whatever or wherever life may be, there will always be the chance for that marriage to take place" (*TT*, 166). James's third theme pertains to the generation and sustenance of that "endurance," the work pursuant of an ideal that differentiates "morally exceptional individuals . . . from the rest" (*TT*, 161).

James holds that "the difference between willing and merely wishing, between having ideals that are creative and ideals that are but pinings and regrets, . . . depends solely either on the amount of steam-pressure chronically driving the character in the ideal direction, or in the amount of ideal excitement transiently acquired" (*VRE*, 215). He does not mean that there is some optimal amount of energy to aim for but that there is some level of "excitement" that enables one to maintain concentration, overcome physical tiredness, ignore distractions, and so forth: "Every individual soul, in short, like every individual machine or organism, has its own best conditions of efficiency. A given machine will run best under a certain steam-pressure, a certain amperage; an organism under a certain diet, weight, or exercise. . . . And it is just so with our sundry souls: some are happiest in calm weather; some need the sense of tension, of strong volition, to make them feel alive and well" (*VRE*, 241).[87]

As we saw earlier, James complained about the anxiety and excessive tension and excitement that he noticed in the American culture of his day, and the "absence of repose" that might serve as their antidote. Such characteristics interfere not only with physical movement, but with such other aspects of vitality as healing, concentration, and reflection, making them "the surest drags upon steady progress and hindrances to our success (*TT*, 125). "If . . . living excitedly . . . would only enable us to *do* more, it would be different," he writes (*TT*, 125). He proposed several ways to counter these tendencies so that we might be "calmly ready for any duty that the day may bring forth" (*TT*, 129). The first was to adopt some of the practices of the "mind-cure" movement, a then-new faith in the power of mind over body that included a capacity for self-healing through proper thought. Among these, James focused on techniques that promote mental calm and harmony, including relaxation exercises, cheerful positive thinking, and meditation. Although he acknowledged limits to the efficacy of these methods, he was convinced they would help attain "healthy mindedness," a stronger sense of self, and greater energy.[88]

Later, though, in *Varieties*, James shifted emphasis from mind cure to the benefits of religious spiritualism, his fourth means for improving one's capacity for self-creative ethics (e.g., *VRE*, 118–19). The role that James assigns religion regarding self-transformation is much contested, especially given its importance to his philosophy (and indeed his life) as a whole.[89] Most straightforwardly, he can be read as proposing religion as another way of reducing energy-draining stress and worry, in much the same way as, say, meditation. He writes that we cannot "fail to steady the nerves, to cool the fever, and appease the fret, if one be conscious that, no matter what one's difficulties for the moment may appear to be, one's life as a whole is in the keeping of a power whom one can absolutely trust" (*VRE*, 230). If we are assured that a greater force is "on our side" when facing our moral challenges, we are likely to be more confident and less prone to worry.

For some interpreters, this is enough to indicate a fundamental shift in James's position on moral strenuousness, at least the version expressed in *The Will to Believe*. Gale, for example, insists that James now believes "that our salvation must be found not in living the morally strenuous life but rather in finding an abiding sense of safety and peace through absorption into a higher surrounding spiritual reality"[90] But a recommendation for such passivity would be inconsistent with the moral strenuousness flowing from James's accounts of habit, will, attention, focus, and so on. Nowhere in *Varieties* does James give an alternative theoretical foundation for ethical theory on par with the sophisticated naturalistic ones that informed "Moral

Philosopher." To adopt Gale's interpretation would mean setting aside too much else.

Other philosophers, like Michael Slater, insist that "despite [James's] deep interest in the psychology and practical value of religion, his understanding of the objects of religious belief and his account of religion more generally did not reduce either to human psychology or utility," and that he finds in religion "an objective standard . . . against which we can and, more importantly, should measure our moral values and ideals," and in God, the ultimate unifier of the diverse moral preferences of all people.[91]

Although there is little doubt that James thought religious believers more likely than nonbelievers to lead morally praiseworthy lives, his general antiprescriptivism and the extent to which he integrates discussions of religion and God with the constructive elements of his philosophical psychology, on my view, make Slater's interpretation untenable. To agree with Slater requires that we overlook or downplay the fact that James's principal defense of religion relies "on his view that religion generates human heroic energies and facilitates personal struggle in the world" by letting "loose in us the strenuous mood."[92] James states that "in a merely human world without a God the appeal to our moral energy falls short of its maximal stimulating power" (WB, 160), and he explains several ways in which spiritual belief evokes moral strenuousness. First, it serves as an example of the rich, intense experience that James believes will encourage and reward active self-transformation.[93] Second, religious belief encourages the feeling that one's own moral work and effort is *meaningful*, contributing to a much larger project conducted by God.[94] Third, it encourages the view that human existence generally is purposeful, in contrast, James argues, with materialism, idealism, and determinism (see P, 45–62). Fourth, as Philip Kitcher points out, for all the problems (interpretative and otherwise) of the connection that James proposes between ethical precepts and ideas about God, "one might maintain that, as a matter of fact, the discipline of religious participation provides structures that encourage people to examine their conduct more closely and thus prevent certain types of slackness."[95]

At first glance, James's inclusion of religion among the means for encouraging self-creative ethics seems inconsistent with his intention to help surmount it (together with scientific materialism) because it limits the ways that people make sense of experience and decide on actions. But once it is realized that James finds the advantages of religious belief primarily (though not exclusively) in promoting moral strenuousness, its inclusion makes more sense: it is not that we ought to adopt the ontological, epistemological, or moral claims of a religion as one's own, to be blindly followed on the path to redemption, but rather that we might draw on spiritual belief as an energizing force.[96] This interpretation seems entirely consistent with James's belief that religion is just "*the feelings, acts, and experiences of individual men in their solitude, so far as they apprehend themselves to stand in relation to whatever they may consider the divine*" (*VRE*, 34), that faith is inadequate to be considered as knowledge but can be meaningful nonetheless (*VRE*, 168, 200–201), and that we ought to find room in our explanatory systems for a reality beyond the natural world (*VRE*, 119). It is not that God provides an "objective standard," as Slater would have it, but that *belief* in God promotes moral energy and strenuosity.

James's fifth and final form of practical advice for strengthening the will's efficacy concerns processes of habituation. Although his recommendations are not especially innovative or original from today's perspective, informed as we are by sophisticated psychological studies of habit, they are nonetheless consistent with modern views and provide clear, actionable, and effective steps toward realizing his theoretical recommendations.[97] In short, "the secret of will and energy . . . is in the set of routines that go into discipline, which creates a capability, in our structure of habits, to act successfully."[98] Habituating our routines so as to encourage effective willing will still require mental effort and self-discipline—they are, after all, yet more habits to develop—but they will increase the likelihood of attaining the benefits of other beneficial habits, including self-reflection.

James finds in military training examples of how such discipline and capability are developed by repeated effort over an extended period, helping to make responses more "automatic." It is not just physical habits such as loading a weapon, moving to the correct defensive position, or saluting a superior officer to which he refers. All habits are formed, developed, and used in the same general ways, as we have seen, and so some lessons from military training (especially deliberate and disciplined repetition) can be applied to other areas of life. Each habit, effectively changed and assimilated to the spiritual self, becomes "second nature," and James's adoption of principles from military training is meant to improve that process.

James gives five specific recommendations for changing habits effectively, two drawn from Bain's *The Emotions and the Will* and three of his own. First, we ought to begin the project with a strong desire to improve ourselves, rather than a half-hearted hope, so that initial "momentum" will

delay "the temptation to break down," allowing more time for other practices to take effect. "We must take care to *launch ourselves with as strong
and decided an initiative as possible*," he writes, and we should "re-enforce
the right motives" by using such devices as "a public pledge" and "making
engagements incompatible with the old" (*PB*, 134). Second, "*never suffer
an exception to occur till the new habit is securely rooted in life*" because "a
single slip undoes more than a great many turns will wind again" (*PB*,
134); "without *unbroken* advance, there is no such thing as *accumulation*
of the ethical forces possible" (*PB*, 135). James makes an exception in cases
of addiction, where "tapering off" might be appropriate, and he warns that
we need to be realistic about the task we set ourselves ("We must be careful
not to give the will so stiff a task as to insure its defeat at the very outset"),
but generally "a sharp period of suffering, and then a free time, is the best
thing to aim at" (*PB*, 135).

James's third maxim, intended like the first two to build "momentum"
and confidence in one's capabilities, is to "*seize the very first possible opportunity to act on every resolution you make and on every emotional prompting you
may experience in the direction of the habits you aspire to gain*" (*PB*, 135–36).
The fourth is to avoid talking about or preaching one's intentions in the
abstract but instead to remain alert for opportunities to act. "No matter
how full a reservoir of *maxims* one may possess, and no matter how good
one's *sentiments* may be, if one has not taken advantage of every concrete
opportunity to *act*, one's character may remain entirely unaffected for the
better. With mere good intentions, hell is proverbially paved" (*PB*, 136).

The final maxim is different, directed at the general capacity for habit
formation rather than pursuit of any particular habit, and is intended to
counter the human tendency toward conservative inertia:

> *Keep the faculty of effort alive in you by a little gratuitous exercise
> every day.* That is, be systematically ascetic or heroic in little
> unnecessary points, do every day or two something for no other
> reason than that you would rather not do it, so that when the
> hour of dire need draws nigh, it may find you not unnerved
> and untrained to stand the test. . . . [T]he man who has daily
> inured himself to habits of concentrated attention, energetic
> volition, and self-denial in unnecessary things . . . will stand like
> a tower when everything rocks around him, and when his softer
> fellow-mortals are winnowed like chaff in the blast. (*PB*, 137–38)

Deliberate cultivation of willed conscious attention ensures that it is strong and reliable when needed, such as with deliberate self-transformation, and capable of advancing James's other recommendations for effective habit formation.

With consistent and sustained attention pursuant to our interests, we gradually accrue those distinctive, deeply embedded, and reliable inclinations that James thinks define our character: "A 'character,' as J.S. Mill says, 'is a completely fashioned will'; and a will, in the sense in which he means it, is an aggregate of tendencies to act in a firm and prompt and definite way" (*TT*, 50).[99] Consequently, what is at stake in willing is whether or not one is committed to self-transformation, "less what act he shall now choose to do than what being he shall now choose to become" (*PB*, 158).

The relationship between character and action is not, then, omni-directional. It is just as true that one's character enables and guides the creation of habits as it is that accumulation of habits defines character. As Ruth Anna Putnam points out, "A life is not a string of actions chosen one by one. A life has a shape, a coherence due to the character and the aims of the person whose life it is."[100] James's recovering alcoholic, referred to previously, is defined as a drunkard by his habitual drinking (and the persistent temptation to drink) but simultaneously as a noble soul struggling to reform himself by trying to keep before his mind the repellent image of the wayward drunk. To the extent that James accounts for both one's character as it is defined by actions to date *and* prospects for amending habits in pursuit of other goals, his ethics is even more clearly melioristic and future-oriented: wherever one must "choose which *interest* out of several, equally coercive, shall become supreme," the "choice really lies between one of several equally possible future Characters. What he shall *become* is fixed by the conduct of this moment" (*PP*, 276). The moral good is not located in one's eventual destiny or even the habits that lead to it but in the energetically demanding processes of character formation: the development of "a completely fashioned will," that give form to one's life according to one's own interests and efforts rather than preconceptions, gospel, or science (*TT*, 50).

For James, self and character are defined by relational habits, and we literally re-create ourselves over time by accumulating, altering, and entrenching habits, a project deserving significant effort and training of will. As James puts it, "The daily drill and the years of discipline end by fashioning a man completely over again, as to most of the possibilities of his conduct" (*PP*, 125). There is an unavoidable obligation to decide in each moment how to exercise our freedom; whether to take the easier path and be guided by existing habits or to follow the more difficult one and pursue new ideas, actions, and interpretations. Effectively, the latter was James's recommendation to those of his compatriots locked into the received views offered by religion and science: to "avoid a life lived by formulas, by definition, and seek instead the fringe, the novel, the unspoken, the secret and the hidden recesses of being, which speak only to those who know how to listen."[101] The reward will be a richer, freer, more energetic life, and a more exploratory, more active, and increasingly inventive character.

Conclusion

Recovering James's Therapeutic Ethics

Although classical pragmatism was distinctively a product of its time (who knows how the Golden Age figures might have responded to robotics, nanotechnology, gene therapies, space warfare, and "big data"?), its experimental, hopeful attitude seems ready-made for our own age, "one that eschews tradition and superstition but desperately craves existential meaning; one that is defined by affluence but also depression and acute anxiety; one that valorizes icons who ultimately decide that the life of fame is one that really ought to be cut short prematurely," as John Kaag puts it.[1] The pragmatist commitment to the significance of experience, practice, and context for assessing meanings and determining actions indicate that its "spirit" is peculiarly well suited to a world of rampant changes (political, social, economic, institutional, technological, legal, . . .), where the notion of moral absolutes seems quaint and spiritual certainties have largely been superseded.

James's version of pragmatism embodies a "spirit" relevant to contemporary times, "its unashamedly moral emphasis and its unequivocally ameliorative impulse" meeting "a longing for norms and values that can make a difference, a yearning for principled resistance and struggle that can change our desperate plight."[2] It encourages hope, realizable in tangible action, in a manner unachievable by traditional modernist ethics, postmodern alternatives, and the explanatory Peircean pragmatism of Brandom, Misak, and Price: a set of concrete proposals for making the best of an uncertain world, drawn from a sophisticated philosophy and psychology. As Koopman deftly expresses it, "Making oneself at home in a world of chance would presumably be well facilitated by founding a form of freedom as self-transformation. Herein lies the ongoing importance of James's contributions."[3] Just as James's melioristic

159

voluntarism was acclaimed for its uplifting qualities in the early twentieth century, so ought it to be more than a hundred years later.

James's various workings-out of the human condition constitute a vital response to the abstract intellectualism of much of the philosophy of his time, and of our time, too. His focus on individual agency counters postmodernism's virtual dismissal of it, and his introspective account of experience offers an accessible alternative to the cognitive and linguistic preoccupations that have helped to draw philosophy away from a wider public. Most significant for this work, his theory of self-transformation centers on an account of the good life that chimes with the ups and downs, constraints, and possibilities of human experience. It denotes a practical way of living rather than offering specific rules or ideals and emphasizes the diverse implications of our ideas, patterns of thought, and actions. It acknowledges the need to decide and act in response to complicated and ever-changing circumstances, sometimes with consequences for a whole life, without either a definitive guiding principle or unqualified confidence in a successful outcome. James's account of character development as contingent on one's own decisions and the inevitable plurality of ideals exceeds the descriptive and normative resources of virtue ethics, and his experimentalism and context-sensitivity surpass rule- and consequence-based ethics. As such, we ought not to be surprised at the recent rise in scholarly interest in James's theory, whether focused on the existential themes first pursued in the two decades before Rorty's *Philosophy and the Mirror of Nature*, or some other aspect, such as energy, will, or habit.

This book seeks to establish the ideological and methodological connections between elements of James's works that explain and justify his ethics of self-transformation. Robert Richardson has claimed that "for all his grand accomplishments in canonical fields of learning, James's best is often in his unorthodox, half-blind, unpredictable lunges at the great question of how to live."[4] The task here was to make some of those lunges more obvious and less blind. Because James's ideas and approaches are so multidimensional, his reader can often *feel* as though there is an important link (or distinction) to be found between disparate ideas or works without it being altogether clear, and so the intention was to map a productive and defensible path toward a therapeutic ethics suitable for a wider public. The approach taken here frames James's ethics historically, in terms of both his departure from Peirce (specifically, his deployment of pragmatist principles to theorize first-person meaning) and his bid to relieve his peers of the symptoms of a passive, purposeless life brought on by radical socioeconomic changes and the absence of spiritual and intellectual resources offering sufficient succor and appropriate guidance. Although his ethics as usually conceived (and as laid out in "Moral Philosopher") speaks effectively against traditional moral systems and in favor of the importance of individual agency for determining one's own destiny, it lacked explanatory specificity and seemed to raise as many questions as it answered.

To understand James's positive ethics means engaging with the specifics of his philosophy of experience. By utilizing his relational metaphysics to explore the productive intersection between the conscious self and the world, we realize the full extent of the ambiguity and relational complexity to which we respond and that we seek to resolve by creating patterns of meaning and habits of thought and action (the "flights" as well as the "perchings"). In this way, too, we become aware of the range of possibilities coming into and going out of existence in every moment—interests and ideas, cares and capabilities, motivations and regrets, and stimuli of all kinds—together with our capacity to focus attention. Experience is, then, the field of possibility for ethics. We attend to one idea over others and decide on this course of action rather than that, and so we gradually forge the habits that define our moral identity and tendencies, or character.

As Koopman writes, "The active practice of reflexively remaking our-selves, what we might also call *the conduct of our conduct*, is the central idea in James's moral philosophy and psychology."[5] To conduct self-reflexive review is no easy task, at least not initially, as it requires deliberate attentive effort, over and over again, to surmount and replace old, deeply engrained habits with new ones. Given the effort required and the risk of failure, James describes his pedagogical recommendations—exercises in discipline and self-control that encourage effective habit-formation—in terms of "heroism" and "risk." His focus is practical and existential, and he hopes that, with the success of small, incremental changes, people might go on to take greater control of their lives—even making a habit of reviewing their own habits—and so realize more of the rich potential evident in experience than if they continued following the same path. Each small change is an expression of freedom: the pursuit of an ideal or goal, however small or large, framed by that tiny moment of choice between stimulus and response. "There *is* a 'drama' of freedom and responsibility, and there is a problem of training the will," writes Edie, "but 'the whole drama is a mental drama. The whole difficulty is a mental difficulty.'. . . . To bridge the chasm between the possibility and actuality, to make what 'could be' become real, is, for James, the ethical problem *par excellence*."[6] Although we cannot control every aspect of life, neither is our future entirely out of our hands, or, more precisely, our heads.

Without the kind of detailed explication provided here, James's therapeutic, self-help philosophy can appear simplistic and "old hat." With it, though, the theory assumes a different character, as a sophisticated and self-contained ethics with profound implications for our conception of the possibilities of self and world. As McDermott has written, "James's pragmatic temper is the proper mood for contemporary society. His stress on the experience of relations and connections provides us with the metaphysical subtlety necessary as an antidote to the single vision which dominates so many of our endeavors. James's spiritual vision is also of note, for he insists that we celebrate the affairs of ordinary experience and that we realize it is we, and we alone, who are responsible for the course of human history."[7]

Notes

Preface

1. Dewey, *Middle Works*, 92.
2. Perry, *Faith and Morals*, vi.
3. Perry, *Faith and Morals*, vi.
4. Brennan, *Ethics of William James*; Roth, *Freedom and the Moral Life*.
5. Seigfried, "Weaving Chaos into Order," 393.

Introduction

1. Westbrook, *Democratic Hope*, ix.
2. Fish, *Trouble with Principle*, 299.
3. Bernstein, "American Pragmatism," 64.
4. Rescher, "Pragmatism," 747.
5. Lovejoy, "Thirteen Pragmatisms I," 5.
6. Lovejoy, "Thirteen Pragmatisms I," 5.
7. Peirce, "What Pragmatism Is," 162–63.
8. Cotkin, *Reluctant Modernism*, 31.
9. Menand, *Metaphysical Club*, 438–41; cf Kloppenberg, *Uncertain Victory*.
10. Misak, *American Pragmatists*.
11. This tradition has its contemporary incarnation in such thinkers as Simon Blackburn, Robert Brandom, Arthur Fine, Susan Haack, Ian Hacking, John McDowell, Misak, Huw Price, and Hilary Putnam. It is well represented in Brandom, *Perspectives on Pragmatism*; Malachowski, *New Pragmatism*; Misak, *New Pragmatists*; Misak, *American Pragmatists*. Misak's version, in particular, has its critics. Larry Hickman rejects her antieclipse views as incomplete and simplistic, and proposes four alternative accounts informed in part by the perspectives of those who lived through the period. See Hickman, "Shedding Light on the 'Eclipse' Narrative."
12. Alexander, "Mythos and Polyphonic Pluralism," 7.

13. West, *American Evasion*, 194.

14. See, for example, McDermott, *Streams of Experience*.

15. See, for example, Wilshire, *Fashionable Nihilism*.

16. See, for example, Edie, *William James and Phenomenology*.

17. Linschoten, *Phenomenological Psychology*.

18. Roth, "Talking About Religion," 12; Roth, emails to author, 14 and 17 January 2015; Westphal, "Introduction," 1.

19. See, for example, McDermott, *Streams of Experience*; Lachs, *Stoic Pragmatism*; Smith, *Spirit of American Philosophy*.

20. Thayer, *Meaning and Action*, 5.

21. Rorty, *Consequences of Pragmatism*, 217.

22. Dewey, "Need for a Recovery," 66–67.

23. Dewey, *Essays in Experimental Logic*, 303.

24. See Cotkin, *Public Philosopher*, 13–16.

25. On James's activism, see Coon, "One Moment.'" On his anti-imperialism and political thought, see Livingston, *Damn Great Empires*.

26. Rorty, *Contingency, Irony, and Solidarity*, 40.

27. Unger, *Self Awakened*, 38.

28. There have been a number of notable exceptions, such as Suckiel, *Pragmatic Philosophy of William James*; Seigfried, *Radical Reconstruction of Philosophy*; Gale, *Divided Self of William James*; Bordogna, *William James at the Boundaries*.

29. Campbell, "Ethics of Fullfillment," 224.

30. West, *American Evasion*, 54, 55.

31. Brennan, *Ethics of William James*, 9.

32. Brennan, *Ethics of William James*, 10.

33. Roth, *Freedom and the Moral Life*, 57.

34. Roth, e-mails to author, 14 and 17 January 2015.

35. Roth, *Freedom and the Moral Life*, 7.

36. Roth, *Freedom and the Moral Life*, 14.

37. Roth, *Freedom and the Moral Life*, 13.

38. These other philosophers could well be classified among the more influential figures, too. James Albrecht explains how the intricacies of James's philosophy and psychology underpin his ethics (Albrecht, *Reconstructing Individualism*). Sergio Franzese studies James's ethics in terms of the organization of energy, particularly how habits serve to direct one's attentive focus toward whatever one takes to be "good" in the conduct of life (Franzese, *Ethics of Energy*). Todd Lekan distinguishes two distinct but related aspects of James's moral philosophy, one focused on a more inclusive ethics based on sympathetic appreciation of others' ideals and the other concerned with addressing existential doubts in a world of fate and suffering (Lekan, *William James and the Moral Life*). James Pawelski takes a physiological approach, arguing that James's various conceptions of individuality turn on the relative emphasis that

he accords perception, conception, and volition (Pawelski, *Dynamic Individualism of William James*). Mark Uffelman agrees with Marchetti that self-cultivation is an aspect of the melioristic orientation of classical pragmatism toward the unavoidable and ongoing development of one's self (Uffelman, "Forging the Self"). He traces development of a distinctive pragmatist theory of self-cultivation as describing "a lifestyle that imbues the individual's existence with ever-increasing richness and coherence by providing a directional guide to the process of living, rather than a nomological maxim" (Uffelman, "Role of Self-Cultivation," 206). Jennifer Welchman's account of "self-experimentation" focuses more on epistemology rather than ethics (Welchman, "William James's 'The Will to Believe'"). Also noteworthy are contributions by John Kaag, who describes in two personal narratives the kind of therapeutic and ameliorative benefits of James's pragmatism that this book seeks to highlight and explain in detail (Kaag, *American Philosophy* and *Sick Souls, Healthy Minds*). A whole volume of essays on James's moral philosophy has been released recently; see Goodson, ed. *Moral Philosophy and the Ethical Life*. Most of the essays draw out and expand upon moral themes introduced in, or suggested by, James's better-known works.

39. Marchetti, *Ethics and Philosophical Critique*, 49–50.

40. Marchetti, *Ethics and Philosophical Critique*, 49–50.

41. Marchetti, "Unfamiliar Habits," 102.

42. Koopman, "Transforming the Self"; "The Will."

43. Koopman, "The Will," 291; "Transforming the Self," 42–44.

44. Koopman, "Transforming the Self," 47.

45. McGranahan, *Darwinism and Pragmatism*.

46. McGranahan, *Darwinism and Pragmatism*, 11.

47. McGranahan, *Darwinism and Pragmatism*, 71.

48. Throntveit, *Ethical* Republic, 11.

49. McDermott, *Drama of Possibility*, 132.

50. James, *Letters*, 2:355.

51. Wild, *Radical Empiricism*, 265.

52. Unger, *Self Awakened*, 1.

53. Unger, *Self Awakened*, 1.

54. Henry James, *Letters*, 2:270.

Chapter 1

1. Halliwell and Rasmussen, "Introduction," 5.

2. Croce, *Science and Religion*, 6–10, 227.

3. Letter from James quoted in John Dewey, "The Philosophy of William James," in *Problems of Men* (New York: Philosophical Library, 1946), 390.

4. Gerald Stanley Lee, *Inspired Millionaires: A Forecast* (New York: Mount Tom Press, 1908), 49.

5. Croce, *Science and Religion*, 16–17.

6. Perry, *Thought and Character*, 1:654.

7. Cotkin, *Public Philosopher*, 8.

8. Cotkin, *Public Philosopher*,10.

9. One expert of the day, George Miller Beard, defined neurasthenia as a "family of functional nervous disorders that are increasingly frequent among the indoor classes of civilized countries, and that are especially frequent in the northern and eastern parts of the US," most prevalent in "brain-working households." Beard, *Practical Treatise*, 23.

10. There is another side to this condition, for as Cotkin notes, "For young men dissatisfied with their anticipated careers or frustrated by their failure to choose a calling, neurasthenia provided an agreeable moratorium, an excuse for inactivity on account of physical or mental infirmity." Cotkin, *Public Philosopher*, 27.

11. Henry James (William's son) wrote that "bad health, a feeling of the purposelessness of his own particular existence, his philosophic doubts and his constant preoccupation with them, all these combined to plunge him into a state of morbid depression." James, *Letters*, 1:145.

12. Croce, *Science and Religion*, 229–30.

13. Kuklick, *Rise of American Philosophy*, xvii.

14. For a full account, see Sklansky, *Soul's Economy*, 137–70.

15. Dooley, "James, William: Pragmatism," 417.

16. See for example Parker, *Mind Cure*, 91, 160. James once wrote to his wife with ironic glee at having encountered a woman with his "portrait in her bed-room with the words written under it, 'I want to bring a balm to human lives'!!!!! Supposed to be a quotation from me!!!" James, *Letters*, 2:43.

17. Bjork, *Center of His Vision*, 261.

18. Kloppenberg, *Uncertain Victory*, 37; Perry, *Thought and Character*, 1:324.

19. James T. Kloppenberg, "Pragmatism," 137.

20. Croce, "Non-Disciplinary William James," 8.

21. Kitcher, *Preludes to Pragmatism*, 4.

22. McDermott, *Drama of Possibility*, 153.

23. Quoted in Cotkin, *Public Philosopher*, 54.

24. Wilhelm Dilthey, Thomas Hill Green, Henry Sedgwick, and Albert Rouille were involved in similar undertakings.

25. Talisse and Hester, *On James*, 44.

26. I acknowledge the traditional demarcation between the fields of "ethics" and "morals," but will use the terms interchangeably.

27. For an early critique of Perry's interpretation, see Wild, *Radical Empiricism*.

28. Perry, *Thought and Character*, 2:263; *Faith and Morals*, vi. However, Perry acknowledges that the essays "Is Life Worth Living?" and "On a Certain Blindness in Human Beings" contain "forceful statements" of James's "own moral attitudes."

29. Edie, *William James and Phenomenology*, 43.

30. Perry, *Thought and Character*, 2:263.

31. Marchetti, *Ethics and Philosophical Critique*, 49.

32. Perry, *Thought and Character*, 2:263.

33. That James proposes such "general rules" throughout "Moral Philosopher" has led some philosophers to downplay its main and unifying themes in favor of reading it as a predominantly deontological treatise. See, for example, Ruth Anna Putnam, "The Moral Life of a Pragmatist."

34. Perry, *Thought and Character*, 2:264.

35. Perry, *Thought and Character*, 2:265.

36. Hilary Putnam, "Philosophy as a Reconstructive Activity," 34.

37. Those who have downplayed James's critical project include Suckiel, *Pragmatic Philosophy*; Bird, "Moral Philosophy"; Boyle, "William James's Ethical Symphony"; Cooper, "William James's Moral Theory,"; Gale, *Divided Self*; Lekan, "James's Normative Ethics."

38. Roth, *Freedom and the Moral Life*, 62.

39. Slater, *Ethics and Faith*, 80–81.

40. McGranahan, *Darwinism and Pragmatism*, 130.

41. Leary, "Visions and Values," 135.

42. As Abraham Edel puts it, the "deceptively diffuse but actually tight-packed pages" of "Moral Philosopher" "carry us father than we may think, but much less than we need or hope" and "beyond that we have to look elsewhere." Edel, "Search for a Moral Philosophy," 245.

43. Franzese, *Ethics of Energy*, 3.

44. Roth, *Freedom and the Moral Life*, 7.

45. Roth, *Freedom and the Moral Life*, 62.

46. Croce, *Science and Religion*, 5.

47. Seigfried, "Phenomenological Methodology," 73.

48. Cormier, "Comment on Talisse and Aikin," 14.

49. Hilary Putnam, *Pragmatism*, 7, 57.

50. Dewey, "The Moral Self," 353.

51. For a catalogue, see Uffelman, "Forging the Self," 323.

52. Unger, *Self Awakened*, 130.

53. Robert J. Roth, "Morality and Obligation," 23.

54. Smith, *Spirit of American Philosophy*, 58.

55. Of course, James's is not the only self-creative ethics. The same general approach was anticipated by the Stoics, developed variously by Spinoza, Hume, Mill, and Nietzsche, and taken up subsequently by Dewey, Foucault, Gilles Deleuze, Stanley Cavell, Bernard Williams, and Rorty, among others.

56. Dewey, "Self-Realization," 652–53.

57. Dewey, "The Moral Self," 341–42.

58. Marchetti, *Ethics and Philosophical Critique*, 41–42.

59. Quoted in Shusterman, *Practicing Philosophy*, 39.

60. McDermott, "Life Implicitness"; "A Lost Horizon"; "Promethean Self and Community."

61. Edel, "Search for a Moral Philosophy," 257–58, 46–47.

62. Edel, "Search for a Moral Philosophy," 246.

63. Marchetti, "Unfamiliar Habits," 105.

64. McDermott, "Promethean Self," 90.

Chapter 2

1. McDermott, *Drama of Possibility*, 149.

2. Marchetti, *Ethics and Philosophical Critique*, 62.

3. James's theories of truth are perhaps his best-known and most contested engagements with questions from traditional philosophy. Since he conceives of the self-creative project in terms of repeated and deliberate deciding and acting, and "true" beliefs are those on which one is prepared to act, James's theorization of truth is implicated in his ethics, though not overtly.

4. Marchetti, *Ethics and Philosophical Critique*, 75, 80.

5. West, *American Evasion*, 58.

6. Perry, *Thought and Character*, 2:383.

7. Bordogna, "Selves and Communities," 32, 33.

8. William James to Josephine Lowell, December 6, 1903, James Papers, Harvard Library Archive, cited in Coon, "'One Moment,'"91.

9. Roth, "Introduction," 8.

10. Marchetti, *Ethics and Philosophical Critique*, 65.

11. John Dewey, *Experience and Nature*, 38.

12. McDermott, "Classical American Philosophy," 668.

13. Taylor, "Humanistic Implications," 410.

14. "It is interesting that James's *Principles*, even today, is sometimes represented as being an experimental psychology. It was not. It was a scientific, nonmetaphysical psychology but not an experimental one. It was science based on observation but not necessarily on experimentation." Evans, "William James and His *Principles*," 28.

15. This suggests that James was, in contemporary parlance, a philosopher *of* psychology. See, for example, Reck, "Philosophical Psychology of William James."

16. Marchetti, *Ethics and Philosophical Critique*, 125.

17. Marchetti, *Ethics and Philosophical Critique*, 125–26.

18. Evans, "William James and His *Principles*," 28.

19. In *Principles*, James was determined to focus on psychology to the exclusion of metaphysics, writing, "As *psychologists*, we need not be metaphysical at all. The phenomena are enough, the passing Thought itself is the only *verifiable* thinker, and its empirical connection with the brain-process is the ultimate known law" (*PP*, 328).

20. Throntveit, *Ethical Republic*, 101.

21. Marchetti, *Ethics and Philosophical Critique*, 124.

22. Marchetti, *Ethics and Philosophical Critique*, 129.

23. McDermott, "Introduction," *ERE*, xxi.

24. See Shook, "Introduction," 10; Powell, "William James," 171.

25. Crosby and Viney, "Recapturing the Vision," 102.

26. Perry, *Spirit of William James*, 100.

27. For a clear account of experience as an ontological category, see Smith, *America's Philosophical Vision*, 75. For a summary of James's various uses of the term, see Suckiel, "William James," 75.

28. Smith, *Purpose and Thought*, 33.

29. We ought to remain mindful that even the notions of concreteness and immediacy are problematic. Smith (among others) "is deeply suspicious of appeals to immediacy" because "what appears to be absolutely immediate turns out to be . . . in some typically disguised and thus unnoticed manner mediated" and "the very attempt to identify concrete particularly in its absolute concreteness depends upon the most abstract of 'concepts' (e.g., this, here, now)." Colapietro, "Critic of Abstractions," 122.

30. Bergson, *Creative Mind*, 290 n. 32.

31. McDermott, *Drama of Possibility*, 82.

32. Commager, *American Mind*, 93. Commager adds: "Practical, democratic, individualistic, opportunistic, spontaneous, hopeful, pragmatism was wonderfully adapted to the temperament of the average American," 97.

33. McDermott, "Foreword," ix.

34. Note, however, that Kant's account of experience, like James's, emphasizes the role of an embodied subject interacting with the world, rather than relying solely on formal conditions of knowledge.

35. McDermott, "Foreword," xxix.

36. Although James's most considered attempts to address this deficiency came in the series of essays from 1904–5 collected as *ERE*, there is evidence that it had troubled him for more than twenty years. This quote comes from an 1884 article.

37. For a pithy account of this point, see John E. Smith, "Experience, God," 122–23.

38. Hare, "Introduction," xxiv.

39. James's criticism is not limited to Humean associationists. As McDermott explains, James identifies a tendency for metaphysicians generally to overemphasize "those discrete particulars for which we have assigned a 'name'" so that "the leap from name to name has become the equivalent to the leap from thing to thing and the relations which bind them are hereby held to be primarily next to that, that is, relations of simple 'contiguity.'" McDermott, "Introduction," xx. Some versions of psychology had the same problem. For example, Wundt too conceived of consciousness in terms of discrete, atomistic sensations.

40. Leary, "Psychological Roots," 42.

41. The temporal aspect of this account is often underemphasized by James scholars (an odd tendency given James's engagements with Kant). James writes, "According to my view, experience as a whole is a process in time, whereby innumerable particular terms lapse and are superseded by others that follow upon them by transitions which . . . are themselves experiences" (*MT*, 65).

42. Smith, "Experience, God," 121.

43. Uffelman, "Role of Self-Cultivation," 46.

44. See Barzun, *Stroll with William James*, 37–39.

45. Powell, "William James," 170.

46. Myers, "Pragmatism and Introspective Psychology," 12.

47. Giorgi, "Phenomenological Reinterpretation," 134.

48. Giorgi, "Phenomenological Reinterpretation," 134.

49. Doyle, "Jamesian Free Will," 9.

50. Myers, "Pragmatism and Introspective Psychology," 12, 20.

51. Myers, "Pragmatism and Introspective Psychology," 11–12.

52. Roth, *Freedom and the Moral Life*, 24.

53. Roth, "Introduction," 2.

54. Perry, *Thought and Character*, 2:386.

55. Ayer, *Origins of Pragmatism*, 292.

56. Banks, "Neutral Monism Reconsidered."

57. Stevens, *James and Husserl*, 19.

58. Seigfried, "Concrete Analysis," 539.

59. Seigfried, "Concrete Analysis," 540.

60. See Seigfried, "World We Practically Live In," 85.

61. McDermott, "Promethean Self," 87; "Pragmatic Sensibility," 80–81.

62. Menand, *Metaphysical Club*, 88.

63. Quoted in Perry, *Thought and Character*, 2:347.

64. Smith, "Being and Willing," 27.

65. McDermott, "Promethean Self," 99. Dewey for example wrote that "relationships which are produced by the fact that interests are formed in their social environment are far more important than are the adjustments of isolated selves," and "to a large extent, the emphasis of theory upon the problem of adjustment of egoism . . . took place at a time when thought was decidedly individualistic in character." Dewey, "The Moral Self," 348–49.

66. Rorty, "Eliminative Materialism," 202.

67. Rorty, "Eliminative Materialism," 205.

68. Sellars, *Empiricism and the Philosophy of Mind*.

69. Malachowski, "Imagination Over Truth," 212.

70. Rorty, *Consequences of Pragmatism*, xix.

71. Rorty, *Consequences of Pragmatism*, xx.

72. Rorty, *Philosophy and Social Hope*, 95.

73. Johnson, "Experiencing Language," 15.

74. Not all neo-pragmatists argue for a wholly linguistic pragmatism. Misak, for example, criticizes Rorty and Brandom for "setting up a false choice between language or experience" when in fact "language and experience cannot be pulled apart." Misak, "Language and Experience for Pragmatism," 29. On the other side of the debate, some classical pragmatists have proposed a form of pragmatism that mediates the two (e.g., Koopman, *Pragmatism as Transition*).

75. Koopman, "Language is a Form of Experience."

76. Johnson, "Experiencing Language," 19.

77. Johnson, "Experiencing Language," 17.

78. Hookway, "Pragmatism and the Given," 271.

79. Wilshire, *Fashionable Nihilism*, 11–12.

80. Regarding intentionality in Jamesian pragmatism, see Rosenthal, "Pragmatic Reconstruction," 134. Linschoten contends that while James's psychology "is phenomenological by intention," it did not become so explicitly because he "did not succeed in developing a clear concept of intentionality." Linschoten, *Phenomenological Psychology*, 307. By contrast, Reck holds that there are in fact two relatively well-developed versions of intentionality in James's philosophy, which are "cognitive and volitional. In cognition consciousness refers to objects that exist independently of it. Moreover, the objects with which it deals depend, in part, on its own selections; they are the objects to which it attends, and attention is a volitional act." Reck, "William James's *Principles of Psychology*," 8. I am inclined toward Reck's view, as will be evident from the account that follows.

81. Pihlström, "Naturalized Transcendental Subjectivity," 5.

82. For example, Eugene Taylor holds that James's 1901 lectures, documented *in The Varieties of Religious Experience*, were "clearly a phenomenological study" and identify James as "a first-generation phenomenologist." Taylor, "Phenomenological Psychology," 126. Like Wilshire, Russell Goodman calls James a "proto-phenomenologist." Goodman, "William James." There is evidence that Husserl read *Principles* and several of James's essays.

83. For examples of critical pioneering work, see Edie, "William James and Phenomenology" and *William James and Phenomenology*; McDermott, "Editor's Introduction"; Wild, *Radical Empiricism*; Wilshire, *William James and Phenomenology* and "Phenomenology and Pragmatism." On similarities between James's project and Husserl's, see Seigfried, "Phenomenological Methodology," 62–63 and "World We Practically Live In," 84.

84. Smith, "Experience, God," 122.

85. Uffelman, "Role of Self-Cultivation," 205, 210.

86. On James's development of the field model, see Taylor, "Humanistic Implications," 414.

87. James quoted in Perry, *Thought and Character*, 2:700.

88. See Watzl, *Structuring Mind*, 183–84.

89. Wilshire, *Fashionable Nihilism*, 11.

90. Lamberth, *Metaphysics of Experience*, 90 provides an intricate account of such experiments.

91. James's 1895–96 notebooks, quoted in McDermott, "Introduction," xxv.

92. Albrecht, *Reconstructing Individualism*, 150.

93. McDermott, "Lost Horizon," 11.

94. The stream model is especially effective for conveying the continuous, dynamic nature of consciousness, whereas the field model is best for describing and assessing the relational properties associated with, and leading to, particular states of consciousness. James provides no direct guidance on this matter.

95. Ford, *William James's Philosophy*, 19.

96. See for example Flanagan, *Problem of the Soul*, 232.

97. James, *Letters*, 2:141.

98. Shook, "Introduction," 25.

Chapter 3

1. Dewey, "Self-Realization," 663.

2. Gale, "Self Identity Over Time."

3. See, for example, Edie, *William James and Phenomenology*; Gurwitsch, "Transitive Parts,"; McDermott, *Drama of Possibility*; Smith, *Purpose and Thought*.

4. Stevens, *James and Husserl*, 127.

5. For a summary of James's changing views, see Shea, "Self in William James," 326–30. Inukai advances the contrary view that James's views are actually continuous; see "James and Hume," 5–6.

6. Dewey, "Vanishing Subject," 398–99.

7. On this point James's discussion is highly reminiscent of Hume.

8. Fen, "Has James Answered Hume?," 161.

9. For Kant, all human experience, including experience of the self, is a product of successive acts of synthesis that are not themselves experienced. He calls construction of coherent consciousness from disparate experiences "transcendental apperception."

10. Shook, "Introduction," 15.

11. Myers, "Pragmatism and Introspective Psychology," 21.

12. Czerwionka, "The Self," 203.

13. Inukai, "James's Answer to Hume."

14. Myers, *William James*, 78.

15. Dewey, "Vanishing Subject," 408.

16. Wild, *Radical Empiricism*, 311.

17. Edie, "William James and Phenomenology," 514.

18. This is not always the case. For a discussion of the extent to which James seems to find a unifying metaphysical role for the body, see Ayer, *Origins of*

Pragmatism, 78. For the role that James granted the body in staving off idealism, see Myers, *Life and Thought*, 351–52.

19. Crosby, *Philosophy of William James*, 36.

20. Bailey, "Beyond the Fringe," 152.

21. McDermott, *Streams of Experience*, 53.

22. Smith, *Spirit of American Philosophy*, 41.

23. Not all scholars agree. Seigfried has written that "those who call James a voluntarist fail to realize the extent to which he has reconstructed rationality." Seigfried, "Concrete Analysis," 543. Shook considers "voluntarism" to be the wrong word, preferring "functionalism" because it "replaces the notion of an unnatural free will with voluntary control: a natural capacity for humans to make deliberate decisions and regulate their habitual behavior." Shook, "Introduction," 9.

24. Parker, "Experience and Creative Growth," 210.

25. Doyle, "Jamesian Free Will," 7.

26. James quoted in Perry, *Thought and Character*, 1:682.

27. Koopman, "The Will," 504.

28. Rosenthal, "Pragmatic Reconstruction," 132.

29. Ralph W. Emerson, "The Infinitude of the Private Man" (Chicago: Maurice York, 2008). For an example of this view, see Commager, *American Mind*, 98.

30. West, *American Evasion*, 58; Bacon, *Richard Rorty*, 84.

31. McDermott, *Drama of Possibility*, 378; "Promethean Self," 91. It is difficult to consider James over-optimistic after reading this: "The normal process of life contains moments as bad as any of those which insane melancholy is filled with, moments in which radical evil gets its innings and takes its solid turn. The lunatic's visions of horror are all drawn from the material of daily fact." (*VRE*, 136–37).

32. Allen, *William James*, 499.

33. Quoted in Seigfried, "Phenomenological Methodology," 69–70.

34. Suckiel, *Pragmatic Philosophy*, 14–15.

35. Dewey draws an important distinction, often unrecognized in discussions of the active self, between "interests" (which are internal to and constitutive of the self) and "motives" (which are external to the self but might *arouse* one's interest). Dewey, "The Moral Self," 344, 347.

36. Perry, *Thought and Character*, 1:301.

37. Although James uses "ideals" quite frequently in his discussions of ethics and character development, it is only in *Talks to Teachers* that he discusses these characteristics explicitly, and then only briefly.

38. For a detailed account of James's Darwinism, see McGranahan, *Darwinism and Pragmatism*.

39. Roth, *Freedom and the Moral Life*, 77. See James's essay "On a Certain Blindness in Human Beings" (*TT*, 132–49).

40. Suckiel, *Pragmatic Philosophy*, 2.

41. Smith, *Spirit of American Philosophy*, 54.

42. McDermott, *Drama of Possibility*, 137.

43. Smith, *Experience and God*, 32.

44. Kolenda, *Rorty's Humanistic Pragmatism*, 38.

45. Roth, *Freedom and the Moral Life*, 46–47.

46. Crosby, *Philosophy of William James*, 33.

47. Crosby, *Philosophy of William James*, 34.

48. Bordogna, *William James at the Boundaries*, 203.

49. Uffelman, "Jamesian Self-Cultivation," 9.

50. McDermott, *Drama of Possibility*, 147.

Chapter 4

1. McDermott, *Culture of Experience*, 106–7.

2. Marchetti, *Ethics and Philosophical Critique*, 105.

3. Roth, "Introduction," 5.

4. Roth, "Introduction," 17.

5. Koopman, "Conduct Pragmatism," 6.

6. Albrecht, *Reconstructing Individualism*, 158.

7. Albrecht, *Reconstructing Individualism*, 159.

8. James refers to Bain's *The Emotions and the Will* (1859) and *Mental and Moral Science* (1868), and Carpenter's *Principles of Mental Physiology* (1874).

9. Quoted in Thomas, "Figures of Habit," 9.

10. John Locke, *An Essay Concerning Human Understanding* (London: Routledge, 2000), 121.

11. Quoted in Rosenbaum, *Reflective Life*, 120.

12. McGranahan, *Darwinism and Pragmatism*, 71.

13. Quoted in Shade, *Habits of Hope*, 25.

14. Talisse and Hester, *On James*, 22.

15. Reflex arc theory describes automatic neuromuscular activity as a product of the neural circuit comprising incoming sensory nerves and outgoing motor nerves, in conjunction with the spinal cord and/or the brain.

16. On this point, James is following George Henry Lewes and others. In 1860, Lewes had noted that new skills were initially difficult to learn but became easier (even "automatic") once channels for sensations were established.

17. Barzun, *Stroll with William James*, 76.

18. Franzese, *Ethics of Energy*, 126. For an account of James's relationship to contemporary neuroscience, see Sheets-Johnstone, "Legacy of William James."

19. See Norman Doidge, *Brain That Changes Itself*, 209–10.

20. Menand, *Metaphysical Club*, 354.

21. Marchetti, *Ethics and Philosophical Critique*, 146.

22. Marchetti, "Unfamiliar Habits, 1.

23. Franzese, *Ethics of Energy*, 127.

24. McDermott, *Culture of Experience*, 107–8.

25. McDermott, *Culture of Experience*, 105.

26. Unger, *Self Awakened*, 130.

27. For examples of data exploring James's claim, see Antonio Terracciano, Paul T. Costa Jr., and Robert R. McRae, "Personal Plasticity After Age 30," *Personality and Social Psychology Bulletin* 32, no. 8 (2006): 999–1009, and Rodica Ioanna Damian et al., "Sixteen Going on Sixty-Six: A Longitudinal Study of Personality Stability and Change Across 50 Years," *Journal of Personality and Social Psychology* 117, no. 3 (2019): 674–95.

28. Brennan, *Ethics of William James*, 139–40. Perry writes of James's "Habit" chapter, "It is not without bearing on its success that it should have sprung from an early and lifelong faith of his own in the benign effect of routine and the cumulative significance of little acts." Perry, *Thought and Character*, 2:90.

29. McDermott, *Culture of Experience*, 106.

30. Albrecht, *Reconstructing Individualism*, 157.

31. Dewey, *Theory of the Moral Life*, 173–74.

32. McDermott, *Drama of Possibility*, 384.

33. Scheffler, *Four Pragmatists*, 122.

34. Koopman, "The Will."

35. Eldridge and Pihlström, "Glossary," 33–34.

36. Craig, "Habit," 176.

37. Craig, "Habit," 176.

38. The transformation cannot be so radical and complete that the self becomes entirely "new," as it were. The balance of our interests ensures that "we cannot wilfully ignore that which has the sting of reality for us. Although we may be able to open up the possibility of other kinds of feelings, other patterns of attention, we cannot wilfully and voluntarily choose not to believe in verisimilar concernful construals." Janack, "Epistemological and Psychological Subject," 169.

39. James, *Letters*, 1:119.

40. James, *Letters*, 1:148.

41. The reference is to the editorial list of "James's Annotations of His Private Copy."

42. See Myers, *Life and Thought*, 198.

43. McGranahan, *Darwinism and Pragmatism*, 81.

44. Craig, "Habit, Relaxation," 178–79.

45. Marchetti, *Ethics and Philosophical Critique*, 150.

46. Parker, "Experience and Creative Growth," 217.

47. James, *Letters*, 1:147. In considering this philosophically romantic tale of James's recovery, we ought not to overlook the impact of changes in his personal and professional life, too; see Bjork, *Center of His Vision*, 228–29; Cotkin, *Public Philosopher*, 9–10; Kuklick, *Rise of American Philosophy*, 165.

48. Perry, *Thought and Character*, 1:655.

49. James's five kinds of volitional decision are reasonable deliberation, acquiescence, recklessness, changes of heart, and decision through effort (*PP*, 1138–42). Among the first four, James includes cases where a decision is made prior to discovery of a compelling reason to favor one path over another.

50. Myers, *His Life and Thought*, 203.

51. Gale, *Philosophy of William James*, 44. For James, "the very first actions made by an organism" must have been of this reflex kind, having "been built into its biological and physiological structures as instinctive or reflexive movements." Rychlak, "Concept of Free Will," 324.

52. As an alternative to differentiating "simple" from "complex" cases on a kind of continuum, Franzese holds that "will" is "a name for two distinct things: 1) the entire capacity for impulsive and active life, including instinctive reactions and habitual, automatic, or semiconscious acts; and 2) acts that are deliberately performed. The latter are acts that require a distinct idea of what they are and a focussed attention on the part of the mind." Franzese, *Ethics of Energy*, 121. However, Franzese's reading does not do justice to the rich plurality of cases "between" the wholly reflex and the wholly deliberate, or to the way in which cases that initially required close and conscious attention become, with sufficient practice, more akin to reflexes.

53. Michael Tunnecliffe (Clinical Psychologist, Ashcliffe Psychology), in discussion with the author, December 2020.

54. Gale, *Philosophy of William James*, 47.

55. As Stevens writes, "Attention is the index of the mobile mastery of consciousness and the entire cycle of its activity: a) in the perceptual structuring of the flow of experience; b) in the projection of patterns of meaning; c) in the not natural combination of these projects in concrete corporeal activity." Stevens, *James and Husserl*, 148.

56. Stevens, *James and Husserl*, 144.

57. If the effort of attention brings with it exertion in the *body* (James mentions "tense muscles, strained ligaments, squeezed joints, fixed chest, closed glottis, contracted brow, clenched jaws, etc. etc."), then this ought to be understood as evidence of an *unintentional* response to stimuli best left to physiology and physics for an explanation, James thinks, and ought not to be confused with the act of willing itself, which remains always "a psychic or moral fact pure and simple" that "is absolutely completed when the stable state of the idea is there" (*EPs*, 85; *PB*, 385).

58. Stevens notes that "traditional psychological studies of attention have concentrated upon the subjective feeling of effort which accompanies voluntary focus upon an object. As a consequence, the objective direction of attention . . . tends to be subordinated to the mental-fact of attending. This is, in fact, the usual result of the methodology of introspective psychology which ironically objectifies the

activities of subjectivity in the very effort to reflect upon them." Stevens, *James and Husserl*, 150.

59. James's more detailed account of the will comes in the crucial chapter of *Principles* called "Will" (*PP*, 1098–1193). His phenomenological approach keeps his philosophy immune from some recent scientific challenges to traditional conceptions of the will and willing. For example, there is evidence that brain activity occurs *before* one is aware of willing an action, so that although we might feel as though an action originated from our conscious decision about it and our commitment to it, that might be an error: the decision was perhaps already made. See, for example, Daniel M. Wegner, *The Illusion of Conscious Will* (Cambridge, MA: MIT Press, 2002. Yet we do still seem to experience various connections between attention, decision, commitment, and action that are indicative of willing. Using phenomenological psychology, James illuminates such experiences without begging the question of whether will is causally efficacious or a mere epiphenomenon. See Blok, "Contesting the Will."

60. The comment "when it is most voluntary" is meant to differentiate between the more active and passive of the five types of decision discussed earlier.

61. Gale, *Divided Self*, 76.

62. Smith, *Spirit of American Philosophy*, 67.

63. Koopman, "The Will," 499.

64. This from Koopman is indicative of James's general position: "Wherever he wrote of freedom, James refused to offer an argument on behalf of the existence of our freedom. As he put it in *Principles*, 'the question of free-will is insoluble on strictly psychologic grounds,' and so it is on ethical grounds that we must answer the question without any direct backing from, but also without conflicting with, moral psychology." "The Will," 503.

65. Smith, "Being and Willing," 29.

66. Smith, "Being and Willing," 29.

67. Ayer, *Origins of Pragmatism*, 206, 205.

68. Stevens, *James and Husserl*, 148, 149.

69. Flower, "Unity of Knowledge and Purpose," 191.

70. One of James's brothers struggled with addiction to alcohol, and James saw it as a product simultaneously arising from and exhibited in a failure of will that could only be overcome through a "turn" that bridged the gap between "knowing" (or "realizing") the problem and acting on it.

71. Putnam, "Moral Life," 74.

72. Gale, *Divided Self*, 74.

73. Stevens, *James and Husserl*, 133.

74. Stevens, *James and Husserl*, 133.

75. Wild, *Radical Empiricism*, 311.

76. McDermott, *Culture of Experience*, 106.

77. McDermott, "Experience as Freedom," 250.

78. Aikin and Talisse, "Three Challenges," 5.

79. McDermott points out the profound epistemological connotations of this final point: "Granted that it is impossible to predict safely or accurately all of the implications of any decision, far greater attention must now be paid to future fallout. . . . [so that] it would be far better if we were to develop an epistemology which accepted surprise, novelty, and potential mishap as permanent ingredients of human inquiry. In so doing, our decisions would be more tentative, less absolute, and consequently truer to the actual situation in which we find ourselves." McDermott, *Drama of Possibility*, 152.

80. Richard M. Gale, "William James and John Dewey," 160.

81. Stuhr, *Future of Philosophy*, 172–73. The point is especially clear in James's distinction between "healthy-minded" people (who consider the world to be basically good and exhibit quite consistent impulses, few regrets, and a stronger will) and "sick souls" (who tend to be weaker in the face of moral responsibilities and exhibit conflicting tendencies and a wish for "incompatibles"). Whereas healthy-minded people are capable of a strenuous ethics, and recognize the risks involved, sick souls are more likely to resort to the consolations of religious faith or "the power of positive thinking." (*ERM*, 62).

82. Albrecht, *Reconstructing Individualism*, 150–52.

83. McGranahan, *Darwinism and Pragmatism*, 86.

84. McGranahan, *Darwinism and Pragmatism*, 91.

85. McGranahan, *Darwinism and Pragmatism*, 84.

86. Koopman, "The Will," 497.

87. In the context of self-transformation, James means by "resistance" the effort involved in maintaining a deliberate grasp of one's experience in the face of those socioeconomic pressures and established ethical norms discussed earlier, and by "steam-pressure," the energy required to sustain that effort.

88. See for example Bordogna, "Selves and Communities," 33; Duclow, "Religion of Healthy-Mindedness," 45. It is noteworthy that aspects of mind-cure are evident in such contemporary approaches as positive psychology, psychology of happiness, various kinds of complementary medicine, and practices that rely on emotional states to aid healing.

89. I am referring here to the influence of James's Swedenborgian father in addition to his evidently conflicted views on religion and its place in his life. James provided no reasons to commit to spiritual realism, and his definition of religion has a markedly psychologistic flavor: "*religion . . . shall mean . . . the feelings, acts, and experiences of individual men in their solitude, so far as they apprehend themselves to stand in relation to whatever they may consider the divine*" (*VRE*, 34).

90. Gale, *Philosophy of William James*, 9.

91. Slater, *Ethics and Faith*, 4, 2, 3.

92. West, *American Evasion*, 66. Alexander Klein argues that James's views on religion entail both a "therapeutic" aim of highlighting the potential benefits of adopting religious beliefs and a "theoretic" one of convincing his "melancholic peers" that such beliefs are epistemically permissible. Klein, "Between Anarchism and Suicide."

93. Gavin, *Reinstatement of the Vague*, 30–33.

94. Talisse and Hester, *On James*, 90.

95. Kitcher, *Ethical Project*, 348 n.8.

96. In *VRE*, James promotes the utility of, and pragmatic justifications for, myriad Christian values but not in the context of either an orienting interest for deliberate self-transformation or a systematic religious ethics.

97. For a scholarly paper on habit that refers explicitly to James's theory, the importance of goals and instrumental learning for habit formation, and the reliance on self-reporting in the study of habit, see Wendy Wood and Dennis Rünger, "Psychology of Habit," *Annual Review of Psychology* 67 (2016): 289–314. For a popular work on habit that employs the same kinds of principles and exercises as James proposed, see Richard Connor, *Rewire: Change Your Brain to Break Bad Habits, Overcome Addictions, Conquer Self-Destructive Behavior* (New York: Plume, 2014).

98. Franzese, *Ethics of Energy*, 203–4.

99. James provides an alternative conception of character, as the "particular mental or moral attitude in which, when it came upon him, he felt himself most deeply and intensely active and alive." James, *Letters*, 1:199.

100. Putnam, "Moral Life," 79.

101. McDermott, "You Are Really Able," 49.

Conclusion

1. Kaag, *Sick Souls*, 5.

2. West, *American Evasion*, 4.

3. Koopman, "Transforming the Self," 54.

4. Richardson, *William James in the Maelstrom*, 6.

5. Koopman, "The Will," 508.

6. Edie, "William James and Phenomenology," 523.

7. McDermott, *Drama of Possibility*, 154–55.

Bibliography

Aikin, Scott F. "Pragmatism, Experience, and the Given." *Human Affairs* 19, no. 1 (2009): 19–27.

Aikin, Scott F., and Robert B. Talisse. "Three Challenges to Jamesian Ethics." *William James Studies* 6 (2011): 3–9.

Albrecht, James M. *Reconstructing Individualism: A Pragmatic Tradition from Emerson to Ellison.* New York: Fordham University Press, 2012.

Alexander, Thomas. "Mythos and Polyphonic Pluralism." *The Pluralist* 15, no. 1 (2020): 1–16.

———. "Richard Rorty and Dewey's Metaphysics of Experience." *Southwest Philosophy Review* 5 (1980): 24–35.

Allen, Gay Wilson, ed. *A William James Reader.* Boston: Houghton Mifflin, 1971.

———. *William James: A Biography.* New York: Viking Press, 1970.

Allen, Michael W. "The 'Bite' of the Existential 'Moment.'" In *Experience as Philosophy,* edited by James Campbell and Richard E. Hart, 84–115. New York: Fordham University Press, 2006.

Anderson, Douglas R. "Old Pragmatisms, New Histories." *Journal of the History of Philosophy* 47, no. 2 (2009): 489–521.

Ayer, Alfred J. *The Origins of Pragmatism: Studies in the Philosophy of Charles Sanders Peirce and William James.* San Francisco: Freeman, Cooper, 1968.

Bacon, Michael. *Richard Rorty: Pragmatism and Political Liberalism.* Plymouth: Lexington, 2007.

Bailey, Andrew R. "Beyond the Fringe: William James on the Transitional Parts of the Stream of Consciousness." *Journal of Consciousness Studies* 6, no. 2–3 (1999): 141–53.

Banks, Erik C. "Neutral Monism Reconsidered." *Philosophical Psychology* 23, no. 2 (2010): 173–87.

Barzun, Jacques. *A Stroll with William James.* Chicago: University of Chicago Press, 2002.

Beard, George M. *A Practical Treatise on Nervous Exhaustion (Neurasthenia).* New York: E. B. Treat, 1905.

Bergson, Henri. *The Creative Mind: An Introduction to Metaphysics*. New York: Dover, 2012.

Bernstein, Richard J. "American Pragmatism: The Conflict of Narratives." In *Rorty and Pragmatism: The Philosopher Responds to His Critics*, edited by Herman J. Saatkamp Jr., 54–67. Nashville: Vanderbilt University Press, 1995.

———. *The Pragmatic Turn*. Cambridge: Polity, 2010.

Bird, Graham. "Moral Philosophy and the Development of Morality." In *The Cambridge Companion to William James*, edited by Ruth Anna Putnam, 260–81. Cambridge: Cambridge University Press, 1997.

———. *William James*. New York: Routledge, 2002.

Bjork, Daniel W. *The Compromised Scientist: William James in the Development of American Psychology*. New York: Columbia University Press, 1983.

———. *William James: The Center of His Vision*. New York: Columbia University Press, 1988.

Blok, Vincent. "Contesting the Will: Phenomenological Reflections on Four Structural Moments in the Concept of Willing." *Journal of the British Society for Phenomenology* 48, no. 4 (2017): 1–18.

Bordogna, Francesca. "Inner Division and Uncertain Contours: William James and the Politics of the Modern Self." *British Journal for the History of Science* 40, no. 4 (2007): 505–36.

———. "Selves and Communities in the Work of William James." *Streams of William James* 6, no. 3 (2004): 30–37.

———. *William James at the Boundaries: Philosophy, Science, and the Geography of Knowledge*. Chicago: University of Chicago Press, 2008.

Boyle, Deborah. "William James's Ethical Symphony." Transactions of the Charles S. Peirce Society 34, no. 4 (1998): 977–1003.

Brandom, Robert B. *Perspectives on Pragmatism: Classical, Recent, and Contemporary*. Cambridge, MA: Harvard University Press, 2011.

Brennan, Bernard P. *The Ethics of William James*. New York: Bookman, 1961.

Bruzina, Ronald, and Bruce Wilshire, eds. *Phenomenology: Dialogues and Bridges*. Albany: State University of New York Press, 1982.

Calcaterra, Rosa M., and Roberta Dreon. "Introduction to Pragmatism and Psychologism." *European Journal of Pragmatism and American Philosophy* 9, no. 1 (2017): 1–9.

Campbell, James. *Experiencing William James: Belief in a Pluralistic World*. Charlottesville: University of Virginia Press, 2017.

———. "John Dewey's Debt to William James." In *The Oxford Handbook of William James*, edited by Alexander Klein. Oxford: Oxford University Press, 2018.

———. "William James and the Ethics of Fulfillment." *Transactions of the Charles S. Peirce Society* 17, no. 3 (1981): 224–40.

Campbell, James, and Richard E. Hart, eds. *Experience as Philosophy: On the Work of John J. McDermott*. New York: Fordham University Press, 2006.

Čapek, Milič. "The Reappearance of the Self in the Last Philosophy of William James." *Philosophical Review* 62, no. 4 (1953): 526–44.

Cobb-Stevens, Richard. "A Fresh Look at James's Radical Empiricism." In *Phenomenology: Dialogues and Bridges,* edited by Ronald Bruzina and Bruce Wilshire, 109–21. Albany: State University of New York Press, 1982.

Colapietro, Vincent M. "It Is Self-Assemblage All the Way Down." *Journal of Speculative Philosophy* 31, no. 1 (2017): 190–206.

———. "John E. Smith: Critic of Abstractions." In *Experience, Interpretation, and Community: Themes in John E. Smith's Reconstruction of Philosophy*, edited by Vincent M. Colapietro, 111–28. Newcastle, UK: Cambridge Scholars Publishing, 2011.

———, ed. *Reason, Experience, and God: John E. Smith in Dialogue.* New York: Fordham University Press, 1997.

Commager, Henry Steele. *The American Mind: An Interpretation of American Thought and Character since the 1880's.* New Haven, CT: Yale University Press, 1950.

Coon, Deborah J. " 'One Moment in the World's Salvation': Anarchism and the Radicalisation of William James." *Journal of American History* 83, no. 1 (1996): 70–99.

Cooper, Wesley. "Pragmatism and Radical Empiricism." *Inquiry* 42, no. 3–4 (1999): 371–83.

———. *The Unity of William James's Thought.* Nashville: Vanderbilt University Press, 2002.

———. "William James's Moral Theory." *Journal of Moral Education* 32, no. 4 (2003): 411–22.

Cormier, Harvey. "Comment on Talisse and Aikin." *William James Studies* 6 (2011): 10–17.

Corti, Walter Robert, ed. *The Philosophy of William James.* Hamburg: Felix Meiner, 1976.

Cotkin, George. *Reluctant Modernism: American Thought and Culture, 1880–1900.* New York: Twayne, 1992.

———. *William James, Public Philosopher.* Baltimore: Johns Hopkins University Press, 1990.

Craig, Megan. "Habit, Relaxation, and the Open Mind: James and the Increments of Ethical Freedom." In *Feminist Interpretations of William James*, edited by Erin C. Tarver and Shannon Sullivan, 165–88. University Park: Pennsylvania State University Press, 2015.

Croce, Paul Jerome. "The Non-Disciplinary William James." *William James Studies* 8 (2012): 1–33.

———. *Science and Religion in the Era of William James: Eclipse of Certainty, 1820–1880.* Chapel Hill: University of North Carolina Press, 1995.

———. "William James's Scientific Education." *History of the Human Sciences* 8, no. 1 (1995): 9–27.

Crosby, Donald A. *The Philosophy of William James: Radical Empiricism and Radical Materialism*. Lanham, MD: Rowman and Littlefield, 2013.

Crosby, Donald A., and Wayne Viney. "Toward a Psychology That Is Radically Empirical: Recapturing the Vision of William James." In *Reinterpreting the Legacy of William James*, edited by Margaret E. Donnelly, 101–18. Washington, DC: American Psychological Society, 1992.

Czerwionka, Felicia. "The Self in William James's Psychology." In *The Philosophy of William James*, edited by Walter Robert Corti, 201–20. Hamburg: Felix Meiner, 1976.

Daniel, Stephen H. "Fringes and Transitive States in William James's Concept of the Stream of Thought." *Auslegung: A Journal of Philosophy* 3, no. 2 (1976): 64–80.

De Waal, Cornelis. On Pragmatism. Belmont, CA: Thomson Wadsworth, 2005.

DeArmey, Michael H., and Stephen Skousgaard, eds. *The Philosophical Psychology of William James*. Washington, DC: Center for Advanced Research in Phenomenology and University Press of America, 1986.

DePaul, Michael R., and William Ramsey, eds. *Rethinking Intuition: The Psychology of Intuition and Its Role in Philosophical Inquiry*. Lanham, MD: Rowman and Littlefield, 1998.

Dewey, John. *The Development of American Pragmatism*. Whitefish, MT: Literary Licensing, 2011.

———. *Essays in Experimental Logic*. Mineola, NY: Dover, 2004.

———. *Experience and Nature*. London: George Allen and Unwin, 1929.

———. *The Influence of Darwin on Philosophy and Other Essays in Contemporary Thoughts*. New York: Peter Smith, 1951.

———. *The Middle Works, 1899–1924*. Vol. 6. Carbondale, IL: Southern Illinois University Press, 1985.

———. "The Moral Self." In *The Essential Dewey: Ethics, Logic, Psychology*, edited by Larry A. Hickman and Thomas M. Alexander, 341–54. Bloomington and Indianapolis: Indiana University Press, 1998.

———. "The Need for a Recovery of Philosophy." In *On Experience, Nature, and Freedom*, edited by Richard J. Bernstein. New York: Liberal Arts Press, 1960.

———. "The Philosophy of William James." In *Problems of Men*, 379–95. New York: Philosophical Library, 1946.

———. "Self-Realization as the Moral Ideal." *Philosophical Review* 2, no. 6 (1893): 652–64.

———. "The Vanishing Subject in the Psychology of James." In *Problems of Men*, 396–409. New York: Philosophical Library, 1946.

———. *Theory of the Moral Life*. New York: Holt, Rinehart and Winston, 1960.

Dickstein, Morris, ed. *The Revival of Pragmatism: New Essays on Social Thought, Law, and Culture*. Durham, NC: Duke University Press, 1998.

Diggins, John Patrick. *The Promise of Pragmatism: Modernism and the Crisis of Knowledge and Authority*. Chicago: University of Chicago Press, 1994.

Doidge, Norman. *The Brain That Changes Itself*. Rev. ed. Melbourne: Scribe, 2010.

Donnelly, Margaret E., ed. *Reinterpreting the Legacy of William James*. Washington, DC: American Psychological Society, 1992.

Dooley, Patrick K. "James, William: Pragmatism." In *American Philosophy: An Encyclopedia*, edited by John Lachs and Robert B. Talisse, 417–18. New York: Routledge, 2008.

———. *Pragmatism as Humanism: The Philosophy of William James*. Totowa, NJ: Littlefield, Adams, 1975.

Doyle, Bob. "Jamesian Free Will, the Two-Stage Model of William James." *William James Studies* 5 (2010): 1–28.

Duclow, Donald F. "William James, Mind-Cure and the Religion of Healthy-Mindedness." *Journal of Religion and Health* 41, no. 1 (2002): 45–56.

Edel, Abraham. *In Search of the Ethical: Moral Theory in Twentieth Century America*. New Brunswick, NJ: Transaction, 1993.

———. "Notes on the Search for a Moral Philosophy in William James." In *The Philosophy of William James*, edited by Walter Robert Corti. Hamburg: Felix Meiner, 1976.

Edie, James M., ed. *An Invitation to Phenomenology: Studies in the Philosophy of Experience*. Chicago: Quadrangle, 1965.

———, ed. *New Essays in Phenomenology*. Chicago: Quadrangle Books, 1969.

———. "William James and Phenomenology." *Review of Metaphysics* 23, no. 3 (1970): 481–526.

———. *William James and Phenomenology*. Bloomington: Indiana University Press, 1987.

Ehman, Robert R. "William James and the Structure of the Self." In *New Essays in Phenomenology*, edited by James M. Edie, 256–70. Chicago: Quadrangle Books, 1969.

Eldridge, Michael. "Pragmatism's Elusive Life-Enhancing Social Philosophy." In *Pragmatism and Values*, edited by John Ryder and Emil Višňovský, 117–24 Amsterdam: Rodopi, 2004.

Eldridge, Michael, and Sami Pihlström. "Glossary." In *The Continuum Companion to Pragmatism*, edited by Sami Pihlström, 29–45. London: Continuum, 2011.

Embree, Lester. "The Project of a Metaphysics of Psychology in William James's Principles of Psychology." In *The Philosophical Psychology of William James*, edited by Michael H. DeArmey and Stephen Skousgaard, 41–56. Washington, DC: Center for Advanced Research in Phenomenology and University Press of America, 1986.

Evans, Rand B. "William James and His Principles." In *Reflections on the Principles of Psychology: William James after a Century*, edited by Michael G. Johnson and Tracy B. Henley, 11–31. Hillsdale, NJ: Lawrence Erlbaum, 1990.

Fen, Sing-Nan. "Has James Answered Hume?" *Journal of Philosophy* 49, no. 5 (1952): 159–67.

Fesmire, Steven. *John Dewey and Moral Imagination*. Bloomington: Indiana University Press, 2003.

Fisch, Max H. *Classic American Philosophers*. New York: Appleton Century Crofts, 1951.

Fischer, Eugen. "How to Practice Philosophy as Therapy: Philosophical Therapy and Therapeutic Philosophy." *Metaphilosophy* 42, no. 1–2 (2011): 49–82.

Fish, Stanley. *The Trouble with Principle*. Cambridge, MA: Harvard University Press, 1999.

Flanagan, Owen. *The Problem of the Soul*. New York: Basic Books, 2002.

Flower, Elizabeth F. "The Unity of Knowledge and Purpose in James's View of Action." In *The Philosophy of William James*, edited by Walter Robert Corti, 179–200. Hamburg: Felix Meiner, 1976.

Flower, Elizabeth F., and Murray G. Murphey. *A History of Philosophy in America*. 2 vols. New York: Capricorn, 1977.

Ford, Marcus. *William James's Philosophy: A New Perspective*. Amherst: University of Massachusetts Press, 1982.

Foust, Mathew A. "William James and the Promise of Pragmatism." *William James Studies* 2, no. 1 (2007).

Franzese, Sergio. *The Ethics of Energy: William James's Moral Philosophy in Focus*. Frankfurt: Ontos Verlag, 2008.

Gale, Richard M. "The Deconstruction of Traditional Philosophy in William James's Pragmatism." In *100 Years of Pragmatism: William James's Revolutionary Philosophy*, edited by John J. Stuhr, 108–23. Bloomington: Indiana University Press, 2010.

———. *The Divided Self of William James*. Cambridge: Cambridge University Press, 1999.

———. "James on Self Identity over Time." *Modern Schoolman* 73, no. 1 (1994): 165–89.

———. *The Philosophy of William James: An Introduction*. Cambridge: Cambridge University Press, 2005.

———. "William James and John Dewey." *Midwest Studies in Philosophy* 28, no. 1 (2004): 149–67.

———. "William James's Ethics of Prometheanism." *History of Philosophy Quarterly* 15, no. 2 (1998): 245–69.

Gavin, William J. *William James and the Reinstatement of the Vague*. Philadelphia: Temple University Press, 1992.

———. "William James on the Richness and Intensity of Life." *Journal of Aesthetic Education* 8, no. 3 (1974): 150–53.

Giannotta, Andrea Pace. "The Concept of Experience in Husserl's Phenomenology and James's Radical Empiricism." *Pragmatism Today* 8, no. 2 (2018): 33–42.

Giorgi, Amedeo. "A Phenomenological Reinterpretation of the Jamesian Schema for Psychology." In *Reinterpreting the Legacy of William James*, edited by Margaret E. Donnelly, 119–36. Washington, DC: American Psychological Society, 1992.

Goodman, Russell B. "Two Genealogies of Action in Pragmatism." *Cognitio* 8, no. 2 (2007): 213–22.

———. "William James." *Stanford Encyclopedia of Philosophy* (Winter 2009 Edition), edited by Edward N. Zalta. https://plato.stanford.edu/archives/win2017/entries/james/.

Goodson, Jacob L., ed. *William James, Moral Philosophy, and the Ethical Life.* Lanham, MD: Lexington, 2018.

Gunnarsson, Logi. "The Philosopher as Pathogenic Agent, Patient, and Therapist: The Case of William James." *Royal Institute of Philosophy Supplement* 66 (2010): 165–86.

Gurwitsch, Aron. *The Collected Works of Aron Gurwitsch (1901–1973): The Field of Consciousness: Phenomenology of Theme, Thematic Field, and Marginal Consciousness.* Vol. 3. New York: Springer, 2010.

———. "William James' Theory of the 'Transitive Parts' of the Stream of Consciousness." *Philosophy and Phenomenological Research* 3, no. 4 (1943): 449–77.

Haack, Susan. "Pragmatism, Old and New." *Contemporary Pragmatism* 1, no. 1 (2004): 3–41.

Halliwell, Martin. "Morbid and Positive Thinking: William James, Psychology, and Illness." In *William James and the Transatlantic Conversation: Pragmatism, Pluralism, and Philosophy of Religion*, edited by Martin Halliwell and Joel D. S. Rasmussen, 97–114. Oxford: Oxford University Press, 2014.

Halliwell, Martin, and Joel D. S. Rasmussen, eds. *William James and the Transatlantic Conversation: Pragmatism, Pluralism, and Philosophy of Religion.* Oxford: Oxford University Press, 2014.

Hare, Peter H. *Introduction to Some Problems of Philosophy*, by William James, xiii–xli. Edited by Frederick H. Burkhardt, Fredson Bowers and Ignas K. Skrupskelis. Cambridge, MA: Harvard University Press, 1979.

Hart, Richard E., and Douglas R. Anderson, eds. *Philosophy in Experience: American Philosophy in Transition.* New York: Fordham University Press, 1997.

Hauskeller, Michael. "The Dramatic Richness of the Concrete World: William James." In *The Meaning of Life and Death: Ten Classic Thinkers on the Ultimate Question*, 133–53. London: Bloomsbury, 2019.

Heney, Diana B. *Toward a Pragmatist Metaethics.* New York: Routledge, 2016.

Herzog, Max. "William James and the Development of Phenomenological Psychology in Europe." *History of the Human Sciences* 8, no. 1 (1995): 29–46.

Hester, D. Micah. "James, William: Radical Empiricism." In *American Philosophy: An Encyclopedia*, edited by John Lachs and Robert B. Talisse, 421–23. New York: Routledge, 2008.

Hickman, Larry A. "Shedding Light on the 'Eclipse' Narrative: Some Notes on Pragmatism in the Twentieth Century." *Pluralist* 17, no. 1 (2022): 1–14.

Hildebrand, David L. "Avoiding Wrong Turns: A Philippic against the Linguistification of Pragmatism." In *Dewey, Pragmatism, and Economic Methodology*, edited by Elias L. Khalil, 73–86. London: Routledge, 2004.

Hobbs, Charles A. "Was William James a Phenomenologist?" *Streams of William James* 5, no. 3 (2003): 8–13.

Hollinger, David A. *In the American Province: Studies in the History and Historiography of Ideas.* Baltimore: Johns Hopkins University Press, 1985.

———. "The Problem of Pragmatism in American History." *Journal of American History* 67, no. 1 (1980): 88–107.

Hollinger, Robert, and David Depew, eds. *Pragmatism: From Progressivism to Postmodernism.* Westport, CT: Praeger, 1995.

Hookway, Christopher. "Pragmatism and the Given: C. I. Lewis, Quine, and Peirce." In *The Oxford Handbook of American Philosophy*, edited by Cheryl Misak, 269–89. Oxford: Oxford University Press, 2008.

Inukai, Yumiko. "James and Hume: Radical Empiricism and the Reality of Relations." In *The Oxford Handbook of William James*, edited by Alexander Klein. Oxford: Oxford University Press, 2018.

———. "James's Answer to Hume: The Empirical Basis of the Unified Self." *British Journal for the History of Philosophy* 20, no. 2 (2012): 363–89.

Jackman, Henry. "William James on Moral Philosophy and Its Regulative Ideals." *William James Studies* 15, no. 2 (2019): 1–25.

James, Henry, ed. *The Letters of William James.* 2 vols. Boston: Little, Brown, and Co., 1926.

Janack, Marianne. "Changing the Epistemological and Psychological Subject: William James's Psychology without Borders." *Metaphilosophy* 35, no. 1/2 (2004): 160–77.

———. *What We Mean by Experience.* Stanford: Stanford University Press, 2012.

Jay, Martin. *Songs of Experience: Modern American and European Variations on a Universal Theme.* Berkeley: University of California Press, 2005.

Johnson, Mark. "Experiencing Language: What's Missing in Linguistic Pragmatism?" *European Journal of Pragmatism and American Philosophy* 6, no. 2 (2014): 14–27.

Johnson, Michael G., and Tracy B. Henley, eds. *Reflections on the Principles of Psychology: William James after a Century.* Hillsdale, NJ: Lawrence Erlbaum Associates, 1990.

Kaag, John. *American Philosophy: A Love Story.* New York: Farrar, Straus and Giroux, 2016.

———. *Sick Souls, Healthy Minds: How William James Can Save Your Life.* Princeton, NJ: Princeton University Press, 2020.

Kallen, Horace M., ed. *In Commemoration of William James, 1842–1942.* New York: Columbia University Press, 1942.

Khalil, Elias L., ed. *Dewey, Pragmatism, and Economic Methodology.* London: Routledge, 2004.

Kitcher, Philip. *The Ethical Project.* Cambridge, MA: Harvard University Press, 2011.

———. *Preludes to Pragmatism: Toward a Reconstruction of Philosophy.* New York: Oxford University Press, 2012.

Klein, Alexander. "Between Anarchism and Suicide: On William James's Religious Therapy." *Philosophers' Imprint* 19, no. 32 (2019): 1–18.

Kloppenberg, James T. "Pragmatism: An Old Name for Some New Ways of Thinking?" *Journal of American History* 83, no. 1 (1996): 100–138.

———. *Uncertain Victory: Social Democracy and Progressivism in European and American Thought, 1870–1920*. New York: Oxford University Press, 1986.

Koczanowicz, Leszek, and Agata Sypniewska. "Aesthetic Ethics: Self-Creation, Community and the Other." In *Pragmatism and Values*, edited by John Ryder and Emil Višňovský, 211–20. Amsterdam: Rodopi, 2004.

Kolenda, Konstantin. *Rorty's Humanistic Pragmatism: Philosophy Democratised*. Tampa: University of South Florida Press, 1990.

Koopman, Colin. "Conduct Pragmatism: Pressing Beyond Experientialism and Lingualism." *European Journal of Pragmatism and American Philosophy* 6, no. 2 (2014): 145–74.

———. "Language Is a Form of Experience: Reconciling Classical Pragmatism and Neopragmatism." *Transactions of the Charles S. Peirce Society* 43, no. 4 (2007): 694–727.

———. "Pragmatism as a Philosophy of Hope: Emerson, James, Dewey, Rorty." *Journal of Speculative Philosophy* 20, no. 2 (2006): 106–16.

———. *Pragmatism as Transition: Historicity and Hope in James, Dewey, and Rorty*. New York: Columbia University Press, 2009.

———. "Transforming the Self Amidst the Challenges of Chance: William James on 'Our Undisciplinables.'" *Diacritics* 44, no. 4 (2016): 40–65.

———. "The Will, the Will to Believe and William James: An Ethics of Freedom as Self-Transformation." *Journal of the History of Philosophy* 55, no. 3 (2017): 491–512.

———. "William James's Politics of Personal Freedom." *Journal of Speculative Philosophy* 19, no. 2 (2005): 175–86.

Kuklick, Bruce. *A History of Philosophy in America, 1720–2000*. New York: Oxford University Press, 2001.

———. *The Rise of American Philosophy: Cambridge, Massachusetts, 1860–1930*. New Haven, CT: Yale University Press, 1977.

Lachs, John. *Stoic Pragmatism*. Bloomington: Indiana University Press, 2012.

Lachs, John, and Robert B. Talisse, eds. *American Philosophy: An Encyclopedia*. New York: Routledge, 2008.

Lamberth, David. *William James and the Metaphysics of Experience*. Cambridge: Cambridge University Press, 1999.

Leary, David E. "The Psychological Roots of William James's Thought." In *The Jamesian Mind*, edited by Sarin Marchetti, 33–48. London: Routledge, 2022.

———. "Psychology and Philosophy in the Work of William James: Two Good Things." In *The Oxford Handbook of William James*, edited by Alexander Klein. Oxford: Oxford University Press, 2018.

———. "Visions and Values: Ethical Reflections in a Jamesian Key." *Journal of Mind and Behavior* 30, no. 3 (2009): 121–38.

———. "William James on the Self and Personality." In *Reflections on the Principles of Psychology*, edited by Michael E. Johnson and Tracey Henley, 101–37. Hillsdale, NJ: Lawrence Erlbaum, 1990.

Lekan, Todd. "The Marriage of Ideals and Strenuous Actions: Exploring William James's Account of Significant Life." *Transactions of the Charles S. Peirce Society* 52, no. 4 (2016): 576–97.

———. "A Reconstruction of James's Normative Ethics." *William James Studies* 9 (2012): 144–68.

———. "Strenuous Moral Living." *William James Studies* 2, no. 1 (2007).

———. "Who Are Moral Philosophers? Ethics William James Style." *Pluralist* 13, no. 1 (2018): 81–96.

———. *William James and the Moral Life: Responsible Self-Fashioning*. New York: Routledge, 2022.

Levine, Steven. "The Identity of Self and Act." In *John Dewey's Ethical Theory: The 1932 Ethics*, edited by Roberto Frega and Steven Levine, 134–55. New York: Routledge, 2021.

———. "James and Phenomenology." In *The Oxford Handbook of William James*, edited by Alexander Klein. Oxford: Oxford University Press, 2018.

Linschoten, Hans. *On the Way toward a Phenomenological Psychology: The Psychology of William James*. Pittsburgh: Duquesne University Press, 1968.

Liszka, James Jakób. *Pragmatist Ethics: A Problem-Based Approach to What Matters*. Albany: State University of New York Press, 2021.

Livingston, Alexander. *Damn Great Empires: William James and the Politics of Pragmatism*. New York: Oxford University Press, 2016.

Livingston, James. *Pragmatism and the Political Economy of Cultural Revolution, 1850–1940*. Chapel Hill: University of North Carolina Press, 1994.

Lovejoy, Arthur O. "The Thirteen Pragmatisms." *Pts. 1 and 2. Journal of Philosophy, Psychology and Scientific Methods* 5, no. 1 (1908): 5–12; 5, no. 2 (1908): 29–39.

Malachowski, Alan R., ed. *The Cambridge Companion to Pragmatism*. Cambridge: Cambridge University Press, 2013.

———. "Imagination Over Truth: Rorty's Contribution to Pragmatism." In *The Cambridge Companion to Pragmatism*, edited by Alan R. Malachowski, 207–28. Cambridge: Cambridge University Press, 2013.

———. *The New Pragmatism*. Montreal: McGill-Queen's University Press, 2010.

———. "Putting Pragmatism into Better Shape: Rorty and James." *Pragmatism Today* 2, no. 1 (2011): 51–55.

Marchetti, Sarin. *Ethics and Philosophical Critique in William James*. London: Palgrave Macmillan, 2015.

———. "James, Nietzsche and Foucault on Ethics and the Self." *Foucault Studies*, no. 11 (2011): 126–55.

———. "Kant, James, and the Practice of Ethics." In *Pragmatist Kant: Pragmatism, Kant, and Kantianism in the Twenty-First Century*, edited by Krzysztof Piotr Skowronski and Sami Pihlström, 213–34. Helsinki: Nordic Pragmatism Network, 2019.

———. "Unfamiliar Habits: James and the Ethics and Politics of Self-Experimentation." In *Proceedings of the American Philosophical Association (Central Division)*. Chicago, 2014.

———. "William James on Truth and Invention in Morality." *European Journal of Pragmatism and American Philosophy* 2, no. 2 (2009): 126–59.

Margolis, Joseph. *Pragmatism's Advantage: American and European Philosophy at the End of the Twentieth Century*. Stanford: Stanford University Press, 2010.

———. *Reinventing Pragmatism: American Philosophy at the End of the Twentieth Century*. Ithaca, NY: Cornell University Press, 2002.

Mathur, Dinesh C. *Naturalistic Philosophies of Experience: Studies in James, Dewey and Farber against the Background of Husserl's Phenomenology*. St. Louis, MO: Warren H. Green, 1971.

May, Todd. "A New Neo-Pragmatism: From James and Dewey to Foucault." *Foucault Studies*, no. 11 (2011): 54–62.

McDermid, Douglas. *The Varieties of Pragmatism: Truth, Realism, and Knowledge from James to Rorty*. London: Continuum, 2006.

McDermott, John J. "All We Seem to Get Is Life Implicitness: The Practical as Ontological." *Southwest Philosophy Review* 11 (Supplement) (1995): 17–26.

———. "Classical American Philosophy: A Reflective Bequest to the Twenty First Century." *Journal of Philosophy* 81, no. 11 (1984): 663–75.

———. *The Culture of Experience: Philosophical Essays in the American Grain*. New York: New York University Press, 1976.

———. *The Drama of Possibility: Experience as Philosophy of Culture*. New York: Fordham University Press, 2007.

———. "Experience as Freedom." In *A Companion to Pragmatism*, edited by John R. Shook and Joseph Margolis, 249–53. Malden, MA: Blackwell, 2006.

———. Foreword to *Chaos and Context*, by Charlene H. Seigfried, ix–xiii. Athens: Ohio University Press, 1978.

———. "The Importance of Cultural Pedagogy." *Thinking* 9, no. 3 (1990): 2–4.

———. Introduction to *Essays in Radical Empiricism*, by William James, xi–xlviii. Edited by Frederick H. Burkhardt, Fredson Bowers and Ignas K. Skrupskelis. Cambridge, MA: Harvard University Press, 1976.

———. Introduction to *The Writings of William James*, xiii–xliv. New York: Modern Library, 1968.

———. "A Lost Horizon: Perils and Possibilities of the Obvious." *Pluralist* 5, no. 2 (2010): 1–17.

———. "A Metaphysics of Relations: James's Anticipation of Contemporary Experience." In *The Philosophy of William James*, edited by Walter Robert Corti, 81–100. Hamburg: Felix Meiner, 1976.

———. "Pragmatic Sensibility: The Morality of Experience." In *New Directions in Ethics*, edited by Joseph De Marco, 113–34. New York: Routledge and Kegan Paul, 1986.

———. "The Promethean Self and Community in the Philosophy of William James." *Rice University Studies* (1980): 87–101.

———. *Streams of Experience: Reflections on the History and Philosophy of American Culture*. Amherst: University of Massachusetts Press, 1986.

———. "William James Presidential Address." *William James Studies* 2, no. 1 (2007).

———. "You Are Really Able." In *Experience as Philosophy*, edited by James Campbell and Richard E. Hart, 237–71. New York: Fordham University Press, 2006.

McGranahan, Lucas. *Darwinism and Pragmatism: William James on Evolution and Self-Transformation*. Abingdon, UK: Routledge, 2017.

Menand, Louis. *The Metaphysical Club: A Story of Ideas in America*. New York: Farrar, Straus and Giroux, 2001.

Misak, Cheryl. *The American Pragmatists*. Oxford: Oxford University Press, 2013.

———. "Language and Experience for Pragmatism." *European Journal of Pragmatism and American Philosophy* 6, no. 2 (2014): 28–39.

———, ed. *New Pragmatists*. Oxford: Oxford University Press, 2007.

———, ed. *The Oxford Handbook of American Philosophy*. Oxford: Oxford University Press, 2008.

Mounce, Howard O. *The Two Pragmatisms: From Peirce to Rorty*. London: Routledge, 1997.

Mullin, Richard P. *The Soul of Classical American Philosophy: The Ethical and Spiritual Insights of William James, Josiah Royce, and Charles Sanders Peirce*. Albany: State University of New York Press, 2007.

Murphy, John P. *Pragmatism from Peirce to Davidson*. Boulder, CO: Westview, 1990.

Myers, Gerald E. "Pragmatism and Introspective Psychology." In *The Cambridge Companion to William James*, edited by Ruth Anna Putnam, 11–24. Cambridge: Cambridge University Press, 1997.

———. "William James and Contemporary Psychology." In *Reinterpreting the Legacy of William James*, edited by Margaret E. Donnelly, 49–64. Washington, DC: American Psychological Society, 1992.

———. *William James: His Life and Thought*. New Haven, CT: Yale University Press, 1986.

O'Connell, Robert J. "The Will to Believe and James's Deontological Streak." *Transactions of the Charles S. Peirce Society* 28, no. 4 (1992): 809–31.

Omelchenko, Nikolay. "Philosophy as Therapy." *Diogenes* 57, no. 4 (2010): 73–81.

Pappas, Gregory F. "The Narrative and Identity of Pragmatism in America: The History of a Dysfunctional Family?" *Pluralist* 9, no. 2 (2014): 65–83.

———. "What Difference Can 'Experience' Make to Pragmatism?" *European Journal of Pragmatism and American Philosophy* 6, no. 2 (2014): 200–228.

Parker, Gail Thain. *Mind Cure in New England from the Civil War to World War I*. Hanover, NH: University Press of New England, 1973.

Parker, Kelly A. "James: Experience and Creative Growth." In *Classical American Pragmatism: Its Contemporary Vitality*, edited by Sandra B. Rosenthal, Carl R. Hausman, and Douglas R. Anderson, 209–23. Chicago: University of Chicago Press, 1999.

Pawelski, James O. *The Dynamic Individualism of William James*. Albany: State University of New York Press, 2007.

Peirce, Charles Sanders. "What Pragmatism Is." *Monist* 15, no. 2 (1905): 161–81.

Perry, Ralph Barton. *Essays on Faith and Morals*. New York: Longmans, Green, 1947.

———. *In the Spirit of William James*. Bloomington: Indiana University Press, 1958.

———. *The Thought and Character of William James*. 2 vols. Boston: Little, Brown, 1935.

Pihlström, Sami, ed. *The Continuum Companion to Pragmatism*. London: Continuum, 2011.

———. "Kant and Pragmatism." *Pragmatism Today* 1, no. 2 (2010): 50–61.

———. *Pragmatic Moral Realism: A Transcendental Defense*. Amsterdam: Rodopi, 2005.

———. "Pragmatism and Naturalized Transcendental Subjectivity." *Contemporary Pragmatism* 6, no. 1 (2009): 1–13.

———. "The Prospects of Transcendental Pragmatism: Reconciling Kant and James." *Philosophy Today* 41, no. 3 (1997): 383–93.

———. *"The Trail of the Human Serpent Is over Everything": Jamesian Perspectives on Mind, World, and Religion*. Lanham, MD: University Press of America, 2008.

Posnock, Ross. "The Influence of William James on American Culture." In *The Cambridge Companion to William James*, edited by Ruth Anna Putnam, 322–42. Cambridge: Cambridge University Press, 1997.

Powell, Thomas C. "William James." In *Oxford Handbook of Process Philosophy and Organization Studies*, edited by Jenny Helin, Tor Hernes, Daniel Hjorth, and Robin Holt, 166–84. Oxford: Oxford University Press, 2014.

Pueyo-Ibáñez, Belén. "The (Very Needed) Experimental Turn in Ethics." *European Journal of Pragmatism and American Philosophy* 13, no. 2 (2021): 1–8.

Putnam, Hilary. "Philosophy as a Reconstructive Activity: William James on Moral Philosophy." In *The Pragmatic Turn: Contemporary Engagements between Analytic and Continental Thought*, edited by William Egginton and Mike Sandbothe, 31–46. Albany: State University of New York Press, 2004.

———. *Pragmatism: An Open Question*. Cambridge, MA: Blackwell, 1995.

———. *Realism with a Human Face*. Cambridge, MA: Harvard University Press, 1990.

Putnam, Hilary, and Ruth Anna Putnam. *Pragmatism as a Way of Life: The Lasting Legacy of William James and John Dewey*, edited by David Macarthur. Cambridge MA: Harvard University Press, 2017.

———. "William James's Ideas." In *Realism with a Human Face*, edited by James Conant. Cambridge, MA: Harvard University Press, 1990.

Putnam, Ruth Anna, ed. *The Cambridge Companion to William James*. Cambridge: Cambridge University Press, 1997.

———. "The Moral Life of a Pragmatist." In *Identity, Character, and Morality: Essays in Moral Psychology*, edited by Owen Flanagan and Amélie Oksenberg Rorty, 67–89. Cambridge, MA: MIT Press, 1990.

———. "Some of Life's Ideals." In *The Cambridge Companion to William James*, edited by Ruth Anna Putnam, 282–99. Cambridge: Cambridge University Press, 1997.

Reck, Andrew J. *Introduction to William James*. Bloomington: Indiana University Press, 1967.

———. "The Philosophical Psychology of William James." *Southern Journal of Philosophy* 9, no. 3 (1971): 293–312.

———. "The Place of William James's Principles of Psychology in American Philosophy." In *The Philosophical Psychology of William James*, edited by Michael H. DeArmey and Stephen Skousgaard, 1–16. Washington, DC: Center for Advanced Research in Phenomenology and University Press of America, 1986.

Rescher, Nicholas. *The Pragmatic Vision: Themes in Philosophical Pragmatism*. Lanham, MD: Rowman and Littlefield, 2014.

———. "Pragmatism." In *Oxford Companion to Philosophy*, edited by Ted Honderich, 747–50. Oxford: Oxford University Press, 2005.

Richardson, Joan. *Pragmatism and American Experience: An Introduction*. New York: Cambridge University Press, 2014.

Richardson, Robert D. *Introduction to The Heart of William James*. Cambridge, MA: Harvard University Press, 2010.

———. *William James in the Maelstrom of American Modernism*. New York: Mariner, 2007.

Robinson, Daniel N. "William James on the Mind and the Body." In *Reinterpreting the Legacy of William James*, edited by Margaret E. Donnelly, 313–22. Washington, DC: American Psychological Association, 1992.

Rohr, Susanne, and Miriam Strube, eds. *Revisiting Pragmatism: William James in the New Millennium*. Heidelberg: Universitätsverlag Winter, 2012.

Romano, Carlin. *America the Philosophical*. New York: Alfred A. Knopf, 2012.

Rorty, Richard. *Consequences of Pragmatism: Essays 1972–1980*. Minneapolis: University of Minnesota Press, 1982.

———. *Contingency, Irony, and Solidarity*. New York: Cambridge University Press, 2009.

———. Introduction to *The Linguistic Turn*, 1–39. Chicago: Chicago University Press, 1967.

———. "In Defense of Eliminative Materialism." In *Mind, Language, and Metaphilosophy: Early Philosophical Papers*, edited by Stephen Leach and James Tartaglia, 199–207. Cambridge: Cambridge University Press, 1970.

———. *Philosophy and Social Hope*. London: Penguin, 1999.

———. *Philosophy and the Mirror of Nature*. Thirtieth anniversary ed. Princeton, NJ: Princeton University Press, 2009.

———. "Some Inconsistencies in James's Varieties." In *William James and a Science of Religions*, edited by Wayne Proudfoot, 86–97. New York: Columbia University Press, 2004.

Rosenbaum, Stuart. *Pragmatism and the Reflective Life.* Lanham, MD: Lexington, 2009.

Rosenthal, Sandra B. "The Pragmatic Reconstruction of Experience: Some Systematic Implications." In *Experience, Interpretation, and Community: Themes in John E. Smith's Reconstruction of Philosophy*, edited by Vincent M. Colapietro, 129–46. Newcastle, UK: Cambridge Scholars Publishing, 2011.

Rosenthal, Sandra B., and Patrick L. *Bourgeois. Pragmatism and Phenomenology: A Philosophic Encounter.* Amsterdam: B. R. Grüner, 1980.

Rosenthal, Sandra B., Carl R. Hausman, and Douglas R. Anderson, eds. *Classical American Pragmatism: Its Contemporary Vitality.* Chicago: University of Illinois Press, 1999.

Roth, John K. *Freedom and the Moral Life: The Ethics of William James.* Philadelphia: Westminster Press, 1969.

———. Introduction to *The Moral Philosophy of William James*, 1–18. New York: Thomas Y. Crowell, 1969.

———. "Possible but Never Finished." *Continental Philosophy Review* 44, no. 3 (2011): 291–95.

———. "Talking About Religion in Public." In *Experience, Interpretation, and Community: Themes in John E. Smith's Reconstruction of Philosophy*, edited by Vincent M. Colapietro, 11–26. Newcastle, UK: Cambridge Scholars Publishing, 2011.

Roth, Robert J. *British Empiricism and American Pragmatism: New Directions and Neglected Arguments.* New York: Fordham University Press, 1993.

———. "Radical Pragmatism and a Theory of Person." *International Philosophical Quarterly* 36, no. 3 (1996): 335–49.

Ryan, Alan J. "Pragmatist Moral Philosophy." In *The Routledge Companion to Ethics*, edited by John Skorupski, 217–29. London: Routledge, 2010.

Rychlak, Joseph F. "William James and the Concept of Free Will." In *Reinterpreting the Legacy of William James*, edited by Margaret E. Donnelly, 323–38. Washington, DC: American Psychological Association, 1992.

Ryder, John. *The Things in Heaven and Earth: An Essay in Pragmatic Naturalism.* New York: Fordham University Press, 2013.

Ryder, John, and Emil Višňovský, eds. *Pragmatism and Values.* Amsterdam: Rodopi, 2004.

Sachs, Carl B. *Intentionality and the Myths of the Given.* Abingdon, UK: Pickering and Chatto, 2014.

Santarelli, Matteo. "The Ethical Consequences of Interests." In *The Jamesian Mind*, edited by Sarin Marchetti. Abingdon, UK: Routledge, 2022.

Scheffler, Israel. *Four Pragmatists: A Critical Introduction to Peirce, James, Mead, and Dewey.* London: Routledge and Kegan Paul, 1974.

Schlecht, Ludwig F. "Mysticism and Meliorism: The Integrated Self of William James." *Philosophical Forum* 32, no. 3 (2001): 253–63.

Schwartz, Robert. *Rethinking Pragmatism: From William James to Contemporary Philosophy.* Malden, MA: Wiley Blackwell, 2012.

Seigfried, Charlene Haddock. *Chaos and Context: A Study in William James.* Athens: Ohio University Press, 1978.

———. "James's Reconstruction of Ordinary Experience." *Southern Journal of Philosophy* 19, no. 4 (1981): 499–516.

———. "On the Metaphysical Foundations of Scientific Psychology." In *The Philosophical Psychology of William James*, edited by Michael H. DeArmey and Stephen Skousgaard, 57–72. Washington, DC: Center for Advanced Research in Phenomenology and University Press of America, 1986.

———. "The Philosopher's 'Licence': William James and Common Sense." *Transactions of the Charles S. Peirce Society* 19, no. 3 (1983): 273–90.

———. "The Structure of Experience for William James." Transactions of the Charles S. Peirce Society 12, no. 4 (1976): 330–47.

———. "Weaving Chaos into Order: A Radically Pragmatic Aesthetic." *Philosophy and Literature* 14, no. 1 (1990): 108–16.

———. "William James's Concrete Analysis of Experience." *Monist* 75, no. 4 (1992): 538–50.

———. "William James's Phenomenological Methodology." *Journal of the British Society for Phenomenology* 20, no. 1 (1989): 62–76.

———. William James's Radical Reconstruction of Philosophy. Albany: State University of New York Press, 1994.

———. "The World We Practically Live In." In *Reinterpreting the Legacy of William James*, edited by Margaret E. Donnelly, 77–90. Washington, DC: American Psychological Society, 1992.

Sellars, Wilfrid. *Empiricism and the Philosophy of Mind.* Cambridge, MA: Harvard University Press, 1997.

Shade, Patrick. *Habits of Hope: A Pragmatic Theory.* Nashville: Vanderbilt University Press, 2001.

Shea, John J. "The Self in William James." *Philosophy Today* 17, no. 4 (1973): 319–27.

Sheets-Johnstone, Maxine. "The Legacy of William James: Lesson's for Today's Twenty-First Century Neuroscience." In *Pragmatist Neurophilosophy: American Philosophy and the Brain*, edited by John R. Shook and Tibor Solymosi, 29–50. London: Bloomsbury, 2014.

Shook, John R. Introduction to *The Essential William James*, 7–45. Amherst, NY: Prometheus, 2011.

———. "The Moral Life as the Basis for Moral Philosophy." In *William James, Moral Philosophy, and the Ethical Life*, edited by Jacob L. Goodson, 97–119. Lanham, MD: Lexington, 2018.

———, ed. *Pragmatic Naturalism and Realism*. New York: Prometheus, 2003.

Shook, John R., and Joseph Margolis, eds. *A Companion to Pragmatism*. Oxford: Blackwell, 2006.

Shook, John R., and Tibor Solymosi, eds. *Pragmatist Neurophilosophy: American Philosophy and the Brain*. London: Bloomsbury, 2014.

Shusterman, Richard. *Practicing Philosophy: Pragmatism and the Philosophical Life*. New York: Routledge, 1997.

Sklanksy, Jeffrey. *The Soul's Economy: Market Society and Selfhood in American Thought, 1820–1920*. Chapel Hill: University of North Carolina Press, 2002.

Slater, Michael R. *William James on Ethics and Faith*. Cambridge: Cambridge University Press, 2009.

Smith, John E. *America's Philosophical Vision*. Chicago: Chicago University Press, 1992.

———. "Being and Willing: The Foundation of Ethics." *Journal of Speculative Philosophy* 1, no. 1 (1987): 24–37.

———, ed. *Contemporary American Philosophy*. London: George Allen and Unwin, 1970.

———. *Experience and God*. London: Oxford University Press, 1968.

———. "Experience, God, and Classical American Philosophy." *American Journal of Theology and Philosophy* 14, no. 2 (1993): 119–45.

———. *Purpose and Thought: The Meaning of Pragmatism*. Chicago: University of Chicago Press, 1984.

———. *The Spirit of American Philosophy*. Rev. ed. Albany: State University of New York Press, 1983.

Sprigge, Timothy. *James and Bradley: American Truth and British Reality*. La Salle, IL: Open Court, 1993.

Stengers, Isabelle. "William James: An Ethics of Thought?" *Radical Philosophy* 157 (2009): 9–19.

Stevens, Richard. *James and Husserl: The Foundations of Meaning*. The Hague: Martinus Nijhoff, 1974.

Stob, Paul. *William James and the Art of Popular Statement*. East Lansing: Michigan State University Press, 2013.

Stroud, Scott R. "William James on Meliorism, Moral Ideals, and Business Ethics." *Transactions of the Charles S. Peirce Society* 45, no. 3 (2009): 378–401.

Strube, Michael J., John H. Yost, and James R. Bailey. "William James and Contemporary Research on the Self: The Influence of Pragmatism, Reality, and Truth." In *Reinterpreting the Legacy of William James*, edited by Margaret E. Donnelly, 189–208. Washington, DC: American Psychological Association, 1992.

Stuhr, John J., ed. *100 Years of Pragmatism: William James's Revolutionary Philosophy*. Bloomington: Indiana University Press, 2010.

———. *Genealogical Pragmatism: Philosophy, Experience, and Community*. Albany: State University of New York Press, 1997.

———. *Pragmatism, Postmodernism, and the Future of Philosophy.* New York: Routledge, 2003.

Suckiel, Ellen Kappy. *The Pragmatic Philosophy of William James.* Notre Dame: University of Notre Dame Press, 1982.

———. "Review of William James on Ethics and Faith, by Michael R. Slater." *Notre Dame Philosophical Reviews*, no. 6 (2010).

———. "William James." In *The Dictionary of Modern American Philosophers*, edited by John R Shook, 1225–32. Bristol: Thoemmes Continuum, 2005.

———. "William James." In *A Companion to Pragmatism*, edited by John R. Shook and Joseph Margolis, 30–43. Malden, MA: Blackwell, 2006.

Talisse, Robert B., and D. Micah Hester. *On James.* Belmont, CA: Thomson, 2004.

Tarver, Erin C., and Shannon Sullivan, eds. *Feminist Interpretations of William James.* University Park: Pennsylvania State University Press, 2015.

Taylor, Eugene. "William James and the Humanistic Implications of the Neuroscience Revolution: An Outrageous Hypothesis." *Journal of Humanistic Psychology* 50, no. 4 (2010): 410–29.

———. "William James on a Phenomenological Psychology of Immediate Experience." *History of the Human Sciences* 23, no. 3 (2010): 119–30.

———. *William James on Consciousness Beyond the Margin.* Princeton, NJ: Princeton University Press, 1996.

Thayer, Horace S. *Meaning and Action: A Study of American Pragmatism.* New York: Bobbs Merrill, 1973.

Thomas, Joseph M. "Figures of Habit in William James." *New England Quarterly* 66, no. 1 (1993): 3–26.

Throntveit, Trygve. *William James and the Quest for an Ethical Republic.* New York: Palgrave Macmillan, 2014.

Uffelman, Mark. "Forging the Self in the Stream of Experience: Classical Currents of Self-Cultivation in James and Dewey." *Transactions of the Charles S. Peirce Society* 47, no. 3 (2011): 319–39.

———. "Jamesian Self-Cultivation: Meliorism in the Double-Barreled Stream of Experience." Paper presented at the 41st Annual Meeting of the Society for the Advancement of American Philosophy, Denver, CO, 2014.

———. "The Role of Self-Cultivation in Classical Pragmatism." PhD diss., Temple University, 2005. ProQuest (AAT 3176856).

Unger, Roberto M. *The Self Awakened: Pragmatism Unbound.* Cambridge, MA: Harvard University Press, 2007.

Voparil, Christopher J. "Rorty and James on Irony, Moral Commitment, and the Ethics of Belief." *William James Studies* 12, no. 2 (2016): 1–30.

Watzl, Sebastian. *Structuring Mind: The Nature of Attention and How It Shapes Consciousness.* Oxford: Oxford University Press, 2017.

Weinberger, Joel. "William James and the Unconscious: Redressing a Century-Old Misunderstanding." *Psychological Science* 11, no. 6 (2000): 439–45.

Welchman, Jennifer. *Dewey's Ethical Thought*. Ithaca, NY: Cornell University Press, 1995.

——. "William James's *The Will to Believe* and the Ethics of Self-Experimentation." *Transactions of the Charles S. Peirce Society* 42, no. 2 (2006): 229–41.

West, Cornel. *The American Evasion of Philosophy: A Genealogy of Pragmatism*. Madison: University of Wisconsin Press, 1989.

Westbrook, Robert B. *Democratic Hope: Pragmatism and the Politics of Truth*. Ithaca, NY: Cornell University Press, 2005.

Westphal, Merold. Introduction to *Reason, Experience, and God*, edited by Vincent M. Colapietro, 1–5. New York: Fordham University Press, 1997.

White, Heidi E. "William James's Pragmatism: Ethics and the Individualism of Others." *European Journal of Pragmatism and American Philosophy* 2, no. 1 (2010): 1–11.

White, Morton. *Pragmatism and the American Mind: Essays and Reviews in Philosophy and Intellectual History*. New York: Oxford University Press, 1973.

Wild, John D. "Authentic Existence." *Ethics* 75, no. 4 (1965): 227–39.

——. *Existence and the World of Freedom*. Englewood Cliffs, NJ: Prentice-Hall, 1963.

——. *The Radical Empiricism of William James*. Garden City, NY: Doubleday, 1969.

Wilshire, Bruce W. *Fashionable Nihilism: A Critique of Analytic Philosophy*. Albany: State University of New York Press, 2002.

——. "Protophenomenology in the Psychology of William James." *Transactions of the Charles S. Peirce Society* 5, no. 1 (1969): 25–43.

——. *William James and Phenomenology: A Study of "The Principles of Psychology."* Bloomington: Indiana University Press, 1968.

——. "William James, Phenomenology and Pragmatism: A Reply to Rosenthal." *Transactions of the Charles S. Peirce Society* 13, no. 1 (1977): 45–55.

——. "William James's Pragmatism: A Distinctly Mixed Bag." In *100 Years of Pragmatism: William James's Revolutionary Philosophy*, edited by John J. Stuhr, 96–107. Bloomington: Indiana University Press, 2010.

Index

Milton Keynes UK
Ingram Content Group UK Ltd.
UKHW011125080124
435661UK00006B/615

9 781438 493275